Human Capital in Gender and Development

Human Capital in Gender and Development addresses timely feminist debates about the relationship between feminism, neoliberalism, and international development. The book engages with human capital theory, a labour economics theory associated with the Chicago School that now animates a wide range of political and economic governance. The book argues that human capital theory has been instrumental in constructing an economistic vision of gender equality as a tool for economic growth, and girls and women of the global South as the quintessential entrepreneurs of the post-global financial crisis era.

The book's critique of human capital theory and its role in Gender and Development gives insights into the kinds of development interventions that typify the 'Gender Equality as Smart Economics' agenda of the World Bank and other international development institutions. From the World Bank, to NGOs, and private businesses, discourses about the economic benefits of gender equality and women's empowerment underpin a range of development interventions that aim to unlock the 'untapped' potential of the world's women. Its implications are both conceptual and material, producing more interventionist forms of development governance, increased power by private sector actors in development, and the de-politicization of gender equality issues.

Human Capital in Gender and Development will be of particular interest to feminist scholars in Politics, International Relations, Development Studies, and Human Geography. It will also be a useful resource for teaching key debates about feminism, neoliberalism, and international development.

Sydney Calkin is Assistant Professor (Research) and Leverhulme Early Career Fellow in Human Geography at Durham University. Her research addresses questions at the intersection of political economy, reproductive justice, and international relations.

Routledge Studies in Gender and Global Politics

This series aims to publish books that work with, and through, feminist insights on global politics, and illuminate the ways in which gender functions not just as a marker of identity but also as a constitutive logic in global political practices. The series welcomes scholarship on any aspect of global political practices, broadly conceived, that pays attention to the ways in which gender is central to, (re)produced in, and is productive of, such practices.

There is growing recognition both within the academy and in global political institutions that gender matters in and to the practices of global politics. From the governance of peace and security, to the provision of funds for development initiatives, via transnational advocacy networks linked through strategic engagement with new forms of media, these processes have a gendered dimension that is made visible through empirically grounded and theoretically sophisticated feminist work.

Series Editor: Laura J. Shepherd, UNSW Australia

Masculinity and New War
The gendered dynamics of contemporary armed conflict
David Duriesmith

Why Women Rebel
Understanding Women's Participation in Armed Rebel Groups
Alexis Leanna Henshaw

Feminism, Prostitution and the State
The Politics of Neo-Abolitionism
Edited by Eilís Ward and Gillian Wylie

Gender, Governance and Feminist Analysis
Missing in Action?
Edited by Christine Hudson, Malin Rönnblom and Katherine Teghtsoonian

Marriage Trafficking
Women in Forced Wedlock
Kaye Quek

Human Capital in Gender and Development
Sydney Calkin

For more information about this series, please visit: https://www.routledge.com/Routledge-Studies-in-Gender-and-Global-Politics/book-series/GGP

Human Capital in Gender and Development

Sydney Calkin

Routledge
Taylor & Francis Group
LONDON AND NEW YORK

First published 2018
by Routledge
2 Park Square, Milton Park, Abingdon, Oxon OX14 4RN

and by Routledge
711 Third Avenue, New York, NY 10017

Routledge is an imprint of the Taylor & Francis Group, an informa business

British Library Cataloguing in Publication Data
A catalogue record for this book is available from the British Library

Library of Congress Cataloging in Publication Data
A catalog record for this book has been requested

ISBN: 9781138697348 (hbk)
ISBN: 9781315522098 (ebk)

Typeset in Times New Roman
by Taylor & Francis Books

Contents

Illustrations

Figures

Tables

Box

Acknowledgements

This book began in my doctoral research. It has been supported by numerous colleagues and friends at York, Durham, and many places in between. I am so grateful to my PhD supervisors Audra Mitchell and Carole Spary for their guidance and wisdom during that long process. I was lucky to meet Audra when I was still an undergraduate, and she has inspired and encouraged me in my academic career ever since. During the PhD, and in the years since, Juliana Bidadanure has been an enormous source of support, friendship, and insight for this project; she has helped with the development of the ideas along the way and challenged me to think in new ways. Holly Steel has also been a treasured source of friendship and support since our PhD days. At Durham, several colleagues have kindly read and commented on chapters from this book: thanks to Divya Tolia-Kelly, Siobhan McGrath, Oliver Belcher, Phil Steinberg, Gavin Bridge, Lizzie Richardson, and Grace Garside, among others. Ben Anderson and Noam Leshem generously gave their time to read the entire manuscript and provide helpful comments that improved the work immensely. The intellectual generosity, friendship, and outstanding scholarship of my colleagues at Durham continually pushes me to become a better researcher, writer, and thinker.

In the field of Feminist Political Economy, it has been a joy to work among women who have dedicated their lives to feminist research and the cause of gender equality, because the environment is one of productive engagement and collaboration with special generosity for junior scholars. I know this is not the case in every academic field! I'm very grateful to Marysia Zalewski, Sylvia Chant, Spike Peterson, Kate Bedford, Lisa Prügl, Jacqui True, Juanita Elias, Adrienne Roberts, Catia Gregoratti, Jemima Repo, Penny Griffin, and many others for their support and intellectual engagement with my research.

Many thanks to Laura Shepherd and the anonymous reviewers who gave advice that helped to improve this manuscript, and to Nicola Parkin, Lydia de Cruz and Lucy Frederick at Routledge for their assistance with the publication process. Earlier research associated with this project has been published in *Third World Quarterly, Progress in Development Studies, Globalizations, International Feminist Journal of Politics,* and *New Formations.* Text and images from the World Bank's World Development Report 2012 are republished here under a Creative Commons license.

I'm so lucky to have the support of a wonderful family that extends across two continents. Thanks to Ben for his kindness, support and Skype chats. Thanks to the Higginsons for welcoming me into their family and making Scotland feel like a second home. I am so grateful to Harry Higginson, who has seen me through this project and encouraged me to keep faith in it. He is changing the world with his own work and he inspires me to try to do the same. For so many reasons, I feel lucky every day that he is my partner. My parents, Jean and Mark, have been a continuous source of love and encouragement throughout my life. They have made every opportunity possible for me, for which I'm so grateful. This book is dedicated to them, with love.

List of Abbreviations

BoP	Bottom of the Pyramid
CSR	Corporate Social Responsibility
GAD	Gender and Development
GAP	Gender Action Plan
GEA	Girl Effect Accelerator
GPSLF	Global Private Sector Leaders Forum
IFC	International Finance Corporation
WID	Women in Development
WDR	World Development Report

Introduction

At Kiva.com, users can browse listings of entrepreneurs across the globe and contribute $25 towards a micro-loan for their business. As Kiva's lending portfolio expanded, its co-founder Matthew Flannery observed "an unusual cross-cultural form of competition" on the site:

> "Our users, given an array of choices, voted with their wallets. Every business on the site thus far has been funded at an average rate of 2.2 days per business, but with significant variance. Lenders showed unambiguous preferences according to region, gender, and business type: Africans first, women first, and agriculture first. A female African fruit seller? Funded in hours. A Nicaraguan retail stand? Funded in days. A Bulgarian taxi driver? Funded in weeks."
>
> (2007: 50)

Flannery makes this point to emphasize the diversity of Kiva's global community, and the choice available to the site's users, but it reveals something deeper about public perceptions of development, poverty, and empowerment. Development provides a potent geographical imaginary that is deeply internalized and reproduced: when asked to select a deserving recipient of their dollars, Kiva's users echoed familiar development tropes around the superior productivity and resilience of women. Girls and women today are the faces of global development and calls to recognize their potential fill the campaigns and policy documents of institutions across the world. This is notable for a few reasons: first, because it has not always been this way. The consensus around the importance of gender equality is a relatively new, and hard-won, gain. Second, it is notable because the role of women in global development agendas is a fiercely contested topic, tied to broader public debates about gender equality and its relationship to public policy. The Kiva anecdote above alludes to this ambivalence: the girls and women who have achieved the greatest visibility in these public discourses are those who conform to pre-set narratives about for whom development exists, what it does, and how it works. The women whose economic empowerment is held up as the most powerful driver for future growth are imagined as being "constantly, diligently, and happily engaged" in labor for global markets (Wilson 2011: 323). Does development now work for women, or is it the other way around?

For decades, women were considered marginal actors in the development process, either as victims of "underdeveloped" cultures, passive recipients of aid, or reproductive vessels for overpopulation. The policy and discursive processes by which women have become visible actors in development spans decades and demonstrates the shifting (and overlapping) subject positions they have occupied: oppressed wife, dutiful mother, empowered entrepreneur. Today, the dominant discourses of "Gender Equality as Smart Economics" and the "Business Case for Gender Equality" represent the primary modes by which girls and women visibility and agency in global governance. For decades, feminist advocates worked to put gender on the agenda by convincing policy makers that they would ignore gender inequalities at their peril. Efforts to demonstrate the intrinsic and instrumental value of gender have been ongoing for years in development, with mixed success and slow transformation in mainstream institutions. In the last twenty years, narratives emphasizing the efficiency of gender equality for states and corporations have caught on and spread rapidly, as have arguments about the altruistic and efficient economic behavior of women, who are represented as unique drivers of shared growth. Today, the role of gender equality is widely recognized in governmental institutions and celebrated by policy makers, who promise to deliver growth by empowering women. The rationale tends to emphasize instrumental benefits of gender equality: the instrumental case stresses that gender equality produces a range of other beneficial outcomes, rather than advocating for gender equality on the basis of its intrinsic importance. This mode of instrumental advocacy of gender equality now dominates the discourse, most notably in the years following the 2007–2008 global financial crisis. The issue of low female labor force participation, for instance, is recognized in terms of national productivity and planning inefficiency. The recognition of gender inequality as a producer of economic, social, and political inefficiencies has animated a new political discourse around the need to "tap in" to women's power, to "unlock" their economic potential, and to educate and empower girls in order to produce profitable returns on their human capital in the long run. Rhetorical consensus on the issue of gender equality is now so widely shared across institutions and regions that it appears as a common-sense feature of mainstream development discourse.

The unprecedented attention accorded to gender issues on the international stage signals a "strategically crucial moment" for feminists (Harcourt 2012: 308). And yet, this recognition also presents a serious challenge. These ostensible gains are complex and ambiguous because much of the gender equality policy discourse is so closely tied to the advancement of a neoliberal economic policy agenda characterized by market fundamentalism, deregulation, and corporate-led development. Recognition of feminist success has been tempered by worries that the newfound visibility of girls and women in development is symptomatic of something else: not a genuine engagement with feminist political and economic critique, but rhetorical and visual uptake of girls and women as symbols to legitimize other agendas. Does this newfound visibility reflect less a feminist infiltration of politico-economic power structures than "neoliberalism with a woman's face" (Prügl 2017)? Anxieties over the visibility and significance of popular representations of gender equality in political and development discourse stems from the concern that feminism has been selectively appropriated, watered down, and re-purposed to provide a pseudo-feminist gloss to neoliberalism.

The intellectual driver of these changes has been, however, under-recognized in feminist debates. Women's current visibility in development discourses has been made possible by the rise of human capital theory in development governance, and its promotion of girls and women as untapped human capital resources. Human capital theory is an innovation in economic theory that allows policymakers to calculate the value of things like education, health, and other dimensions of life in terms of their effect on productivity. Human capital theory re-imagines humans as a form of capital and re-imagines wages as return on capital. Using this theoretical approach, policymakers have increasingly come to understand state provision of education, health, or social services as investments in citizens' capital. It introduces a new social classification that transcends all others: individual "human capitalist(ists)" are in perpetual competition with each other to improve themselves and generate future gains (Fleming 2017: 175). Human capital theory underpins broad paradigmatic shifts around the meaning of work and life. In the global North, it lies behind the proliferation of low-skilled, precarious, and flexibilized work. In global development policymaking, human capital theory has been central to the newfound visibility of women and girls, through the contention that investment in their capital promises the most profitable return on investment. The re-imagination of girls and women as human capital means that forms of gender oppression like discrimination and violence can be re-written in terms of inefficiencies or obstacles to realization of investment. Indeed, this is precisely the narrative form that much of the dominant "Gender Equality as Smart Economics" agenda takes to gender inequality, economizing all dimensions of life and gender power relations.

Human Capital in Gender and Development introduces a feminist critique of human capital theory. I intend this feminist critique to demonstrate the gendered logic that underpins human capital theory, but also to highlight the way that human capital theory has been deployed in Gender and Development governance. Using this feminist critique of human capital, the book makes three main arguments. First, I argue that the puzzle of women's visibility in development must be understood in the context of human capital theory, which enabled the newfound recognition of women as development agents while legitimizing new forms of intervention to "develop" women into idealized entrepreneurial subjects. Women's position as development agents hinges on a set of contradictory representations, wherein women are positioned as ideally efficient and productive development agents whose empowerment will unleash a domino-effect of sustainable growth; yet they are also understood as non-market actors who are trapped by reproductivity and must be socialized into market attitudes to unleash their entrepreneurship. Second, I argue that human capital theory animates the dominant "Gender Equality as Smart Economics" agenda in development today. But I caution against the perception that Smart Economics discourse represents a mere co-optation of feminism that uses its rhetoric for an agenda of privatization and deregulation: I argue that we should look for the ways that the Smart Economics agenda works as a tool of neoliberal governance in the Foucauldian sense. Gender and Development governance cannot be understood simply as a faux-feminist façade used by neoliberal institutions to mask capitalist agendas; feminist efforts to engage with these institutions has authorized new understandings of female agency, but also permitted a range of development interventions to transform women. Third, the gendered logic of human capital theory operates beyond the conventional limits of Gender and Development policy in mainstream development institutions. It also underpins new power structures in development that legitimize a range of new non-state, private actors as sources of funding and authority. Public-private partnerships and hybrid governance initiatives in Gender and Development are bound up with the logic of human capital and the convergences between gender equality and profit that it constructs. Taken together, these three strands of the argument provide an account of Gender and Development governance that offers fresh insights on the most important conceptual and material trends in the field.

Position and aims

Feminist knowledge building is a collective project, and as such this book is situated in a wider body of feminist literature that has shaped my orientation to research, the questions I address, and the arguments I make. Feminist knowledge building in political economy challenges us to recognize gender's function as a "governing code" that shapes what we value and how we value it. This knowledge building process is incremental, as Spike Peterson shows us: it starts by exposing masculinist bias in political economy, adding women and gender to existing conceptual frameworks, and proceeds through the process of politicizing the gendered hierarchies that underpin it (Peterson 2003; 2005). This book intervenes in a few ongoing debates in the feminist literature: the power relationships and politics of the "Gender Equality as Smart Economics" development agenda; the relationship between feminism and neoliberalism as it plays out in mainstream development institutions; and the usefulness of a Foucauldian feminist critique for feminist political economy. *Human Capital in Gender and Development* is pitched at the intersection of these debates, bringing a Foucauldian feminist analysis of human capital to push forward existing debates about feminism, neoliberalism, and co-optation in the age of Smart Economics.

The ascendance of the "Gender Equality as Smart Economics" policy agenda has provoked debates among feminist scholars, many of whom see Smart Economics as merely another neoliberal effort to capture and appropriate feminism for conservative ends. If this is the case, what is the substance of the Smart Economics agenda and what are its effects? A body of feminist historical materialist writing has articulated the connections between Smart Economics development agendas and the emergence of a "Transnational Business Feminist" class of elites and corporations who aim to entrench corporate power and increase private profit through this agenda (Roberts 2012; 2015a; 2015b). This feminist historical materialist approach locates this phenomenon within the broader processes of capitalist accumulation and suggests that it represents a response to the crisis of capitalism, whereby pseudo-feminist rhetoric provides a survival strategy for neoliberalism to smooth over its contradictions (Dauvergne and Lebaron 2014; Roberts and Soederberg 2012; Elias 2013; Sato 2016). This literature tends to understand manifestations of "business feminism" as efforts to commodify feminist resistance and entrench corporate power through co-opting feminist causes. By contrast, on the question of co-optation, analysis of the Smart Economics agenda from feminist development studies has approached this question from a desire for institutional change and skepticism about the possibilities of transformative feminist change. Given the long and troubled history of feminists working for change inside (and outside) development institutions, does the Smart Economics agenda represent an opportunity or a crisis? Is feminist change possible within mainstream institutions, or does this represent a futile effort that will inevitably end in feminism's co-optation? In this debate, the optimists see Smart Economics as potentially providing space to challenge existing economic development wisdom, most notably by providing a framework in which women's care work can be recognized at the level of the household (Bergeron 2016; Prügl 2015; 2017; Harcourt 2012; Evans 2012). The pessimists see the recognition of female labor and agency as providing the impetus for policies that overburden women with work: Sylvia Chant has called this the "feminization of responsibility" in anti-poverty policies (Chant 2008; 2013; 2016; Cornwall and Rivas 2015; Ferguson 2014; Chant and Sweetman 2012; Prügl and True 2014).

The visibility of girls and women on the Smart Economics development agenda is frequently treated with ambivalence, and usually overlaid with concerns about the co-optation of feminism by neoliberalism. This book starts from the point of the co-optation debate, and seeks to offer a way around it: it argues that Smart Economics is not a rhetorical façade for ideological neoliberalism, nor is it simply a mask for corporate power, but it represents the extension of particular forms of neoliberal governance in the lives of girls and women. We cannot disregard as corrupted the forms of feminism that are used to brand development interventions, because they are the product of contestation within institutions and create some spaces for feminist knowledge to inform the project of development. This is not an endorsement: the forms of development power that operate here deserve scrutiny, because they tend to reinforce patriarchal gender structures and neo-colonial power relations.

Disagreement over the substance of Smart Economics and its political potential speaks to a broader debate in development and global governance around neoliberalism and its many faces. The crisis of development and backlash against Washington Consensus policies of the 1980s has led to the emergence of a post-Washington Consensus agenda and human development models that emphasize poverty reduction. Critical political economy scholarship has demonstrated the persistence of neoliberalism as the foundational policy paradigm in the post-Washington Consensus era, albeit a reformed neoliberalism that is embraced in mainstream development institutions (Fine 2001; Babb 2013). In relation to gender in the development agenda, what is the substance of the post-Washington Consensus for gender equality concerns? The most important contributions in this debate have come from post-structural feminist political economists, like Kate Bedford and Penny Griffin, who have brought the tools of post-structuralism – primarily Butler and Foucault – to the question of global economic governance. These works emphasize sexuality as an under-recognized element of development policy and argue that neoliberal governance must be analysed through its management of sexed bodies and its reliance on heterosexual family models (Griffin 2007; 2009; 2010; Bedford 2005; 2007; 2009). This body of work has informed the broader orientation of post-structural feminist political economy, by demonstrating that the operation of gender in the global economy highlights the privileging of heterosexual masculinity, its equation with economic productivity, and the devaluation of female bodies, subjectivities, and skills that underpin these discourses. Post-structural feminist accounts of the post-Washington Consensus development landscape help us see past the cycle of reform, failure, and critique: reformed neoliberalism cannot realistically produce different results because it is underpinned by gendered hierarchies that have harmful effects on girls and women, no matter how it is re-labelled.

Analysis of global governance and political economy that aims to de-construct the gendered codes of economic governance has opened up a productive line of research for feminist political economy: which bodies and social relations are seen to matter in the global economy, as it is constructed/ produced by development institutions? Which bodies and social relationships are excluded from dominant visions of the economy? This is a line of questioning I take up and extend through this book, through the conceptual lens of human capital theory. Feminist work on heteronormativity takes inspiration from Foucault's understanding of sexuality as a "dense transfer point for relations of power" (Foucault 1998) and uses this framework to argue that neoliberal governance operates through the regulation and management of sexuality and the production of binary male/female bodies to perform different forms of work. *Human Capital in Gender and Development* also draws inspiration from Foucault, but argues that his critique of human capital theory provides the most significant starting point for a feminist analysis, because it allows us to trace the relationship between gender, sex, modes of economic subjectivity, and neoliberal governance interventions. The role of human capital in undergirding politico-economic governance today is increasingly being recognized. Recent work on the topic has shown: how human capital theory is bound with up data collection and financialization of development (Murphy 2017); its role in reconciling economic neoliberalism and moral conservatism to legitimize patriarchal family structures in economic terms (Cooper 2017); and its driving force in labor market structures today, characterized by on-demand and flexibilized work (Fleming 2017). However, human capital theory remains largely unexplored from a feminist perspective (Foucauldian or otherwise) although it presents an essential site of analysis if we are to understand the conceptual basis and power operations of the current Smart Economics development agenda. Foucault's critique of neoliberalism presents the most important, and under-recognized, work on the theory because of his insistence of placing human capital theory in a broader context of neoliberal governance and demonstrating its role in *producing* neoliberal subjects.

Feminist engagement with Foucault's work has produced path-breaking scholarship, but the relationship is still fiercely contested. Throughout researching, writing, and presenting the work in this book, I have been challenged by my feminist colleagues to justify the usefulness of Foucault: why must we always rely on the "big name" male theorists? Wasn't Foucault guilty of his own sexism and/or sympathy for neoliberalism? What can Foucault tell us that other feminist work has not already shown? I maintain that engagement with Foucault can still yield important feminist insights. To this end, there are two points to draw out: first, Foucault's thought merits feminist engagement because his diagnosis of the operation of power as *constitutive* allows us to develop a more nuanced account of the subject. Power does not merely act on the body of the subject, to discipline or restrict, but it actively constitutes the subject and works from a distance to instil an ethos of self-governance. In this way, Foucault's account allows us to see how feminine subjects are shaped by patriarchal and disciplinary practices, with significant impact on their status as political subjects (Oksala 2011; 2013). Second, and by extension, this approach allows us to see how neoliberalism operates as a governing rationality *through* the social body, with significant feminist implications. With a more nuanced account of power, Foucauldian tools can help us see contemporary forms of neoliberal governance that work through gender categories and gender equality policy structures (Repo 2015). Foucault's account of capillary power in social relationships, practices of self-surveillance and self-management, and disciplinary power have been embraced in feminist political theory, where they provide influential accounts of how gender norms operate and are internalized (see Deveaux 1994; McNay 1992; Sawicki 1991; Hekman 2007). By extension, this work has informed development studies scholarship: post-development theorists have employed a Foucauldian approach to biopower in order to illuminate new technologies of development governance and to make links between the sovereign power of the colonial with the biopower of the post-colonial (Brigg 2001; Miraftab 2004). This perspective is particularly evident in literature that grapples with financialized development, illuminating the production of (feminized) neoliberal subjects in the areas of remittances (Kunz 2012), microcredit (Rankin 2001; Brigg 2002; Aitken 2010; Shakya and Rankin 2008), conditional cash transfers (Molyneux 2006; Ballard 2013), and public-private partnerships (Bexell 2012). Foucauldian tools in development studies are essential because they move us away from the terrain of binary North/South relations of domination or accumulation: development governance and knowledge production result in more fragmented and contested power relations. For these reasons, Foucauldian insights can inform feminist and political economy scholarship in new ways, particularly in uncovering the role of human capital theory in Gender and Development knowledge.

Human Capital in Gender and Development sits at the intersection of these ongoing debates in the feminist literature. It provides a feminist critique of human capital theory in order to draw together, explain and analyse some of the most significant trends in the field of Gender and Development. The aims of the book are as follows:

- To map the visibilities of girls and women on the development agenda through human capital theory and the evolution of "Gender Equality as Smart Economics"
- To provide a feminist critique of human capital theory that illuminates the function of human capital as a strategy of neoliberal governance, and in doing so to demonstrate the conceptual and material implications of human capital theory for girls and women in development policy agendas
- To employ a feminist critique of human capital in development to push debates about feminism and neoliberalism beyond the narrative of co-optation of feminism

Organization of the argument

In *Human Capital in Gender and Development,* I aim to provide new conceptual tools to make sense of wide set of trends in the field. The book's argument proceeds through six chapters, roughly divided into three parts: Chapters 1–2 outline the conceptual problem at hand and propose a new approach by introducing the feminist critique of human capital theory. Chapters 3–4 take the World Bank as an empirical focus, exploring human capital theory in the Bank's past and present gender work. Chapters 5–6 look to the broader development context, addressing the implications of human capital logics in "girl-power" development campaigns and public-private development partnership for gender equality.

The book starts with a widely contested question: has feminism been co-opted by neoliberal capitalism? Debates about feminism's relationship to these forces continue to animate feminist conversations in scholarship, media, and public policy. In the field of feminist development studies, this debate has been the focal point of years of scholarship. Feminists working in development studies are confronted by a dilemma of visibility: girls and women are today widely recognized as central to global development, and calls to empower women in order to promote growth are heard across institutions. Yet, this policy agenda gives girls and women visibility as economic agents by inserting them into familiar narratives of market-led growth and neoliberal re-structuring. As such, the status of Smart Economics is a major source of debate in feminist literature. Does it represent the co-optation of feminism by neoliberalism? This is the wrong question to ask, I argue in Chapter 1. Debates about co-optation of feminism by neoliberalism provide a convincing explanation for some processes of neoliberal re-structuring and state roll-back that have been legitimized in the language of women's economic empowerment. But the co-optation narrative does not provide us with the necessary tools to understand a broader function of the Smart Economics agenda. Smart Economics, I demonstrate, is doing something different: it has made women the conceptual centre of development in order to legitimize further interventions to construct ideal neoliberal subjects and shape their behavior. Smart Economics works through gender equality discourses, by presenting women as saviours of global development, but it does so in a way that authorizes extensive neoliberal interventions beyond processes of economic re-structuring. This is part of a broader turn to post-structural economy that starts from the feminist contention that gender is an organizing principle in economies at all scales and examines the role played by gender, race, sexuality (and their intersections) in neoliberalism.

In order to understand the Smart Economics agenda and its policy implications, we must start with the conceptual framework that underpins it: this is human capital theory. Human capital theory has acquired enormous popularity as a conceptual framework for politico-economic policymaking, in part because it advances a broader ideological project of extending market logic into all realms of human life. Human capital theory posits that human capabilities can be understood as a form of capital that generates income in the form of wages: investments in health or education, for instance, can therefore be understood in terms of their impact on economic productivity of individuals and communities. Human capital theory has been especially important in the increased visibility of women and girls as agents of development because it has provided a way for their skills to become legible as tools for future growth. In Chapter 2, I argue that human capital theory presents the most important site of analysis for understanding the field of Gender and Development today. To this end, I provide a feminist critique of human capital theory, drawing in part on Foucault. Foucault provides an essential critique of human capital because he identifies it as a tool of governance in the broader context of neoliberalism; he shows that human capital theory provides policymakers with a set of categories to identify economically productive subjects and to prescribe a range of interventions to shape the behavior of those subjects. I demonstrate that these categories are at work in Gender and Development policy, where girls and women are attributed a set of essentialized traits, imagined as ideally productive and altruistic development subjects, and set up as dormant sources of power to be harnessed through development interventions.

Human capital theory has been influential in development policy thinking since the 1980s, although it has achieved the most widespread notoriety as part of the post-Washington Consensus and human development paradigm. Backlash against market-led structural adjustment reforms prompted a turn to integrating social dimensions of development back in and re-asserting a role for the state; in this context, human capital theory gained significant popularity. In leading development institutions like the World Bank, human capital theory spurred the growth and institutionalization of Gender and Development in policy and lending. It often did this by drawing on familiar ideas about girls and women as investments and sources of economic growth for the state: today it represents the dominant conceptual frame through which girls and women are visible in Smart Economics policies today. But their visibility on these terms has not occurred through a simple process of co-optation by mainstream institutions or corruption by anti-feminist forces. In fact, the process by which gender has gained status in development institutions has been characterized by a more complex process of cooperation, contestation, and strategic participation. In Chapter 3, I examine the politics of knowledge production on gender in the World Bank and address the process through which gender equality came to occupy the position of "common sense" economics at the Bank. I use the 2012 World Development Report on Gender equality to highlight the power struggles behind the production of gender knowledge at the Bank. As a founder and leading promoter of the "Gender Equality as Smart Economics" agenda, the World Bank has been at the forefront of a range of new gender policy approaches in development, not least in promoting the role of the private sector in Gender and Development governance.

A feminist critique of human capital theory demonstrates the effects of women's policy position in development: it highlights the way that particular gender essentialisms have granted women status as productive and altruistic drivers of development, while advancing the idea that they require interventions to harness their capacities and instil them with the appropriate skills for full market participation. In Chapter 4, I undertake a close textual analysis of the 2012 World Development Report to examine the frames through which women are granted economic agency in the document, and the kinds of interventions that are authorized to empower them. The WDR is the World Bank's flagship report; the 2012 report laid out the Bank's vision for the future of Gender and Development governance. Human capital theory is the conceptual framework that structures the 2012 WDR, and I employ a feminist critique of human capital to understand the economic logic at work in the report through the policies it prescribes to activate female potential. I demonstrate that the categories that the report relies on to understand productivity and market-compatibility produce important exclusions, rely on gendered tropes about supposedly intrinsic female behavior, and prescribe a range of tools to access women's entrepreneurial abilities and train them for full productivity.

Among the forms of economic agency that are highlighted in Smart Economics development discourses, adolescent girls and young women are especially visible as anti-poverty agents. They are especially celebrated for their status as investment opportunities, although they are also identified as risky subjects whose life choices can cement development achievements or compound development failures. As such, the supposed "discovery" of girls' power has generated a range of public policies, public-private partnerships, NGO campaigns, and corporate social responsibility projects that aim to empower girls. In Chapter 5, I examine four girl-power development campaigns that advance a narrative of girls as poverty-eradication solutions. I argue that girls' visibility through human capital theory has given rise to a new range of private sector development interventions that propose to reap financial rewards through investment in girls. These initiatives advance a vision of girls as future mothers and future workers whose productive potential must be reconciled with their reproductive capacities. As such, the kinds of development solutions proposed to harness the power of girls tend to reproduce familiar interventions designed to empower girls by raising their aspirations and activating their productive potential through skills training. Much of the emphasis on unlocking girl-power across the world reproduces familiar civilizational hierarchies that ask empowered, Western girls to pity and save girls across the global South. I show that Smart Economics authorizes a new visibility for girls as development agents, but does so through a familiar set of interventions to transform girls into entrepreneurial subjects.

The embrace of a human capital approach to gender has allowed girls and women to be understood as sites of investment and economic growth, because it has permitted their lives to be calculated in terms of investments in their capital and the ripple effect of its returns. This increased visibility of gender equality as a development issue has occurred alongside increased corporatization of development and growing power for private-sector partners. The growing expectation that leading firms will demonstrate their Corporate Social Responsibility, coupled with the Smart Economics push to demonstrate the value of investment in girls and women, has produced a new trend in development for public-private partnerships that focus on women's empowerment. In Chapter 6, I address this as a further implication of the human capital turn in Gender and Development. The equation of gender equality with profit, situated in the broader context of growing corporate power in development, has given rise to a new regime of private governance in Gender and Development. I address the implications of this turn through three initiatives that represent Corporate Social Responsibility, cause-related marketing, and Bottom of the Pyramid development. The kind of development agency accorded to girls in the Smart Economics agenda depends on the association of gender equality outcomes with economic growth and private profit; moreover, it does so through a critique of public development failures that provides private sector actors with increased authority to position themselves as leaders in Gender and Development. In a brief conclusion, I draw together the book's arguments and broader implications.

References

Aitken, Rob. 2010. "Ambiguous Incorporations: Microfinance and Global Governmentality." *Global Networks* 10(2): 223–243.

Babb, Sarah. 2013. "The Washington Consensus as Transnational Policy Paradigm: Its Origins, Trajectory and Likely Successor." *Review of International Political Economy* 20(2): 268–297.

Ballard, Richard. 2013. "Geographies of Development II: Cash Transfers and the Reinvention of Development for the Poor." *Progress in Human Geography* 37(6): 811–821.

Bedford, Kate. 2005. "Loving to Straighten Out Development: Sexuality and Ethnodevelopment in the World Bank's Ecuadorian Lending." *Feminist Legal Studies* 13(3): 295–322.

Bedford, Kate 2007. "The Imperative of Male Inclusion: How Institutional Context Influences World Bank Gender Policy." *International Feminist Journal of Politics* 9(3): 289–311.

Bedford, Kate 2009. *Developing Partnerships: Gender, Sexuality, and the Reformed World Bank.* Minneapolis, MN: University of Minnesota Press.

Bergeron, Suzanne. 2016. "Transgressing Gender and Development: Rethinking Economy Beyond 'Smart Economics.'" In *Social Sciences for an Other Politics*, edited by Ana Cecilia Dinerstein, 65–77. New York: Springer.

Bexell, Magdalena. 2012. "Global Governance, Gains and Gender: UN–Business Partnerships for Women's Empowerment." *International Feminist Journal of Politics* 14(3): 389–407.

Brigg, Morgan. 2001. "Empowering NGOs: The Microcredit Movement through Foucault's Notion of Dispositif." *Alternatives* 26: 233–258.

Brigg, Morgan 2002. "Post-Development, Foucault and the Colonisation Metaphor." *Third World Quarterly* 23(3): 421–436.

Chant, Sylvia. 2008. "The 'feminisation of Poverty' and the 'feminisation' of Anti-Poverty Programmes: Room for Revision?" *The Journal of Development Studies* 44(2): 165–197.

Chant, Sylvia. 2013. "The Long Shadow of 'smart Economics': The Making, Methodologies and Messages of the World Development Report 2012." In *The International Handbook on Gender, Migration and Transnationalism*, edited by Laura Oso and Natalia Ribas-Mateos, 97–126. Cheltenham: Edward Elgar.

Chant, Sylvia. 2016. "Galvanising Girl for Development? Critiquing the shift from 'smart' to 'smarter economics.'" *Progress in Development Studies.* 16(4): 314–328.

Chant, Sylvia, and Caroline Sweetman. 2012. "Fixing Women or Fixing the World? 'Smart Economics', Efficiency Approaches, and Gender Equality in Development." *Gender & Development* 20(3): 517–529.

Cooper, Melinda. 2017. *Family Values: Between Neoliberalism and the New Social Conservatism.* Cambridge, MA: MIT Press.

Cornwall, Andrea, and Althea-Maria Rivas. 2015. "From 'gender equality and women's empowerment' to Global Justice: Reclaiming a Transformative Agenda for Gender and Development." *Third World Quarterly* 36(2): 396–415.

Dauvergne, Peter, and Genevieve Lebaron. 2014. *Protest Inc.* Cambridge: Polity Press.

Deveaux, Monique. 1994. "Feminism and Empowerment: A Critical Reading of Foucault." *Feminist Studies* 20(2): 223–247.

Elias, Juanita. 2013. "Davos Woman to the Rescue of Global Capitalism: Postfeminist Politics and Competitiveness Promotion at the World Economic Forum." *International Political Sociology* 7(2): 152–169.

Evans, Alice. 2012. "World Development Report 2012: Radical Redistribution or Just Tinkering within the Template?" *Development* 55(1): 134–137.

Ferguson, Lucy. 2014. "This Is Our Gender Person." *International Feminist Journal of Politics* 17(3): 380–397.

Fine, Ben. 2001. "Neither the Washington nor the Post-Washington Consensus: An Introduction." In *Development Policy in the 21st Century: Beyond the Post-Washington Consensus*, edited by Ben Fine, Costas Lapavitsas, and Jonathan Pincus, 1–27. Abingdon: Routledge.

Flannery, Matt. 2007. "Kiva and the Birth of Person-to-Person Microfinance." *Innovations: Technology, Governance, Globalization* 2(1–2): 31–56.

Fleming, Peter. 2017. *The Death of Homo Economicus: Work, Debt and the Myth of Endless Accumulation*. London: Pluto Press.

Foucault, Michel. 1998. *The History of Sexuality: The Will to Knowledge: The Will to Knowledge Volume 1*. Translated by Robert Hurley. London: Penguin.

Griffin, Penny. 2007. "Sexing the Economy in a Neo-liberal World Order: Neo-liberal Discourse and the (Re) Production of Heteronormative Heterosexuality." *The British Journal of Politics & International Relations* 9(2): 220–238.

Griffin, Penny. 2009. *Gendering the World Bank: Neoliberalism and the Gendered Foundations of Global Governance*. Basingstoke: Palgrave Macmillan.

Griffin, Penny. 2010. "Gender, Governance and the Global Political Economy." *Australian Journal of International Affairs* 64(1): 86–104.

Harcourt, Wendy. 2012. "Review Essay: Beyond 'Smart Economics': The World Bank 2012 Report on Gender and Equality." *International Feminist Journal of Politics* 14(2): 307–312.

Hekman, Susan J. 2007. *Feminist Interpretations of Michel Foucault*. College Station, PA: Penn State Press.

Kunz, Rahel. 2012. *The Political Economy of Global Remittances: Gender, Governmentality and Neoliberalism*. Abingdon: Routledge.

McNay, Lois. 1992. *Foucault and Feminism: Power, Gender and the Self.* Oxford: John Wiley.

Miraftab, Faranak. 2004. "Making Neo-Liberal Governance: The Disempowering Work of Empowerment." *International Planning Studies* 9(4): 239–259.

Molyneux, Maxine. 2006. "Mothers at the Service of the New Poverty Agenda: Progresa/ Oportunidades, Mexico's Conditional Transfer Programme." *Social Policy & Administration* 40(4): 425–449.

Murphy, Michelle. 2017. *The Economization of Life*. Durham, NC: Duke University Press.

Oksala, Johanna. 2011. "The Neoliberal Subject of Feminism." *Journal of the British Society for Phenomenology* 42(1): 104–120.

Oksala, Johanna. 2013. "Feminism and Neoliberal Governmentality." *Foucault Studies* 16: 32–53.

Peterson, V.Spike. 2003. *A Critical Rewriting of Global Political Economy: Integrating Reproductive, Productive, and Virtual Economies.* Abingdon: Routledge.

Peterson, V. 2005. "How (the Meaning Of) Gender Matters in Political Economy." *New Political Economy* 10(4): 499–521.

Prügl, Elisabeth. 2017. "Neoliberalism with a Feminist Face: Crafting a New Hegemony at the World Bank." *Feminist Economics* 23(1): 30–53.

Prügl, Elisabeth, and Jacqui True. 2014. "Equality Means Business? Governing Gender through Transnational Public-Private Partnerships." *Review of International Political Economy* 21(6): 1137–1169.

Rankin, Katharine. 2001. "Governing Development: Neoliberalism, Microcredit, and Rational Economic Woman." *Economy and Society* 30(1): 18–37.

Repo, Jemima. 2015. *The Biopolitics of Gender.* Oxford: Oxford University Press.

Roberts, Adrienne. 2012. "Financial Crisis, Financial Firms… And Financial Feminism? The Rise of 'Transnational Business Feminism' and the Necessity of Marxist-Feminist IPE." *Socialist Studies/Études Socialistes* 8(2): 85–108.

Roberts, Adrienne. 2015a. "Gender, Financial Deepening and the Production of Embodied Finance: Towards a Critical Feminist Analysis." *Global Society* 29(1): 107–127.

Roberts, Adrienne. 2015b. "The Political Economy of 'Transnational Business Feminism.'" *International Feminist Journal of Politics* 17(2): 209–231.

Roberts, Adrienne, and Susanne Soederberg. 2012. "Gender Equality as Smart Economics? A Critique of the 2012 World Development Report." *Third World Quarterly* 33(5): 949–968.

Sato, Chizu. 2016. "Two Frontiers of Development?: A Transnational Feminist Analysis of Public-Private Partnerships for Women's Empowerment." *International Political Sociology* 10(2): 150–167.

Sawicki, Jana. 1991. *Disciplining Foucault: Feminism, Power, and the Body.* Abingdon: Routledge.

Shakya, Yogendra, and Katherine Rankin. 2008. "The Politics of Subversion in Development Practice: An Exploration of Microfinance in Nepal and Vietnam." *Journal of Development Studies* 44(8): 1214–1235.

Wilson, Kalpana. 2011. "'Race', Gender and Neoliberalism: Changing Visual Representations in Development." *Third World Quarterly* 32(2): 315–331.

1 Feminism, Neoliberalism, and Development

Introduction

Is feminism a victim of its own success? Has it been co-opted by conservative and neoliberal forces? This debate has been provoked by a profound sense of alienation from the kind of nominally "feminist" successes we see today in politics, economics, and culture. It is provoked by the worry that feminism has been taken up in service of some unrecognizable conservative agenda. It is driven by the perception that the language of feminism has been adopted to give legitimacy to a set of profoundly anti-feminist policies and people. These anxieties are encapsulated in the concept of empowerment: while empowerment once referred to a grassroots movement for collective political action through Consciousness Raising, today it provides products with a fuzzy feminist glow to appeal to female consumers. Journalist Andi Zeisler captures this ambivalence in her book *We Were Feminists Once*, in which she laments the rise of "market feminism" in pop culture and advertising:

> "Over the past two decades, a partial list of everything that has been deemed empowering by advertising campaigns, pop culture products, and feminist rhetoric includes the following: High heels. Flats. Cosmetic surgery. Embracing your wrinkles. Having children. Not having children. Natural childbirth. Having an epidural. Embracing fat positivity. Embracing anorexia. Housework. Living like a slob. Being butch. Being femme. Learning self-defence. Buying a gun. Driving a truck. Riding a motorcycle. Riding a bike. Walking. Running. Yoga. Pole dancing classes …"
>
> (2016: 169–170)

The coupling of supposedly "empowering" opposites here shows the ubiquity and meaninglessness of pseudo-feminist rhetoric in advertising, but it also signals wider tensions. It relates to much broader feminist debates and anxieties about co-optation, revolving around the question of the relationship between feminism and various conservative ideologies. Co-optation is a process in which the "initial meaning" of a concept is "transformed and used in the policy discourse for a different purpose than the original one," although the initial meaning is not rejected outright (Stratigaki 2004: 36). Anxieties about the co-optation of feminism are frequently revived by political discourses that purport to embrace feminism in service of economic neoliberalism, militarism, white supremacy, and beyond. Rhetorical appeals to gender equality have become a favourite tool for legitimizing various political projects, whether that means George W. Bush re-labelling American military interventions in the Middle East as battles for women's rights, or right wing, racist and anti-immigrant political forces claiming to defend women's rights by opposing the re-settlement of Muslim refugees. Central to this book is a similar ongoing debate about the re-purposing of feminist rhetoric to legitimize neoliberal economic policies in Gender and Development. This debate asks whether feminism has been employed as a rhetorical façade for a range of economic policies that have widened wealth inequality, entrenched gender inequalities, and reproduced neo-colonial power relations.

This chapter provides an introduction to the debates around feminism, neoliberalism, and co-optation in Gender and Development today, in order to lay out the conceptual framework for the remainder of the book. In doing so, it argues against the prevalent notion that feminism has been fully co-opted by neoliberalism: the chapter argues that the co-optation debate traps us in a circular mode of discussion, engaged in the futile task of trying to determine what is authentic feminism while ignoring some of the most important political and economic trends of the current era. It demonstrates that co-optation critiques have contributed essential criticisms of economic neoliberalism and convincingly shown us the way that pseudo-feminist rhetoric has been taken up in service of exploitative and harmful policy agendas. Yet, it shows that co-optation narratives have limited usefulness for understanding more complex dimensions of ideological neoliberalism, insofar as it aims to shape subjectivities and modes of conduct. The policy agenda of "Gender Equality as Smart Economics" that currently dominates the field of Gender and Development should not be understood as an example of feminist co-optation, but as a governance strategy that authorizes a range of interventions to govern girls and women. The chapter argues that we require a post-structural account of power and governance in order to understand how neoliberalism works through gender equality governance; to this end, it advocates for the use of Foucauldian conceptual tools in a feminist analysis of Gender and Development.

From "Women in Development" to "Gender Equality as Smart Economics"

Debates about feminism's co-optation are not new to the movement: before neoliberalism was the primary suspect, there was imperialism, capitalism, or statism. Debate about feminism's relationship to institutions and ideologies is an ever-present feature of its discourse. This is not a criticism of the movement, but a reflection of its position in broader social structures. The issue of feminism's relationship to other social structures has been at the center of decades-long debates: can we speak of women as a single group? Do women in the global South share more in common with the men in their own communities than they do with wealthy women in the global North? Can feminism claim to work as a singular movement or are women's interests too diverse? Feminism has always been constituted in relation to other institutions or movements, rather than sustaining itself as a fully-fledged movement linked only to female solidarity: it is "constantly vexed by its desire for the autonomous" (Grewal quoted in Roy 2017: 255). As such, is important to situate debates about feminism, neoliberalism, and development in a brief historical context. Although gender equality is the headlining feature in development discourse today, this has not always been the case. For decades, women were considered marginal actors in the development process, either as victims of "under-developed" cultures, passive recipients of aid, or vessels for overpopulation and its Malthusian consequences. The discursive process by which women have become visible actors in development spans decades and demonstrates the shifting (and overlapping) subject positions they have occupied: oppressed wife, dutiful mother, empowered entrepreneur. The shifting visibility of women in development discourses– and the process by which they moved from margin to center – provides essential context for understanding the salience of particular narratives that dominate in the current moment of the "Gender Equality as Smart Economics" agenda.

At its inception, the set of institutions, policies, and discourses that we know as international development were understood as a value-neutral, gender-neutral, and technical enterprise delivering economic expertise to countries in the global South. Within this enterprise, the concept of gender was seen as irrelevant, and women as marginal to development economics. Women were largely invisible to early development planners of the 1950s and 60s and, when made visible, discussed largely in passive, welfarist terms (Kabeer 1994). Representations of women were characterized by passivity and based in the assumption that while women could not contribute to growth, once growth was achieved, they too would progress along the trajectory of modernization towards a Western model of womanhood, thereby identifying gender oppression in outmoded and traditional forms of pre-development (Escobar 1995). Early development models, centered around relief work and "welfarism", primarily envisioned a role for women as the recipients of aid (Moser 1993; Rai 2002). These efforts focused on traditionally "feminine" areas closely related to the reproductive sphere (health, nutrition, family planning) with a focus on social welfare. Women first became visible as targets of development interventions in terms of their biological reproductivity. Beginning in the mid-1970s, international efforts to cut population growth through family planning acknowledged the centrality of women to any effective policy (Pietila and Vickers 1990; Joachim 2007). Efforts to curb population growth formed part of an overall economic growth strategy that identified a "conceptual link" between women, development, and economic growth

(Kabeer 1994: 4). The agency ascribed to women during this early phase of development interventions was heavily circumscribed as it was limited to their involvement in biological and social reproduction, and was therefore largely negative or preventative. This included violent and coercive interventions to curb women's fertility through enforced birth control or sterilization on women across the global South (Wilson 2012). Broadly, women's visibility in development discourses as instruments of biological reproduction prompted greater efforts to engage them for child and family welfare, though not in terms of women's own rights, choices, or capabilities.

Early feminist gains were consolidated during the 1970s, when feminist economists working in development institutions designed the Women in Development (WID) framework. The first generation of WID analysis began in 1970 with Esther Boserup's groundbreaking work *Women in Economic Development.* Boserup's study focused on the mechanisms by which women's productivity could be mobilized for more modernized and "productive" work than the typically feminine sectors to which they were confined: she argued that women's labor was generally underreported and therefore invisible to policy planners, drawing on a comparative analysis of women's agricultural work. WID marked an important turning point in the place that women occupied in development policy makers' minds and ushered in the (still dominant) emphasis on women as resources to be utilized for better development outcomes. Where once women had been understood as potential beneficiaries of development – but peripheral to the process itself – they were now conceptualized as an important and under-utilized resource whose integration was essential to the success of the development enterprise. WID advocates and practitioners strategically seized on efficiency arguments to advance their cause within gender-skeptic institutions (Tinker 1990). WID advocates created a powerful and influential liberal feminist paradigm that continues to influence development policy, not least because it was underpinned by the claim that women could improve the function of existing development models and institutions (Kabeer 1994; Razavi and Miller 1995; Rai 2002). WID frameworks, although introducing critical new analysis into development studies, operated largely within the development-as-economic growth paradigm that characterized the field. Women's development "problem" was identified as a lack of productive capacity within capitalism, rather than gendered capitalist relations that depended upon women's subordination.

For WID's critics, its modernization framework endorsed an unproblematic association between improvements in women's status and economic growth, without considering structural critique of harmful gendered implications of capitalism (Benería and Sen 1981; Jaquette 1990; Sen and Grown 1985). Women's status could not be transformed within a capitalist system, socialist feminists argued, because their subordination is so integral to the working of capitalist regimes of accumulation (Sen and Grown 1985; Benería and Sen 1981).

These critiques gave rise to a new iteration of the policy framework called Gender and Development (GAD), advocated by grassroots women's groups in the global South, which sought to introduce a more critical and relational approach. Central to GAD is the shift from a focus on women (and women's group interests) to gender, meaning both gender as a social construction and gender relations between men and women. Derived from socialist and Third World feminist perspectives, GAD contested the premise that women were excluded from development and should be integrated into its structures. Women's subordination, GAD proponents argued, is inbuilt and naturalized within capitalist growth models where unequal distribution of power makes substantive equality impossible. GAD cast a focus on the gendered division of labor within the household, differential access to and inequality within wage work, access to and control over resources, and the social status of men and women (Rai 2002: 71). It therefore sought to move beyond a focus on women's absolute status (i.e. access to paid work and the status accorded to that work) towards an appreciation of their relative state (i.e. social status in the household, work, and community) and the gendered structures that enabled and constrained transformation (Ibid.). In the short term, GAD sought to promote women's education, access to credit, and improved access to the legal system; in the long term it focused on transformative challenges to gender ideologies and institutions that reproduced subordination, embodied in dominant norms and structures of development governance (Parpart 1995).

The Gender and Development framework was itself subject to criticism, particularly in terms of its implementation in the form of Gender Mainstreaming inside institutions. Critiques of GAD comprise two main strands: the first reflects a debate among feminists about the relative merits of a woman or gender focus, given the difficulties of articulating a unified set of "women's interests" and the likelihood that introducing "gender" concerns will shift focus onto men. The second reflects ongoing concerns about rhetorical co-optation and the suspicion that, regardless of the specific terms employed, feminist language will be appropriated for other purposes (see Prügl 2009; Moser and Moser 2005; Rao and Kelleher 2005). Overall, feminist appraisal of GAD has recognized its potentially transformative elements but noted that it has largely been embraced in terminology but not in policy terms; instead of instituting a new development paradigm, GAD language has been used interchangeably with WID (Rai 2002: 73; see also Baden and Goetz 1997). "Gender" might have replaced "women," but familiar policy agendas persisted. Gender discourse has been, in many ways, "overtaken by its own success" as donors are eager to present their own gender sensitivity and gender focused programs, though this often results in the uptake of language that has been stripped of critical focus on power relations between groups (Porter and Verghese 1999: 132). The policy frameworks outlined here, the critiques levelled at them, and the debate between proponents of various approaches is by no means a historical debate confined to the literature. The themes outlined here continue to animate development policy and have enormous significance for feminist action.

The "Gender Equality as Smart Economics" policy agenda today represents the dominant iteration of Gender and Development in mainstream institutions. Broadly it, advances the case that the goal of gender equality should be embraced by development institutions because gender equality has beneficial economic results, like increased GDP and productivity. Gender equality, the story goes, is not only the right thing to do, but it is also the "smart thing". The political salience of the Smart Economics agenda can be directly attributed to the legacy of efficiency narratives that began in WID policy discourses. The WID-GAD debate still strongly resonates here because, although its two main positions were staked out years ago, they have been broadly institutionalized in powerful development and global governance institutions (WID) and feminist development and political economy research and activism (GAD). Smart Economics claims are underpinned by an efficiency rationale, rather than an equality rationale, although the intrinsic importance of gender equality is more frequently acknowledged than in the past. Much of this centers on arguing that women are uniquely suited to advance development goals. Where WID aimed to show the under-recognized economic potential of women to contribute to their local economies when given appropriate training, Smart Economics similarly advances the argument that women could be made more productive if their unpaid contributions were recognized (and better managed). Their role as mothers, for instance, is held up as a development good. Smart Economics proposes that we re-interpret women's role in development, holding up female values of care and cooperation as fundamental to development goals, rather than inimical to them (Bergeron 2016). Human capital theory plays a central role here, because it has provided an appealing cross-sector rationale for investment in women (discussed in Chapters 2–3). Just as WID sought to show that women were development agents, not passive recipients of development benefits, so too Smart Economics depends on the idea that women possess uniquely cooperative characters that can be translated into greater productivity. WID's legacy is clear here, and so too is the ongoing debate with GAD-oriented advocates who endorse a much more critical account of gender inequality in relation to neoliberal capitalism, rather than gender equality in service of capitalist goals.

The "Gender Equality as Smart Economics" agenda has emerged since the mid-1990s and is linked to an expanding range of international development and financial institutions, NGOs, and governments. Sylvia Chant attributes the origins of the Smart Economics agenda origins to the 1995 United Nations World Conference on Women in Beijing, where the language of the "pay-offs to investing in women" first crystallized (2012: 200). Since then, it has spread widely cross public and private sector discourses: for example, it is deployed by governments to highlight the returns on investment available to firms who empower women, global institutions advising investors to see women as an "untapped development resources" (UN Women 2011) and by private firms like Goldman Sachs whose "Womenomics" research assesses the economic gains of female employment. Box 1.1 demonstrates the widespread use of Smart Economics messages across public and governmental bodies, international financial institutions, corporations, and civil society organizations.

Box 1.1 "The Spread of Smart Economics"

"The business case for investing in [Millennium Development Goal 3 on gender equality] is strong – it is nothing more than smart economics."

(World Bank 2007: 145)

"Women may well be the dominant source of economic growth in the near future – and organizations that are able to capitalize on the roles women play as economic actors will most likely have a competitive advantage as the world pulls out of the global recession."

(Deloitte 2011)

"The [World Economic Forum Global Gender Gap] index continues to track the strong correlation between a country's gender gap and its national competitiveness. Because women account for one-half of a country's potential talent base, a nation's competitiveness in the long term depends significantly on whether and how it educates and utilizes its women."

(World Economic Forum 2013)

"When you lend to a woman you can set off an amazing chain reaction ... Invest in her potential. She will do the rest."

(Kiva n.d.)

"Investment in women has a multiplier effect... called Women Effect Investment. Notice I used the phrase 'invest in women' not donate to charities supporting women [sic]. Donating is important, but sometimes you want/need a financial return. Investing for both return and social good is called impact investing. You're getting a two-for: financial and social return."

(Stengel 2012, published in the "ForbesWoman" section of Forbes Magazine)

"Investing in women is smart economics, and investing in girls, catching them upstream, is even smarter economics. If you invest in girls, if you educate girls, if you get girls into jobs, you solve so many problems."

(Ngozi Okonjo Iweala, former Managing Director of the World Bank; World Bank 2009)

"We know that educating girls is the smartest investment of our time. When girls are educated, communities thrive and economies grow. Yet 66 million girls are missing from classrooms worldwide, and tremendous opportunities are lost."

(Girl Rising 2014)

As is evident in the samples above, the Smart Economics discourse is underpinned by a series of "clever conflations" of gender equality and neoliberal development (Chant 2013: 205). This tactic has long been employed in efforts to sell gender to economistic institutions by emphasizing gender equality as a win-win for development institutions and, presumably, women. Part of the reason that such emphasis on the *smart* decision of gender equality has been so effective is its strategic re-framing of gender issues: where once women were understood in development as recipients of welfare or philanthropy, Smart Economics re-imagines investment in women as the best business decision a firm or state could make. It therefore works to widen the constituencies for gender equality, with important implications for knowledge production and development authority in Gender and Development.

The co-optation blues

"Gender Equality as Smart Economics" is the dominant narrative currency for gender equality in global political and economic institutions today. Will Smart Economics advance feminist goals, or produce familiar policy solutions that do little to advance women's equality? Feminist literature on the topic is suffering from the "co-optation blues" (Smith 2006 quoted in de Jong and Kim 2017: 186) because it seems that apparent feminist successes are so routinely transformed into ambiguous or anti-feminist political realities. In development, this debate has often been framed in terms of the question of whether to engage with mainstream development or stay outside it. Can feminist change be achieved within mainstream institutions? Why and how has feminism been co-opted by neoliberalism?

This is a difficult question, and any attempt to answer it must start with an essential caveat: it depends on how we understand neoliberalism. Neoliberalism has a well-observed tendency to be employed broadly as a "one size fits all" diagnosis for every political, economic, or cultural malady; for this reason, it is essential to precisely specify what it means. Neoliberalism is variegated and can be defined in many different ways, often depending on disciplinary conventions. Here I approach neoliberalism as a concept with two dominant (and linked) interpretations: economic and ideological. As a set of economic policies, neoliberalism reflects a shift from state to market where welfare provision withdrawn and public serviced privatized. *Neo*liberalism, reflecting a new orientation to liberalism, comprises a set of economic principles that center around free-markets and de-regulation. In an ideological sense, neoliberalism reflects the expansion of market logic into all areas of life and governmental efforts align all individual and institutional behavior with market norms (Larner 2000). Although we can separate out economic and ideological forms of neoliberalism, in practice they are closely linked. Peck and Tickell provide a useful framework for understanding different forms of neoliberalism and the relationship between them, identifying two distinct forms of neoliberalism. Economic neoliberalism is the process Peck and Tickell label "roll-back neoliberalism", as it involves the roll back of state welfare provision (2002: 384). By contrast, ideological neoliberalism is a distinct phase termed "roll-out neoliberalism", characterized by the creation of new governance forms, including socially interventionist policies and the delegation of authority to non-governmental agents (Ibid.). Roll-back neoliberalism centers on the dismantling of the welfare state and destruction of collective social institutions, while roll-out neoliberalism involves the construction of neoliberal institutions and modes of governance. Against those who identify neoliberalism as being a project wholly focused on deregulation and institutional dismantling, Peck and Tickell show that ideological neoliberalism requires the active construction of institutions to bolster neoliberalism against crisis. This is achieved, for instance, through new forms of governance that take the social as their focal point: in urban governance, they point to the roll-out of new interventions to manage crime, immigration, policing, and welfare (Ibid.: 390). These two forms of roll-back and roll-out neoliberalism are conceptually linked, but also temporally linked in the sense that ideological neoliberalism is the successor to earlier forms of economic neoliberalism. The distinction between them provides a useful heuristic tool, rather than a clear-cut method for distinguishing two entirely distinct phenomena. Neoliberalism therefore includes both economic policy and ideological dimensions, both of which are relevant to a feminist critique of neoliberalism and its embrace of gender equality politics. The distinction between roll-back and roll-out neoliberalism can be mapped on to gendered economic governance, and has implications for debates about feminism's co-optation. I argue here that dominant narratives of co-optation provide a convincing explanation of feminism's role in roll-back neoliberalism, but do less to help us understand the relationship between feminism and roll-out neoliberalism.

The co-optation debate has many voices, but this chapter prioritizes a few of the most widely discussed and cited entries, centred on Nancy Fraser, Hester Eisenstein, and Angela McRobbie. Nancy Fraser has written perhaps the most influential account of feminism's co-optation by neoliberal capitalism. She identifies the crux of the problem as the "cultural turn" that feminism underwent in the 1990s, severing its links to Marxism and centering its analysis on cultural theory (2013: 159–60). At issue, she argues, is feminism's turn away from concrete politics of redistribution towards a cultural emphasis on politics of recognition and identity, which poses little concrete challenge to neoliberal capitalism. Fraser argues that the cultural turn has been key to feminism's co-option: by abandoning a Marxist critique and reducing feminism to a set of identity claims, it has "dovetailed all too neatly" with neoliberalism (Ibid.: 160). Recognition of identity claims can be granted without material change, and severing demands for recognition from demands for redistribution can serve the interests of the powerful. As such, Fraser argues that second-wave feminism reflected certain "elective affinities" with neoliberalism, which have allowed feminist critiques of the welfare state to be taken up and re-purposed in service of neoliberal state rollback. Neoliberalism, she explains:

> "… cloaks its depredations beneath an enchanting, charismatic veil: invoking the feminist critique of the family wage, it promises liberation through waged labor in the service of capital."
>
> (Fraser 2013: 240)

In particular, Fraser highlights the way certain feminist critiques have proven amenable to co-option by neoliberalism, over and above the claim that an emphasis on recognition has weakened feminism's political force. Feminist critiques of the welfare state, for example, embody this process. The critique of androcentric economic structures – the family wage and the male-breadwinner model – sought to properly value female labor and unpaid care. Instead, the second wave critique was interpreted (and adopted) in order to lament women's confinement to the home, valorize wage labor, and free up women to serve as a flexible labor source. The supposed emancipation of women through wage work has therefore served to invest labor flexibilization and state re-structuring with a "moral point" (Fraser 2009: 109–11). Similarly, feminist critique of the paternalistic welfare state has been embraced as part of a broader neoliberal project of state withdrawal that seeks to shrink the state's capacity and rollback social provision. The feminist critique of the welfare state is re-interpreted as a condemnation of state assistance and a call for women's emancipation from dependence through individual market participation (Ibid.: 111–112), with which neoliberal governments are only too happy to comply. As a result, Fraser argues, second-wave feminism was not attuned to the risks of neoliberalism, or to the possibility that its critique of the welfare state would lend such support to marketization. Feminism thus provided a new rationale for neoliberal capitalism, unwittingly endorsing the extension and intensification of marketization. Stripped of a class analysis that foregrounds unpaid labor, Fraser argues that the feminist pursuit of recognition has overshadowed its politics of redistribution, and thus turned feminism into its own "uncanny double" that legitimizes neoliberal economics in the name of individual liberty, agency, and difference (Ibid.: 114).

Co-optation accounts argue that feminism has been reduced to an individualistic conception of gender equality as women's full market participation and as such, it has been emptied of transformative potential. Furthermore, it is corrupted and re-purposed for exploitative ends. Hester Eisenstein argues, for example, that feminism has been "seduced" by "corporate leaders and elites" and that the movement has become irreparably fragmented in the process. Women have been incorporated into the economy but split into high-wage managers and low-wage, flexibilized, precarious workers which widens inequalities between them and creates obstacles to collective feminist action (2009; 2010). Eisenstein argues that the emphasis on the liberatory power of wage work, and on the goal of women's career success, has converged with employers' interests in exploiting female labor. This means that while some women enjoy career success in elite, well-paid positions, many more serve as a cheap labor force for global capital's race to the bottom. Capitalism has proved welcoming to women because it has allowed them the ability to earn income, become financially independent, and control their fertility, among other things; but it does so at the cost of the recognition of women's roles as wives or mothers (and therefore the economic roots of their subordination).

Eisenstein argues that this fragmentation is partly the result of the intersection of class, race, and gender inequalities: different feminist agendas developed on either side of this divide. White, middle-class women identified the oppressions of marriage and exclusion from the workplace as their most significant problem, and therefore welcomed the opportunity to enter professional jobs. Black women often did not have the choice *not to work* and therefore did not experience wage work as liberatory; moreover, they identified the most important struggles as those against racism and for education, housing and healthcare (Eisenstein 2010: 416–9). The kinds of opportunities afforded to women by business leaders and elites allowed a narrow demographic of women to achieve professional success and cultural status. Corporate feminism is well and good for elite, white women in the global North. However, fragmentation produces difference, and the flip side to the (exceptional) female CEO or President is the marginalized woman working in a garment factory in the global South, in dire conditions and poor wages. A popular "pseudo-feminist ideology" has served to erase the role of institutions in development and posit, in its place, the power of individual girls and women to access education and work so they can transform their societies (Eisenstein 2015). This amounts to what she calls "sweatshop feminism", because it is so committed to the idea that wage work liberates, it welcomes the severe exploitation of women's labor by global capital (Eisenstein 2017; Berik 2017). From this perspective, the process of co-optation has proceeded with the full cooperation of elite, white women in the global North who benefit from these forms of exploitation that they have re-branded as empowering.

Accounts of feminism's co-optation are not limited to political economy analysis of the state and labor; theorists of culture and media also identify the co-optation of feminism as a pernicious cultural discourse to valorize individualism and inequality. Angela McRobbie introduces a cultural studies approach to this question, theorizing an era of post-feminist politics in which particular forms of "faux-feminism" are permitted, but separated from feminist calls to political action. Post-feminism describes a prevailing cultural discourse in which feminism is understood to have achieved success, giving women access to specific forms of economic and sexual "empowerment", and is therefore no longer relevant as a political movement (2009). McRobbie's account of co-optation, like those discussed above, stresses that post-feminism works to transform structural issues into individual, apolitical problems with private solutions. In 2009, McRobbie observed numerous ways in which feminism as a political movement was "fiercely repudiated, indeed almost hated" (2009: 12), although more recently she has noted feminism's "unexpected rehabilitation" in the form of a "symbiotic relationship" between neoliberalism and liberal feminism (2013: 120). This rehabilitation has moved the terrain from post-feminism to neoliberal feminism in service of capitalism. If post-feminism was premised on allowing women access to a conservative form of empowerment as consumers and entrepreneurs, the new neoliberal feminism is premised upon cementing and celebrating the gains of middle class women exclusively. Although once thoroughly repudiated, feminism has recently been re-animated through its "articulation with a specific range of values" associated with white, middle-class motherhood (McRobbie 2013: 120). As with so many recent accounts of neoliberal feminism, Facebook CEO Sheryl Sandberg serves as the quintessential example. Sandberg's best-selling book *Lean In* typifies the tropes of neoliberal feminism, as McRobbie sees it, because the kind of feminism Sandberg endorses is predicated on the idea that what women need is to excel in their careers and in motherhood, by managing and transforming themselves (see also Rottenberg 2013; 2016). These insights from cultural and media studies speak to current trends in development too, because the elite, managerial feminisms McRobbie identifies in American culture characterize an emergent trend of "Transnational Business Feminisms" (Roberts 2015; see Prügl 2015) that spans national governments, international institutions, and global business elites. Such projects increasingly link Euro-American corporate culture and its elite feminisms to development governance in promotion of women's empowerment.

Here, co-optation critiques highlight the easy compatibility between certain feminist themes and roll-back neoliberalism. The idea of co-optation demonstrates the fragmentation and re-definition of feminism that has allowed for its embrace by the right wing. Feminist criticism of welfare-state paternalism has converged with right wing critique of the "nanny state" and therefore colluded in the roll-back of state provision altogether, or to replace state provision with piecemeal funding through non-governmental organizations. With regard to the global South, Eisenstein identifies a different rhetorical guise for the same process: structural adjustment imposed by global financial institutions has mandated a development trajectory that does not replicate the development of industrialized countries during the twentieth century (which created the welfare state). Instead, the kind of so-called development imposed is neoliberal state-restructuring and austerity which harms women and children the most (Eisenstein 2010: 421). Women in these countries are offered access to low-paid, highly exploitative jobs in special economic zones where they comprise a cheap workforce for global capital. Most significantly, these kinds of reforms are undertaken in the name of gender equality, because development rhetoric has come to represent the exploitation of women's labor, as a "substitute for state-led economic development" in the global South (Ibid.: 422). Such programs of state roll-back disguise themselves as projects of empowerment to unleash the talents of the world's poor women. The critics of feminism's co-optation plainly demonstrate how, across the world, the deleterious effects of neoliberal social and economic policies are dressed up in the language of freeing women from the shackles of state over-regulation.

The above accounts of co-optation are convincing at one level, because they capture the alienation from feminism that comes from seeing it re-purposed to give support to neoliberalism. They capture the frustration at seeing the political substance of feminism cut away, leaving a fuzzy set of buzzwords that are then used to endorse precisely the opposite of the social justice vision that feminists envision. The "uncanny double" of feminism not only presents an individualized account of elite female career success as feminist victory, but also gives ideological support to a particular worldview and program of neoliberal politico-economic reform. It demonstrates the ease with which profoundly anti-feminist policy can be genuinely positioned as brave, forward thinking, consensus-challenging feminism: feminism re-born as a flexible and business-friendly vision of women working harder, longer, and for less. The strength of the co-optation accounts is their ability to capture this dynamic, and thereby illuminate the ways in which feminism has been selectively appropriated by capitalism. In particular, they account for the way that feminism has given legitimacy – and indeed, a vague flavor of "empowerment" – to a particular vision of state, society, and market. They are especially adept at demonstrating how feminism has been taken up in service of the process of roll-back neoliberalism, constituted by the twin projects of marketization and deregulation, which aimed to dismantle the Keynesian-welfare state since the early 1970s. The move to rollback the state emerged from a context of perceived over-regulation, where political forces advocating withdrawal of the state could position themselves as radical reformers. The neoliberal narrative promised to restore freedom and self-governance, with a substantial emphasis on asserting "individualized 'opportunity rights' over social entitlements" (Peck and Tickell 2002: 388). This reformulation of state withdrawal as freedom from control is a familiar narrative trope of corporate, neoliberal feminism in which access to opportunities (for the privileged few) comes to occupy more focus than basic provision (for the many). Moreover, the co-optation account demonstrates how the equation of wage labor with empowerment provides a useful tool for business owners and political leaders who sought to promote a libertarian ideal of market participation in place of citizenship rights. In the words of Silvia Federici:

> "There is hardly a politician who dares not to profess eternal devotion to women's rights, and wisely so, since what they have in mind is our 'right to work', for our cheap labor is a cornucopia for the system."
>
> (2012: 62)

Is there feminist life after co-optation?

A few significant areas of concern emerge from the co-optation accounts of feminism and neoliberalism. First, there are problems in the relationship articulated between feminism and neoliberalism. Was the co-optation unwitting? The most influential co-optation accounts often assign partial blame to feminists themselves, who were too naïve to realize their gift to capitalism. Narratives of feminist co-optation often rely on gendered and sexualized imagery of "seduction" by capitalist elites and ideologies (Zalewski and Runyan 2013). However, by insisting that either naïveté or complicity enabled co-optation of feminist principles, we might obscure the possibility of diversity and dissent within the movement, erasing the efforts of liberal feminists and others deliberately working within institutions to effect incremental change. Certainly, to discount the possibility of strategic feminist narratives which position feminist aims *alongside* and *in promotion of* pre-existing institutional goals risks ignoring the substantial impact of feminists in national and global governance institutions (see Miller and Razavi 1998; Rai 2002). Feminist action on public policy can build successful alliances and exert power over strategies, funding, and discourses; the potential for success in this area is evidenced by the work of feminist bureaucrats ("femocrats") who have used power in women's agencies to make important gains (Kantola and Squires 2012). Feminists engaged with public policy can and do take advantage of openings to craft strategic approaches to gender equality, though they inevitably do so in the dominant language of mainstream institutions. This process has been ever-present in Gender and Development. The debate about how to avoid co-optation deflects attention away from the essential question of whether feminists can afford *not to* engage with mainstream institutions (True 2003). Nor is it a simple matter of seeking out "authentic" Southern feminist voices to contest co-opted versions of feminism: processes of professionalization and institutional integration serve to elevate the priorities of elite women in the global South and marginalize the voices of the poorest. The process of professionalization, integration, or co-optation must be read in relation to the numerous forms of difference and inequality that create fissures *within* the category of women (Narayanaswamy 2016; Jad 2004; Alvarez 1999). The equation of institutional participation with co-optation or corruption of feminism imagines forms of authentic, uncorrupted radicalism that do not exist, and are not desirable in the movement, and effectively marks a refusal to engage in centers of policy power.

The second concern addresses the way that accounts of feminism's co-optation presuppose an ideologically purer feminism in a stage before co-optation. This concern is magnified by the tendency to romanticize particular aspects of the feminist movement of earlier eras, or to generalize about what the movement *used to mean* before its entanglement with neoliberalism. If co-optation consists of the transformation of a concept's original meaning, what was the original meaning of feminism which serves as a referent object for analyzing newer, neoliberal versions? Fraser's account in particular risks generalizing about second-wave feminism in such a way that elevates the role of socialist feminists and ignores the prominence of liberal feminists, who sought to change the state but not to dismantle it. Second-wave feminists prioritized many political issues – including equal pay, anti-discrimination, abortion and domestic violence – but the policy changes they advocated were not always incompatible with capitalism (Funk 2013). The wave metaphor itself is contested and problematic in many ways, not least because no "wave" of feminism is monolithic: no matter how we conceptually periodize the movement, divergent ideologies and tactics are always a feature of feminist diversity (Evans 2015). The tendency to over-generalize about the second wave and to assign socialist feminism a defining role therein is a problem for Fraser's account. It requires us to imagine second-wave feminism as a unified, static body of thought that coalesced around a critique of capitalism, until this critique was undermined by the infiltration of post-structuralist feminism and the turn towards identity politics.

The tendency to romanticize past periods of the feminist movement and to imagine the current moment as less radical is an important feature of co-optation narratives. It is especially observable in the longstanding debates between modernist and post-modernist feminisms. In their accounts of co-optation, both Fraser and Eisenstein both lay part of the blame for this co-optation of feminism on the post-structural turn. Post-structuralism, and the turn to identity, has supposedly allowed claims for recognition of difference to overtake claims about egalitarian distribution of resources (Fraser 2013; see also Walby 2011). These critics argue that post-structuralism has emptied feminism of its political content by eroding the basis for a critique of the economic position of women: in other words, the effort to de-construct gender (rather than emphasize gender difference) has also served to undermine feminist politics. Here they echo a familiar modernist feminist claim that post-structuralist feminists have deconstructed the subject so far that there is no basis from which to make political claims or launch political action (Zalewski 2000; Oksala 2013). This points back to the concern that feminists who sought recognition for ever-narrower slices of identity conceded their political ground, destroying the possibility of collective movements by legitimizing inequalities on the basis of identity politics. Such feminist critiques are often couched in terms of "loss", wherein contemporary feminism is imagined as "co-opted, overly professionalized, and [lacking] political practice" (Hemmings 2011: 64). In particular, critiques which lament the post-1990s turn to theory rely on a memory of the 1970s and 80s as more radical, active, and less entangled with power, in comparison to today's technocratic mainstreamed governance feminism (Ibid.: 65). Yet, these narratives should give us pause, not least because they reinforce a notion of feminism unity that mischaracterizes a diverse movement and erase the exclusions that were a part of earlier feminisms.

Dominant co-optation narratives raise a third concern: might co-optation discourses be guilty of inflicting a form of feminist "disciplining violence" in drawing lines around particular theories, chronologies, and voices (Zalewski and Runyan 2013: 310)? One danger of generalizing or waxing nostalgic for the feminism of the 1970s and 1980s is to forget the kinds of exclusions that the second wave performed. Modernist feminist accounts which lament the post-modernist turn and its deconstruction of the subject fail to account for the way that the modernist subject had significant power to dictate whose experiences and whose bodies were the subject of feminist focus. To assign ideological purity to earlier incarnations of feminism is to risk forgetting feminism's own contested history. Feminists of colour long have pointed out the exclusionary effects of the conventional feminist subject, who is (implicitly) a middle-class, white woman in the global North (hooks 1984). Not only were women of colour often absent from the mainstream of feminist theorizing, but their experiences also challenged some of the central principles of feminist theory and highlighted the obstacles to sisterhood (Carby 1996). The narrative construction of radical, uncorrupted feminisms-past performs its own form of deliberate forgetting. As Inderpal Grewal suggests:

> "...the language of co-optation suggests a need for a pure subject of feminism, and a feminism beyond politics, or even a desire for an autonomous movement whose sole vector is gender. Given the long history of feminisms that were nationalist, racialized, classed or connected to particular institutions, the problem we face now is how to address neoliberalism as a problem without producing that pure, prior feminist subject."
>
> (Grewal quoted in Roy 2017: 255)

Acknowledging the problems of the co-optation narrative is not the same as endorsing some of the emergent manifestations of neoliberal feminism that work to advance neoliberal projects. Instead, it is to argue that the assessments of co-opted feminism are liable to over-generalize and smooth out debates and inequalities within the movement. Furthermore, it highlights some questions that cannot be answered by a condemnation of co-opted feminism and a call to "get back" to earlier, more radical forms. The co-optation account may present us with a sharp critique of roll-back neoliberalism, but its analytical purchase beyond that point is somewhat limited (Calkin 2015). Its critique of feminism, moreover, is limited: it serves mainly to set boundaries on "good" and "bad" feminism, and encouraging judgment about where different strategies, actors, or theories fall (Hemmings 2011: 139–140). The continual debate about "to what extent X is feminist" is a severely limiting one that risks re-producing exclusions. Judging the authenticity of various feminisms requires a set of clear boundaries that demarcate feminism from its co-opted doppelganger: who has the authority to draw such boundaries?

A response through post-structuralism

Undoubtedly, the appropriation of feminist language provides a key ingredient to legitimize neoliberal development policies; however, understanding this process through the framework of feminism's co-optation is analytically limited. It is not just that neoliberalism deploys feminist language as a legitimizing tool, or that it promotes women's wage work as a key driver of economic growth. Development governance today involves a more substantial transformation of the role of girls and women in development that promotes a range of interventions to shape, train, and control girls and women so that they can end poverty and develop themselves. This recognition actually prompts a series of much thornier questions. In some ways, the co-optation account is too simplistic: it invites a rejection of any forms of feminism which are diagnosed as "faux" or "neoliberal" feminism. It obscures a discussion of the new iterations of liberal (or perhaps market liberal) feminism that are emergent today. To declare these feminisms are merely co-opted, corrupted remnants of feminism truncates our analysis in many ways, and is not equal to the challenge of the current moment. The visibility of girls and women in global development presents unique dilemma for feminists: the global (rhetorical) consensus around a vague notion of gender equality represents both successes and failures of the feminist movement. Assessment of the current gender and development regime must take these contradictions into account, avoiding the tendency to smooth out the complexities with declarations of co-optation and faux feminism at work.

The critique of feminism's co-optation by neoliberalism presents an incisive account of roll-back neoliberalism which clearly implicates the appropriation of feminist rhetoric in legitimizing state withdrawal, structural adjustment, and the roll-back of social provision; however, it starts from an understanding of neoliberalism which is too limited. Conceptually, the linked projects of roll-back and roll-out neoliberalism capture the distinct version of neoliberalism that have emerged across time and enacted different visions of neoliberal governance. Existing critiques of co-opted feminism explain dimensions of roll-out neoliberal re-structuring, but fail to account for dimensions of roll-out neoliberalism that characterize much of the gender and development landscape today. As the co-optation accounts convincingly demonstrate, feminist language has given economic neoliberalism an "empowering" gloss and allowed it to re-frame a variety of destructive economic policies as pathways to full gender equality. Various aspects of austerity, withdrawal of social provision, de-regulation and liberalization are presented to the public as free-market solutions to usher in women's economic empowerment. Roll-back neoliberalism has acquired a measure of legitimacy through its association with a neoliberal feminist ideology that conflates market access with gender equality. Yet, there is much more to the story. It's not only the case that roll-back neoliberalism has deployed feminist language as a tool of legitimacy. It is also essential to recognize that roll-out neoliberalism uses gender equality as a tool of governance in the current discourse and policy agenda of Gender and Development.

Roll-back neoliberalism has been superseded by roll-out neoliberalism, which refers to both a new temporal phase of neoliberalism and a shift in its governing rationale. Roll-out neoliberalism is not focused exclusively on the extension of market and market logic: it encompasses a new push to re-regulate, discipline, and exert control over populations through social interventions (Peck and Tickell 2002: 389). It is characterized by a focus on building new institutions, designating new sources of governmental authority, designing new interventions to deliver policies, and fostering "new subjectivities" (Ibid.: 389–90). It signals a shift away from efforts to shrink the state and roll-back provision, replacing that approach with ever more interventions to govern numerous aspects of life. In development studies terms, we can see many of these changes in the shift from Washington Consensus to the post-Washington Consensus era that placed a greater emphasis on the role of the social, the role of the state, and the potentially harmful effects of rapidly implementing austere structural adjustment reforms (see Chapter 3). The current regime of Gender and Development governance can best be understood as a regime of roll-out neoliberalism, because its overriding emphasis is on shaping girls and women into entrepreneurial subjects who will conduct themselves as self-governing and productive agents in the marketplace. Its interventions are aimed primarily at developing women's capacities to govern themselves without state intervention or provision, such that they can operate in a context of economic neoliberalism. Its background context is characterized by a renewed emphasis on the social components of economic development, a larger role for the state in social policy, and the recognition that economic reforms alone will not bring about gender equality without wider institutional change. The range of development interventions of the "Gender Equality as Smart Economics" agenda, which will be discussed in detail throughout the book, constitute a range of roll-out interventions delivered by the state and new non-governmental authorities.

I argue that co-optation accounts are limited because they miss out on key features of roll-out neoliberalism: to this end, what can post-structuralism offer us in studying this endeavour? A feminist post-structural analysis of development and political economy starts from an interest in the "gendered norms and identities" that form part of the discursive production of global governance (Elias 2011: 108). It asks us to examine not only the gendered implications of particular policies, but illuminates the way that gender acts as a constitutive and "governing code" in the global political economy (Peterson 2003; Griffin 2009). This approach offers two key advantages. First, a post-structural approach to the subject yields new insight into contemporary forms of gender and development governance. Women – who occupy the role of global anti-poverty protagonist in a neoliberal fairy tale – are not easily identifiable as a single group with a shared set of interests. Lines of race, class, religion, sexuality, ability, and so on fracture this group and position many women across significant socio-political cleavages. More importantly, the figure of "woman" who animates development discourse is not contiguous with the feminist subject of woman: the global woman is a construct of development discourse and should be understood as such. She is a figment who stands for the "visible poor" of the global South whose life is familiar in the global North via her mediation by development and philanthropic organizations whose audio, visual, and textual materials surround us (Roy 2010: 2). How did this figure come to animate development policies? What is smoothed, or elided, in the narratives that produce her? The task is then to investigate the construction of this subject, destabilize the power relations that are at work in its production, and interrogate the policies that are proposed on behalf of the global woman.

Second, the understanding of power and the subject here is too limited. Two of the most influential accounts of co-optation – from Fraser and Eisenstein – both lament the influence of post-structuralism in allowing for feminism's co-optation. Fraser argues that emphasis on recognition of difference eroded the ground for redistributive claims; Eisenstein agrees that by abandoning a Marxist critique, feminism became fragmented into de-politicized post-structural and capitalist strands. Here they echo familiar critiques of post-structural feminism that reflect anxieties that the de-construction of the subject will decimate the potential for political gains. Against this, I argue that post-structuralism has an important contribution to make in advancing our understanding of the current state of gender and development. In order to understand the way that the figure of the "woman" functions in development discourse, we must see power as not only repressive, but also generative of particular social relationships and forms of embodied practice (Griffin 2011). The power relationships that structure Gender and Development governance not only operate in a repressive function, to punish and control women, but also operate in important generative ways to produce particular subjects. A Foucauldian approach to power demonstrates that it functions as a "productive network which runs through the whole social body", over and above a negative, repressive force (1980: 118–9). Emphasis on girls and women does not simply provide rhetorical cover to a pre-existing policy agenda; instead, girls and women animate provide a new spirit to a set of development interventions. The call to "tap" the resources of women and girls translates into a development agenda designed to cultivate their entrepreneurship and neoliberal forms of economic agency. Women occupy the central position of the "ideal neoliberal subject" whose economic agency can revive post-crisis capitalism (Elias 2013: 153), but they acquire this visibility in development through a set of categories that purport to identify and train appropriate subjects. A post-structural account of this process asks us to consider the interventions and technologies of power that are enacted upon women to *actively produce* these neoliberal subjects. We cannot start from a position of assuming that there is a singular "woman" subject upon whom development interventions act, nor can we assess her without understanding the way that she is produced by powerful development discourses.

Foucault's work is useful in this endeavor because it presents a critique of neoliberalism that helps us to understand its short-term political implications and longer term conceptual and paradigmatic implications. His critique of neoliberalism is both specific – addressing the problem of neoliberalism's tendency to signify every possible socio-economic problem – and general – providing a way to imagine neoliberalism that extends beyond the particularities of economic policy. At the core of this critique is the idea of neoliberalism as a governing rationality that produces neoliberal subjects who govern themselves according to its dictates (Foucault 2008). Furthermore, Foucault's account shows us how neoliberalism functions as a normative order and a mode of governing that subsumes all areas of society, even those previously imagined to lie outside the realm of "economy". In doing so, it extends "economic values, practices, and metrics" to all areas of human life and thus changes the logic according to which they operate (Brown 2015: 29). This conceptual framework places exclusive value on economic outcomes, where progressive political goals are subject to market calculations. The implicit understanding is that those progressive values that hinder economic goals will be sidelined. Under this logic, values of justice and equality are marginalized in favor of a complete economization of life. To see the implications of this paradigmatic shift, we need look no further than the "Gender Equality as Smart Economics" agenda introduced above. The claim that women are humans of equal moral worth, and deserving of full political, economic, and social status, is increasingly circumscribed within an economistic framework: gender equality can be recognized as a goal so long as it can be formulated as an economically productive one. Foucault's account of neoliberalism and its interventions to extend the realm of the market into social life also anticipates Peck and Tickell's account of roll-out neoliberalism, because both are based on the notion that neoliberalism produces more, not less, governance. The great irony of neoliberalism's vision of *homo economicus* (the rational economic man) is that this figure must be cultivated and governed in order to sustain this mode of economic self-governance; similarly, neoliberal governance insists on interventions to protect and cultivate markets and market subjects, rather than a wholly free-market approach. Similarly, as I demonstrate throughout this book, the figure of the idealized female entrepreneur is a figure who is "unleashed" through carefully cultivated interventions.

In practical terms, what insights does a post-structural feminist political economy account deliver? Micro-credit provides a useful example to illustrate this debate, and to emphasize the complexities of power/ knowledge at play in roll-out neoliberal development interventions. Micro-credit has been lauded as a "silver bullet" for development, specifically for women's empowerment, despite mixed evidence and sustained criticism (Kabeer 2005). Starting with grassroots NGOs, micro-credit has attracted enthusiasm from major donors and development institutions, becoming increasingly financialized (Roy 2012). Mainstream institutions' passion for micro-credit as a women's empowerment strategy has never been matched with sufficient evidence, however, and feminist literature has treated the topic with skepticism. Nancy Fraser, for instance, identifies micro-credit as a typical example of feminism's co-optation, where feminist critiques of the state were taken up in order to justify the dismantling of the welfare state. Fraser argues that micro-credit has been embraced as an answer to big-government, red-tape failure; employing a discourse of empowerment and grassroots mobilization, it has promised women economic power through enterprise, not entitlement. Such individual-level interventions, delivered by NGOs, have experienced a surge in popularity at the same time that the state has rolled-back its anti-poverty efforts (Fraser 2013: 221–222).

Fraser therefore sees micro-credit as a representative example of roll-back neoliberalism, where a co-opted, neoliberal version of feminism has been used to endorse state withdrawal from social provision and anti-poverty efforts. Her critique takes aim at the shift in scale: critique of state provision translated into enthusiasm for NGO service delivery, and critique of ineffective macro-scale poverty eradication translated into emphasis on individual entrepreneurs who can lift themselves out of poverty.

Yet, a rich body of feminist post-structural literature on micro-credit has provided a more trenchant critique of micro-credit as a technology of power in the Foucauldian sense. This is to say, it is not only that micro-credit envisions individual entrepreneurship as the key to poverty eradication, or that it provides ideological cover for state withdrawal. These are both true. But, more importantly, micro-credit schemes seek to train and transform the (female) borrower at a deeper level so that she functions as a self-governing, responsible entrepreneur whose relationship to the state will be fundamentally transformed. In doing so, it changes the nature of the state, re-structuring it around new forms of consumer citizenship that prioritize access to markets, not entitlements, and the responsibility of the entrepreneur to govern herself (Rankin 2001). Feminist Foucauldian analysis of micro-credit has highlighted the extent to which the schemes rely on interlocking mechanisms to discipline borrowers and coerce repayment. Solidarity borrowing groups, for instance, allow borrowers to access loans without physical asserts for collateral, but are also used to recover loan payments through social pressure (Rankin 2001; Brigg 2001; Lairap-Fonderson 2002). Microfinance schemes have been shown to govern women *through* their social network and existing structures of unequal gender relations, employing local norms of honor and shame to discipline borrowers (Karim 2008). In short, micro-credit not only works to rollback the state, but also constitutes the rolling-out of numerous interventions to shape, train, and inculcate new social subjects. Although microcredit has fallen out of favour in large parts of the development community (see Ghosh 2013), it has been replaced by a wide (and expanding) range of financialized interventions designed to empower women and catalyze their entrepreneurship. This is particularly evident in the wide array of public-private partnerships for gender equality and empowerment that are so popular on the development landscape today. Partnerships between development institutions, philanthropists, and corporations are at the forefront of on-the-ground implementation of the Smart Economics agenda, generally through projects directed at training girls and women in business skills and encouraging their entrepreneurship (see Chapter 6).

It is my contention that roll-out interventions characterize gender and development governance today. Rather than attempting to understand the relationship between feminism and neoliberalism in terms of co-optation, or by assessing the extent to which any particular policy/ institution/ actor is *truly* feminist, I argue that we should ask a different set of questions about power, subjectivity, and agency. We should ask questions about the generative aspects of Smart Economics interventions, not just the repressive dimensions of this trend in development governance. This approach moves us beyond the Marxist feminist critique and, in doing so, better captures the new spirit neoliberal development. As I have argued in this chapter, critiques of feminism's co-optation are limited in part because they imagine that gender equality works primarily as a rhetorical legitimizing device for pre-existing political agendas. Because they tend to imagine co-opted feminism as little more than a disguise for roll-back neoliberalism, they can miss the new power relations produced therein. Rather than seeing the relationship between feminism and neoliberalism as one of co-optation of feminism by neoliberalism, we should be attuned to the ways that neoliberalism works *through* gender. This is an approach developed by Foucauldian feminists, who advance a more nuanced account of power that highlights the ways that power operates through the social body: understanding gender as a biopolitical apparatus can point us to the complex range of political, economic and social forces through which it operates (Repo 2015: 164). Feminist engagement with Foucault has demonstrated the specifically gendered nature of this productive power whereby technologies of governmentality serve to produce gendered subjects of neoliberalism. The ability to see power as productive, rather than repressive, is a key insight that Foucauldian thought contributes: it tracks the shift from sovereign, repressive power to modern incarnations of disciplinary, productive power that shapes the conduct of subjects who internalize and reproduce this governing logic. Against critics like Fraser who fault post-structuralism for feminism's weakness, the Foucauldian feminist orientation demands that we see gender as "merely one of the most recent and intense nodal points of that play of power" (Ibid.). Moving beyond co-optation, a more complex picture of complicity and contestation emerges.

Conclusion

Feminism appears to have a case of the co-optation blues. Books, articles, editorials, and reports abound to detail the appropriation and corruption of feminist ideals by right-wing forces who seize upon them to give legitimacy to anti-feminist conservatism. Exploitative factory bosses and firms use the language of emancipation through income to justify poor work conditions and to stave off pressure to guarantee their workers minimum standards. Billionaire CEOs publish feminist-inflected career manuals for women that reduce a political movement to an individual's journey up the career ladder and into personal wealth. Feminists faced with this reality experience an understandable alienation from this feminist doppelganger. Has feminism become little more than a feel-good brand whose words and images can be appropriated by any interested party? Whose fault is it that feminism's political cache has been diluted in this way?

Feminist theorists, especially Marxist feminists, have developed incisive critiques of the co-optation of feminism by neoliberalism and highlighted the numerous ways that alignment between feminist political goals and neoliberal economic policies have produced harmful policy outcomes. This critique is most notable for its savvy analysis of the way that flexibilization and casualization of work (for the benefit of capital) has been undertaken in the name of freedom for women in the workforce and the dismantling of the welfare state has been given a façade of legitimacy in a similar fashion. Co-optation is a useful lens to understand some of these roll-back processes of neoliberal reform. However, I have argued that the debate about feminism's co-optation is flawed, because it closes off other avenues of investigation through a fixation on declaring various actors, institutions, projects, and trends "neoliberal" or "faux" feminist. The tendency to identify myriad forms of corrupted feminisms, which can then be dismissed as insufficiently radical, fails to advance the conversation about the relationship between feminism and neoliberalism.

This is not to say that we should take "empowerment" language at face value: indeed, the kinds of discourses and policies that Nancy Fraser and others critique are indeed incompatible with a feminist social justice project. Yet, I take issue with the tendency to lay the blame at the feet of feminist post-structuralism and the refusal to engage with potential insights that come from a post-structuralist feminist approach to these questions. Rather than a nihilistic deconstruction of the subject or political action, post-structuralism can open up new analytical ground for us by allowing for a more complex view of power and gender power relations. A Foucauldian feminist approach to these questions is essential: it provides new ways to understand the visibility of girls and women in development and the myriad development interventions proposed to access their productive power. It provides an improved set of conceptual tools to understand the Gender and Development landscape today, both because it provides a more nuanced account of contemporary neoliberalism and because it opens up space to map the gendered origins and effects of neoliberal discourses.

How, then, can we understand the current Smart Economics agenda and the spate of apparently feminist-informed policy discourses? Instead of understanding them merely as strategically calculated rhetoric, an alternative approach can shed more light on the way that development policymaking operationalized gender as a tool of the powerful. In this book, I argue that human capital theory provides the necessary entry point for this debate, because human capital theory has been essential to the current visibilities of girls and women in development. Human capital theory, although it originally emerged as a tool for labor economists in the mid twentieth century, has since gained enormous power as an intellectual movement in development studies. It has also transformed the way that girls and women are understood in relation to development processes. The following chapter introduces human capital theory's historical, intellectual, and current day context, particularly in relation to Gender and Development thinking.

References

Alvarez, Sonia. 1999. "Advocating Feminism: The Latin American Feminist NGO 'Boom.'" *International Feminist Journal of Politics* 1(2): 181–209.

Baden, Sally, and Anne Marie Goetz. 1997. "Who needs [sex] when you can have [gender]? Conflicting discourses on gender at Beijing." *Feminist Review* 56(1): 3–25.

Benería, Lourdes, and Gita Sen. 1981. "Accumulation, Reproduction, and 'Women's Role in Economic Development': Boserup Revisited." *Signs* 7(2): 279–298.

Bergeron, Suzanne. 2016. "Transgressing Gender and Development: Rethinking Economy Beyond 'Smart Economics.'" In *Social Sciences for an Other Politics*, edited by Ana Cecilia Dinerstein, 65–77. New York: Springer.

Berik, Günseli. 2017. "Revisiting the Feminist Debates on International Labor Standards in the Aftermath of Rana Plaza." *Studies in Comparative International Development* 52(2): 193–216.

Brigg, Morgan. 2001. "Empowering NGOs: The Microcredit Movement through Foucault's Notion of Dispositif." *Alternatives* 26: 233–258.

Brown, Wendy. 2015. *Undoing the Demos: Neoliberalism's Stealth Revolution*. Cambridge, MA: MIT Press.

Calkin, Sydney. 2015. "Feminism, Interrupted? Gender and Development in the Era of 'Smart Economics.'" *Progress in Development Studies* 15(4): 295–307.

Carby, Hazel. 1996. "White Woman Listen! Black Feminism and the Boundaries of Sisterhood." *Black British Cultural Studies: A Reader*, edited by Houston Baker, Jr., Stephen Best, Ruth Lindeborg, 61–86. Chicago, IL: University of Chicago Press.

Chant, Sylvia. 2012. "The Disappearing of 'Smart Economics'? The World Development Report 2012 on Gender Equality: Some Concerns about the Preparatory Process and the Prospects for Paradigm Change." *Global Social Policy* 12(2): 198–218.

Chant, Sylvia. 2013. "The Long Shadow of 'Smart Economics': The Making, Methodologies and Messages of the World Development Report 2012." In *The International Handbook on Gender, Migration and Transnationalism*, edited by Laura Oso and Natalia Ribas-Mateos, 97–126. Cheltenham: Edward Elgar.

De Jong, Sara, and Susanne Kim. 2017. "The Co-Optation Of Feminisms: A Research Agenda." *International Feminist Journal of Politics* 19(2): 185–200.

Deloitte. 2011. "The Gender Dividend: The Business Case for Investing in Women." Deloitte. http://www2.deloitte.com/content/dam/Deloitte/global/Documents/Public-Sector/dttl-ps-thegenderdividend-08082013.pdf.

Eisenstein, Hester. 2009. *Feminism Seduced: How Global Elites Use Women's Labor and Ideas to Exploit the World*. Boulder, CO: Paradigm Press.

Eisenstein, Hester 2010. "Feminism Seduced: Globalisation and the Uses of Gender." *Australian Feminist Studies* 25(66): 413–431.

Eisenstein, Hester 2017. "The Sweatshop Feminists." *Jacobin* (June 2015). http://jacobinmag.com/2015/06/kristof-globalization-development-third-world/.

Elias, Juanita. 2011. "Critical Feminist Scholarship and IPE." In *Critical International Political Economy: Dialogue, Debate and Dissensus*, edited by Stuart Shields, Ian Bruff, and Huw Macartney, 99–110. Basingstoke: Palgrave Macmillan.

Elias, Juanita 2013. "Davos Woman to the Rescue of Global Capitalism: Postfeminist Politics and Competitiveness Promotion at the World Economic Forum." *International Political Sociology* 7(2): 152–169.

Escobar, Arturo. 1995. *Encountering Development: The Making and Unmaking of the Third World*. Princeton, NJ: Princeton University Press.

Evans, Elizabeth. 2015. *The Politics of Third Wave Feminisms: Neoliberalism, Intersectionality, and the State in Britain and the US.* Basingstoke: Palgrave Macmillan.

Federici, Silvia. 2012. *Revolution at Point Zero: Housework, Reproduction, and Feminist Struggle.* London: PM Press.

Foucault, Michel. 2008. *The Birth of Biopolitics: Lectures at the Collège de France, 1978–1979*, translated by Graham Burchell. Basingstoke: Palgrave Macmillan.

Fraser, Nancy. 2009. "Feminism, Capitalism and the Cunning of History." *New Left Review* 56 (March/April): 97–117.

Fraser, Nancy. 2013. *Fortunes of Feminism: From State-Managed Capitalism to Neoliberal Crisis.* London: Verso Books.

Funk, Nanette. 2013. "Contra Fraser on Feminism and Neoliberalism." *Hypatia* 28(1): 179–196.

Ghosh, Jayati. 2013. "Microfinance and the Challenge of Financial Inclusion for Development." *Cambridge Journal of Economics* 37(6): 1203–1219.

Girl Rising. 2014. "Fuel the Movement." http://girlrising.com/grow-the-movement/.

Griffin, Penny. 2009. *Gendering the World Bank: Neoliberalism and the Gendered Foundations of Global Governance.* Basingstoke: Palgrave Macmillan.

Griffin, Penny. 2011. "Poststructualism In/ and IPE." In *Critical International Political Economy: Dialogue, Debate and Dissensus*, edited by Stuart Shields, Ian Bruff, and Huw Macartney, 43–55. Basingstoke: Palgrave Macmillan.

Hemmings, Clare. 2011. *Why Stories Matter: The Political Grammar of Feminist Theory.* Durham, NC: Duke University Press.

hooks, bell. 1984. *From Margin to Center.* Boston, MA: South End.

Jad, Islah. 2004. "The NGO-Isation of Arab Women's Movements." *IDS Bulletin* 35(4): 34–42.

Jaquette, Jane. 1990. "Gender and Justice in Economic Development." In *Persistent Inequalities: Women and World Development*, edited by Irene Tinker, 54–69. Oxford: Oxford University Press.

Joachim, Jutta. 2007. *Agenda Setting, the UN, and NGOs: Gender Violence and Reproductive Rights.* Washington, DC: Georgetown University Press.

Kabeer, Naila. 1994. *Reversed Realities: Gender Hierarchies in Development Thought.* London: Verso.

Kabeer, Naila. 2005. "Is Microfinance a 'Magic Bullet' for Women's Empowerment? Analysis of Findings from South Asia." *Economic and Political Weekly of India* 40(45): 4709–4718.

Kantola, Johanna, and Judith Squires. 2012. "From State Feminism to Market Feminism?" *International Political Science Review* 33(4): 382–400.

Karim, Lamia. 2008. "Demystifying Micro-Credit: The Grameen Bank, NGOs, and Neoliberalism in Bangladesh." *Cultural Dynamics* 20(1): 5–29.

Kiva. n.d. "Lend for Free to a Woman on Kiva!" www.kiva.org/women?utm_source=facebook.com&utm_medium=referrer&utm_campaign=fb-share-women.

Lairap-Fonderson, Josephine. 2002. "The Disciplinary Power of Micro Credit: Examples from Kenya and Cameroon." In *Rethinking Empowerment: Gender and Development in a Global/Local World*, edited by Shirin Rai and Kathleen Staudt Jane Parpart, 182–198. London: Routledge.

Larner, Wendy. 2000. "Neo-Liberalism: Policy, Ideology, Governmentality." *Studies in Political Economy* 63: 5–25.

McRobbie, Angela. 2009. *The Aftermath of Feminism: Gender, Culture and Social Change.* London: Sage.

McRobbie, Angela. 2013. "Feminism, the Family, and the New 'Mediated' Maternalism." *New Formations* 80–81: 119–137.

Miller, Carol, and Shahra Razavi, eds. 1998. *Missionaries and Mandarins: Feminist Engagement with Development Institutions.* London: United Nations Research Institute for Social Development.

Moser, Caroline. 1993. *Gender Planning and Development: Theory, Practice, and Training*. Abingdon: Routledge.

Moser, C. and A. Moser. 2005. "Gender mainstreaming since Beijing: a review of success and limitations in international institutions." *Gender & Development* 13(2): 11–22.

Narayanaswamy, Lata. 2016. "Whose Feminism Counts? Gender(ed) Knowledge and Professionalisation in Development." *Third World Quarterly* 37(12): 2156–2175.

Oksala, Johanna. 2013. "Feminism and Neoliberal Governmentality." *Foucault Studies* 16: 32–53.

Parpart, Jane L. 1995. "Deconstructing the Development 'Expert': Gender, Development, and 'Vulnerable' Groups." In *Feminism/postmodernism/development*, edited by M. Marchand and Jane Parpart, 221–243. Abingdon: Routledge.

Peck, Jamie, and Adam Tickell. 2002. "Neoliberalizing Space." *Antipode* 34(3): 380–404.

Peterson, Spike. 2003. *A Critical Rewriting of Global Political Economy: Integrating Reproductive, Productive, and Virtual Economies.* Abingdon: Routledge.

Pietilä, Hilkka, and Jeanne Vickers. 1990. *Making Women Matter: The Role of the United Nations.* London: Zed Books.

Porter, Fenella, and Valsa Verghese. 1999. *Feminists Doing Development: A Practical Critique*. London: Zed Books.

Prügl, Elisabeth. 2009. "Does gender mainstreaming work? Feminist engagements with the German agricultural state." *International Feminist Journal of Politics* 11(2): 174–195.

Prügl, Elisabeth 2015. "Neoliberalising Feminism." *New Political Economy* 20(4): 614–631.

Rai, Shirin. 2002. *Gender and the Political Economy of Development: From Nationalism to Globalization*. Oxford: John Wiley & Sons.

Rao, Aruna, and David Kelleher. 2005. "Is there life after gender mainstreaming?" *Gender & Development* 13(2): 57–69.

Rankin, Katharine. 2001. "Governing Development: Neoliberalism, Microcredit, and Rational Economic Woman." *Economy and Society* 30(1): 18–37.

Razavi, Shahra, and Carol Miller. 1995. "From WID to GAD: Conceptual Shifts in the Women and Development Discourse." Occasional Paper no. 1, Geneva: UNRISD. www.unrisd.org/80256B3C005BCCF9/(httpPublications)/D9C3FCA78D3DB32E80256B67005B6AB5.

Repo, Jemima. 2015. *The Biopolitics of Gender*. Oxford: Oxford University Press.

Roberts, Adrienne. 2015. "The Political Economy of 'Transnational Business Feminism.'" *International Feminist Journal of Politics* 17(2): 209–231.

Rottenberg, Catherine. 2013. "The Rise of Neoliberal Feminism." *Cultural Studies* 28(3): 418–437.

Rottenberg, Catherine. 2016. "Neoliberal Feminism and the Future of Human Capital." *Signs: Journal of Women in Culture and Society* 42(2): 329–348.

Roy, Ananya. 2010. *Poverty Capital: Microfinance and the Making of Development*. Abingdon: Routledge.

Roy, Ananya. 2012. “Ethical Subjects: Market Rule in an Age of Poverty.” *Public Culture* 24 (1 66): 105–108.

Roy, Srila. 2017. “The Positive Side of Co-Optation? Intersectionality: A Conversation between Inderpal Grewal and Srila Roy.” *International Feminist Journal of Politics* 19(2): 254–262.

Sen, Gita, and Caren Grown. 1985. *Development, Crises and Alternative Visions: Third World Women's Perspectives.* London: Earthscan.

Smith, Andrea. 2006. “Without Bureaucracy, Beyond Inclusion: Re-centering Feminism.” *New Left Turn* 20 (June–July): 66–69. www.leftturn.org/without-bureaucracy-beyond-inclusion-re-centering-feminism.

Stengel, Geri. 2012. “Smart Money Says Invest in Women.” *Forbes.* Online. www.forbes.com/sites/geristengel/2012/07/25/smart-money-says-invest-in-women/.

Stratigaki, Maria. 2004. “The Cooptation of Gender Concepts in EU Policies: The Case of ‘Reconciliation of Work and Family.’” *Social Politics: International Studies in Gender, State & Society* 11(1): 30–56.

Tinker, Irene. 1990. *Persistent Inequalities: Women and World Development.* Oxford: Oxford University Press.

True, Jacqui. 2003. “Mainstreaming Gender in Global Public Policy.” *International Feminist Journal of Politics* 5(3): 368–396.

UN Women. 2011. “The Gender Dividend: A Business Case for Gender Equality.” New York: UN Women. www.unwomen.org/en/digital-library/publications/2011/12/the-gender-dividend-a-business-case-for-gender-equality#sthash.Gx44wuwu.dpuf.

Walby, Sylvia. 2011. *The Future of Feminism.* Cambridge: Polity Press.

Wilson, Kalpana. 2012. *Race, Racism and Development: Interrogating History, Discourse and Practice.* London: Zed Books.

World Bank. 2007. “Global Monitoring Report 2007: Millennium Development Goals: Confronting the Challenges of Gender Equality and Fragile States.” Washington, DC: World Bank. http://go.worldbank.org/YG28BS8BG0.

World Bank. 2009. “The World Bank Launches Private-Public Initiative to Empower Adolescent Girls.” Press Release no. 2009/109/PREM. Washington, DC: World Bank. http://go.worldbank.org/83L2MOFND0.

World Economic Forum. 2013. *The Global Gender Gap Report 2013.* Geneva: World Economic Forum. www.weforum.org/reports/global-gender-gap-report-2013.

Zalewski, Marysia. 2000. *Feminism After Postmodernism?: Theorising Through Practice.* Abingdon: Routledge.

Zalewski, Marysia, and Anne Sisson Runyan. 2013. “Taking Feminist Violence Seriously in Feminist International Relations.” *International Feminist Journal of Politics* 15(3): 293–313.

Zeisler, Andi. 2016. *We Were Feminists Once: From Riot Grrrl to CoverGirl®, the Buying and Selling of a Political Movement.* London: Hachette UK.

2 A Feminist Critique of Human Capital Theory

Introduction

Gender equality is a "Smart Economic" solution, so the argument goes, because women represent a pool of labor, knowledge, and talent that is wasted in unequal societies. The argument goes in the other direction, too. We hear often that gender inequality is bad economic policy because it is costly to families, communities, and states. The Smart Economics agenda has not only introduced a popular vocabulary for discussing the economics of gender inequality, but it has made its logic of quantification mainstream. This process is evident in the recent efforts to quantify the public costs of violence against women. In a 2013 BBC editorial, World Bank managing director Caroline Anstey showcased the Bank's effort to quantify the harm of violence:

> "Apart from the obvious physical and emotional toll violence exacts on women and girls, [domestic violence] is destabilising and dehumanising for families and communities. There is also an economic cost to societies and countries that spirals out from that first punch inflicted on a woman or child… It is time now to seize the momentum and demonstrate that violence against women and girls is not only a human rights or public health issue, but an economic and development issue, slowing economic growth and undermining efforts to reduce poverty."
>
> (Anstey 2013)

Anstey argued it is necessary to "put a price tag" on "every punch, kick and rape" in order to generate public action on the issue (Ibid). This kind of quantification of violence against women reflects the broader infiltration of neoliberal economizing discourses into politics and the public sphere, where it is expected that every progressive value should not just be compatible with economic growth but should be a driver of growth (Brown 2015). Every social issue must now be articulated in these terms: domestic violence might be a human rights violation, but what are its costs to the taxpayer? This particular form of quantification is made possible through the embrace of human capital theory, which articulates the analytical link between health and overall economic productivity. In other words, it provides the tools to translate violence against women into the language of public accounts by connecting individual women's health to public expenditure and national economic growth. On the particular issue of quantifying the economic cost of domestic violence, the World Bank has been a leader: in a recent widely-cited paper commissioned by the World Bank, researchers draw on human capital theory to calculate the costs of intimate partner violence on women's human capital formation, which in turn translates into productivity, earnings, and overall economic growth (Raghavendra et al. 2013). This follows a 2009 report in which the Bank employed the metric of "Disability Adjusted Life Years" to calculate the effects of shortened life expectancy and thereby estimate the economic damage caused by violence against women (Skaperdas et al. 2009). Adding up the costs of medical care, costs of the police and justice systems, time lost on the job, and productivity losses, the Bank's findings shore up the Smart Economics narrative: we must act to end violence against women, because ignoring the issue is too costly. This approach is partly strategic, a World Bank staffer involved in this issue explains: economic institutions like the World Bank do not usually pay attention to violence against women, so feminists must be "opportunistic" and raise their issues in the institution's own language (quoted in Mason 2014: 437). Indeed, the strategic effort to render gender equality in the terms of mainstream development institutions is a theme that runs throughout the history of Gender and Development. The current phase of this process is encapsulated in the "Gender Equality as Smart Economics" agenda, whose conceptual substance is human capital theory. The idea of girls' and women's human capital animates Smart Economics because it provides a rubric through which their lives, bodies, and subjectivities can be calculated in economic terms. Women are now at the center of the discourse in development, because ideas about the unrecognized productivity and economic potential of women frame public understanding of development futures.

The previous chapter introduced the "Gender Equality as Smart Economics" agenda and demonstrated the widespread embrace of this policy discourse by mainstream institutions. It contextualized the Smart Economics agenda in relation to broader debates about co-optation: reductive narratives like Smart Economics provide girls and women with an unprecedented level of policy visibility, but at what cost? In this chapter, I argue that Smart Economics is underpinned by human capital theory, and that the re-conceptualization of girls and women through human capital theory has been fundamental to their position in policy today. I provide a feminist critique of human capital theory, drawing on Foucault's engagement with the topic, to show the conceptual and practical implications of this discourse. I argue that human capital theory has made girls and women legible as the most profitable and productive site for development interventions: it has permitted their recognition as development agents, but in such a way that prescribes their transformation into empowered entrepreneurs whose economic power can be harnessed in a global economy.

Such a critique demonstrates that human capital produces new specifically gendered subjectivities that encompass techniques of management and control of girls and women, through the contention that their essential and intrinsic qualities must be activated and cultivated for full economic participation. Girls and women are not only the public faces for a familiar set of roll-back neoliberal policies, but they animate a highly interventionist discourse of entrepreneurship and the empowered self.

From the Chicago School to the post-Washington Consensus

Human capital theory today functions as a popular framework employed by political elites and institutions across the ideological spectrum to make claims about the relationship between social and economic policy. It began in labor economics, as part of a broader effort by the economists of the Chicago School to understand non-market spheres through economic calculations. They sought to solve a few puzzles about the process of economic growth in relation to human and physical resources, when growth outstripped increases in the labor force or technological improvements (see Goldin 2016). What accounted for this growth? Human capital theorists argued that improvements in the composition of the labor force itself – its education and skill – accounted for such improvements (Schultz 1961). The main innovation of human capital theory was to extend the concept of capital from the physical to the human: where physical capital might include tools, land, machines, or other objects used in production, human capital theory includes the human in this framework. Through human capital theory, Chicago School economists – mostly notably Theodor Schultz, Jacob Mincer, and Gary Becker – sought to challenge economists' assumptions that labor was a "given" input in capitalism and could not be augmented. They theorized that labor could itself be a site for market logic to determine outcomes. In this way, humans could be understood as capital because changes to their capacities, such as investments in education, can have effects on them that improve their ability to earn income. This points to a major shift that human capital theory undertakes: it proposes that there is no separation between a human and her capital. In other words, it contests the classical economic notion that the laborer is different from her labor. Rather than selling her labor for a wage, human capital theory imagines that the laborer is earning income off her capital, whose value can be raised or lowered depending on the kinds of investments made therein. Investment in learning new skills might raise the value of one's human capital; chronic illness might lower it. As such, human capital theory introduced the analytical tools for quantifying the economic effects of any social phenomenon: the legacy of this conceptual framework is powerfully evident in the discussion of domestic violence that opens this chapter.

In essence, human capital theory makes the claim that policymakers should understand people as investors who, over the course of their life span, will invest in and profit from their capabilities, skills and attributes. It aims to understand people's personal time and resource allocations as investments in their future productivity, and for this reason, understands expenditure on training, education, or health as an investment rather than an act of consumption. Human capital theory sees the acquisition of skills and knowledge as investments in future earning potential: this includes an individual's investment in her own education, a firm's investment in its employee's skills, or a mother's investment of time in her children's development. Using market logic to theorize human behavior, human capital theorists argued that individuals could, on the basis of cost-benefit analysis, decide how much to invest in their health, education, training, and other inputs (Becker 1993). Although these investments might result in a short-term loss of income, they will result in a future reward in the form of higher long-term incomes (Becker 1976). In this way, the choices made by individuals over the course of the life cycle could factor into broader analysis of economies, by understanding inputs into human capital at a macro level. At first, human capital theorists focused primarily on "inputs" into human capital such as education, health, and job training. Subsequently, the scope of investments in human capital has been broadened to include a range of factors: innate factors like genetic background, contextual factors like social position of one's family, and lifestyle aspects like physical and psychological health. Human capital theorists sought to interpret health, marriage, childbearing, and beyond in terms of the calculations that the "human agent" makes to "protect the value of [his] capital" (Schultz 1981: 13). By extending the economist's tools into areas of life that had not been considered economic, human capital theory also furnished policymakers with the ability to map gender relations, family structures, and household economies onto the same grid of analysis.

Human capital theorists have long sought to employ human capital as an account of gender relations. This was partly made possible by its conceptual orientation to the household: rather than imagining the home as a non-market space where *homo economicus* sleeps at night before returning to the productive sphere, human capital theory created the possibility that the workings of the household could be understood in the same terms as the wider economy. To this end, human capital theory was used to develop an influential account of the family with Gary Becker's New Home Economics, which aimed to understand household-level decision-making in relation to human capital formation. Becker's work applied the economic models of the Chicago School to the family's division of labor and fertility choices.

Given women's lower earnings in the labor market, Becker argued, her decision to leave the workforce and invest her time in child-rearing made long-term financial sense (1976; 1981). By re-imagining time and resource expenditure as an investment in the future productivity and earning potential of children (and therefore the wellbeing of the family), the supposedly irrational time allocation of the family could be explained in terms of capital-building trade-off between short-term loss and long-term gain. Becker's use of human capital theory to theorize gender inequalities in market terms generated significant feminist critique for its application of economic logic to explain complex social norms and gendered power relations (see Jacobsen 1999). Feminist economists have highlighted the "preposterous conclusions" that resulted from Becker's analysis of the economics of the family, because his analysis provided economic modelling that justified (in apparently scientific terms) oppressive family institutions of patriarchal domination. Becker's explanation of the family and its gender division of labour/power assumes it is a "benign" institution populated by loving wives and dutiful husbands (see Bergmann 1996; Woolley 1996; Gardiner 1998). Feminist engagement with Becker has emphasized not only the limitations of his models and their assumptions about human behaviour, but also the political effects of his supposedly apolitical calculations.

Human capital theory, in its application to the family, proved widely influential in the study of labour and population economics. On the population question, an account of human capital formation in the family was used to understand decision-making and fertility, but not only the question of raising or lowering birth rates. They formulated it in terms of the question of quality versus quantity in reproduction, reformulating fundamental ideas in demography by adopting a view of reproduction as accumulation of human capital (Repo 2015). Becker famously argued that with limited resources, parents would have fewer children but invest more in their quality (i.e. productivity and future outputs) through investment in education, health, and leisure time (Becker 1960). For Becker, human capital theory demonstrated the need to roll back public investment in order to incentivize inter-generational investment within the family. The family would only properly invest in children, he argued, if they were required to do so through private credit markets rather than through state provision. Becker's account of the family demonstrates how human capital theory has been imbued from the start with a social conservatism that prioritizes traditional gender roles and patriarchal family structures (Cooper 2017). The application of human capital theory to fertility constituted a new framework for understanding reproductive decision-making, family formation, and gender relations that continues to heavily influence public policy.

Human capital theory emerged in the field of American labor economics, but quickly became a powerful intellectual tool in development planning. When economists first introduced human capital theory in the American context, they did so out of concern about rising costs of education and a shortage of particular skills among workers. The primary emphasis of early human capital theory was related to the costs and benefits of education on workers and implications for growth. At a broader level, human capital theorists argued that differentials in human productive capacity (caused by health and education, among other things) could account for major discrepancies in patterns of national economic growth (Schultz 1981). The interest in the impact of education (and other investments in human capital) on economic growth soon spilled over into the realm of development economics, where it worked to broaden ideas about the drivers and trajectory of economic growth (Arndt

1987). Beginning in the early 1960s, human capital theory was being discussed in development economics conferences and textbooks as a way to re-conceptualize development: rather than focus on wealth creation, it emphasized the capacity to create wealth (Ibid. 60). It was especially influential in the World Bank, which was an early adopter of the theory (Heyneman 2003; Obamba 2013). The theory helped to re-frame economic development questions in terms of skills shortages, technological advances, and the need to invest in technical ability (foreshadowing the preference for development investment in "capacity building").

In development policymaking, human capital theory has subsequently acquired a prominent role in relation to educational investments: after large-scale investment in infrastructure and engineering projects, development lenders identified a need for investment in the technical expertise to maintain such infrastructure. Where there was a lack of local capacity in engineering, development institutions saw a need for investment in physical capital to be matched within investment in *human capital* through education and training (Arndt 1987; Henyeman 2003). Its roots in economic theory made human capital especially suited to this task, because it could be used to translate educational outcomes into hard numbers that policymakers could compare. Human capital allowed for educational investments to be imagined as inputs into people's capacities, from which the rates of return on education could be calculated and compared; this methodology became widespread in the 1970s. This mode of analysis was used to determine, for instance, whether primary or higher education produced a better return on investment for development lenders (Obamba 2013). From its origins in technical training for engineers, a human capital-based rationale for education and methodology for measuring the impact of skills training expanded as a tool for understanding educational investments across the age spectrum and across sectors (Heyneman 2005). It also provided a framework for measuring the impact of education on girls, although they were excluded from the technical skills training: early development education initiative that included girls emphasized the need for "domestic science" skills for girls and theorized the possibility of calculating return on investment in such domestic education (Ibid). The difficulty of translating such domestic skills into economic data was, and remains today, an obstacle to conceptualizing girls as productive. However, the impact of education on girls could be measured through its effect on their fertility decisions and the health of their families (Ilon 1992: 147). Human capital theory provided an important conceptual link between girls, education, and development outcomes, further discussed in Chapter 3.

Human capital theory contributed to what Arturo Escobar (1995) would call the "scopic" regime of development: it brought into being new categories of development and underdevelopment that could be known through their quantification. Through the above methods of quantification, human capital theory helped to render educational investments into development data, so that the value of education could be justified in institutional terms (Klees

2016). When development economists could calculate the rate of return on education, using the tools of human capital theory, they could make its contribution visible and knowable. Human capital theory performed a function of raising visibility for educational issues in development, but also closed off strategic questions. The ability to render development interventions in terms of cost-benefits for economic growth made it attractive to mainstream institutions. On the issue of education, for example, human capital theory provided a rationale for investment linked to economic growth, without bringing in "broader social, cultural and political contexts" that institutions wished to avoid (Ilon 2002: 478). Human capital theory became an important tool in development policy because it performed an economizing function, as well as a de-politicizing function.

Although human capital theory has informed development economics since the 1960s, its ascendance to the status of key development policy discourse can be traced to the discursive and philosophical shift of the 1990s. At this time, the harmful effects of structural adjustment policy during the 1970s and 80s produced a strong backlash from civil society in the global South, which prompted a crisis in development thinking and ushered in efforts to re-imagine a development model that prioritized human wellbeing. This meant the embrace of a new language of "pro-poor" development, an emphasis on partnership rather than donor-recipient hierarchies, a greater role for the state in social protection, and an emphasis on poverty alleviation for the very poorest. This transformation is associated with the rise of Third Way politics in the 1990s, when the state was re-imagined as enabling an environment of private sector growth and non-governmental social provision (Surender 2013; Babb 2013). As a prominent conceptual feature of this policy trend, human capital theory achieved enormous popularity in development policy, promoting the linkage between investment in human capabilities and resources and economic growth, with particular influence on education debates (Mahon 2010). In the context of a political climate where "trickle down" models were under fierce criticism, human capital theory presented a model for development that suggested welfare and economic growth could be complementary, rather than incompatible (Hall 2007: 155). Investment in human capital today stands as a core consensus issue among mainstream development actors in part because it is seen as a politically agreeable middle ground, stopping short of radical proposals for redistribution: it carries the intellectual influence of a "neo-classical revival", in its assumptions about the efficiency of free markets and the harmful effects of too much state intervention in the process of human capital formation, although it also concedes the importance of basic needs provision to generate growth (Hunt 1989). Human capital theory achieved popularity as a rejection of structural adjustment models, although it represented more a reformulation than a total repudiation of this paradigm.

Human capital theory has had far reaching influence in development policy-making, although the theory is not and has never been monolithic. Its different variants have been debated since the 1960s, most tangibly captured in the disagreement between Theodor Schultz and Gary Becker on the question of funding. From its inception, one of the fiercest debates around human capital theory has been the question of who pays for human capital investments: the state, the family or the individual. If the dividends of human capital investments will accrue to the individual, should the state be responsible for making human capital investments? Schultz did not want to concede the role of the state in human capital investments, and so sought to demonstrate how public investment in health and education could impact workers and states. Meanwhile, the variant of human capital theory pioneered by Becker placed more emphasis on private investments by families in their member's human capital: Becker (and their colleague Milton Friedman) argued that because private individuals would reap the benefits of their human capital investments, the state should not subsidize those investments (Becker 1993; Fleming 2017b; Brockling 2011). Schultz's variant of the theory proved more influential in development economics, although not in terms of his defence of public spending. His mode of human capital analysis was attractive to development economists because he stressed the use of human capital theory to estimate the earnings of workers over their lifetime (and the costs needed to sustain that worker). By extension, this allowed for an estimation of national growth in terms of human capital variables (Heyneman 2005). Human capital's different strands have been taken up into development planning by charting a middle course between Schultz's case for public investment and Becker's call for private investment, in the context of this social investment paradigm that emphasizes public spending to bring the most vulnerable up to a minimum standard. Furthermore, this social investment discourse aims to pair public investment with private investment and hybrid forms of public-private provision to make human capital investments (Mahon 2010; Jenson 2010). Its call for recognition of, and investment in, human capital resources proved to be a powerful development discourse in the political context of the 1990s, and dovetailed with concern by mainstream development institutions to demonstrate their attention to gender in development.

Today, human capital theory has taken on a life of its own: much more than just a theoretical tool used by labor and development economists, it animates an "intellectual movement" that is widely influential among policymakers and governments (Fleming 2017a: 695). Human capital theory today forms a core theme of development policy and discourse across major development institutions. To name just a few: at the national level, the UK's Department for International Development assesses human capital as one key asset for sustainable development, alongside social, natural, physical and financial capital (Overseas Development Institute 2000). At the regional level, the Inter-American Development Bank, African Development Bank, and Asian Development Bank all have "human capital development" strategies (African Development Bank 2011; Asian Development Bank 2010; Inter-American Development Bank 2016). The Inter-American Development Bank identifies human capital as one of the main drivers of economic growth and therefore aims to "[help] policy-makers maximize their returns on investment" across the life cycle (Inter-American Development Bank 2016). At the global level, human capital has become a metric for assessing and comparing progress across states. In 2013, and subsequently in 2015–2016, the World Economic Forum published its first Human Capital Report, which aims to measure human capital and the factors that contribute to the development of a "healthy, educated, and productive labor force" (World Economic Forum 2016). The report included a Human Capital Index to rank countries in terms of their investment in the "capacity of the population to drive economic growth", using indicators to evaluate four categories: education, health and wellness, workforce and employment, and enabling environment (legal and physical infrastructure) (World Economic Forum 2013). It has since been updated and re-issued with more detailed data and interactive visualizations to track countries "maximize and leverage their human capital endowment" (World Economic Forum 2016). The logic of human capital embodies a few current trends in development policy planning: emphasis on the state as an enabler of growth, the need to improve national competitiveness, and the re-imagining of social inequalities as economic inefficiencies. Although its historical origins lie in American labor economics of the 1960s, human capital theory has taken on a much bigger role across the world and come to play a major role in development policymaking.

Decades of feminist work in mainstream political and economic institutions have sought to put gender issues on the agenda and contest widely held assumptions about the irrelevance of gender issues in public policy. Given the deeply embedded gender-skepticism of dominant development institutions, gender experts have long recognized the need to "sell" gender to policymakers by stressing the synergies between gender equality and economic growth. To this end, human capital has provided an institutionally salient language and proven a powerful tool for advocates to demonstrate the relevance of gender equality in mainstream development institutions. The re-conceptualization girls and women in human capital terms – as potentially productive economic agents who suffer from under-investment – has prompted a major shift in their visibility as development subjects. In development institutions, the human capital approach has proposed investment specifically in the most disadvantaged groups – girls, indigenous peoples, and the poorest – to allow them to take advantage of economic opportunities. Among these vulnerable groups, women and girls have been particularly targeted for human capital-building interventions: women because they are mothers who shaped the quality of future human capital and girls because they constitute "human capital in the making" (Mahon 2010: 178). Education is one site where human capital addressed gender issue directly, and provided a conceptual lens for gender issues in development (Fine and Rose 2003; Heyneman 2003). Because human capital theory stresses the connection between individual-level inputs (like schooling and training) and macro-level outcomes (like improved productivity and increased growth) it has allowed policymakers to see how educational investments in girls and women could translate into development outcomes. Accordingly, girls and women gained priority in development policies, and particularly in education policy, as ideal targets for interventions to develop their human capital.

Today, human capital theory informs the popular cross-sector discourse on girls and women that stresses their potential, given the right investment and interventions; it therefore forms the bedrock of the "Gender Equality as Smart Economics" discourse. The entire discourse is underpinned by the idea that girls are a site for investment, where resources invested today will produce enormous growth in the future (see Chant 2016; Murphy 2017). The notion that girls and women are "untapped" resources for growth argues that savvy investors can put in the funds now and reap the rewards in the future. Countries with low female labor force participation are frequently urged to develop strategies to better access and investment in women's human capital. Numerous projects and schemes, from across the public, private, and non-profit sectors, propose to empower girls and women in order to grow their human capital and contribute to national GDP (discussed in Chapters 4–6; see also Boyd 2016). Human capital is well and truly arrived as the animating force behind the "Smart Economics" discourse. Although human capital theory has been subject to feminist criticism, both as a specific economic theory and as a feature of the broader neoliberal orthodoxy, feminist economists' criticism has tended to focus on the empirical flaws that human capital models produce, because of the variables they ignore or the problematic assumptions they make (see Jacobsen 1999). A feminist and Foucauldian engagement with human capital theory introduces an alternative view of human capital's effects, pointing to the relationship between the kinds of economic agency it identifies and the modes of development intervention it prescribes.

Foucauldian and feminist engagements with human capital

The influence of human capital theory in policymaking has gained recognition in recent years, and has been the subject of critique by political economists and theorists who have demonstrated that human capital theory fundamentally underpins neoliberal governance as it is practiced today. These contributions have stressed the economizing effect of human capital theory and its implications for the way that life is quantified, calculated, and governed (Murphy 2017; Brown 2015). Feminists critics have pointed to human capital theory's role in shoring up conservative family and gender relations, because policymakers who embraced the theory in the American context tended to interpret it as a call for privatizing investment in education and re-entrenching care responsibility in the home (Cooper 2017). In relation to current labor trends, Fleming (2014; 2017b) traces the role of human capital theory in legitimating a new mode of labor governance that enabled the rise of the so-called "gig economy" of independent contractors who work on-demand. These works enrich our understanding of human capital theory because they lay bare its political implications on the practices of the state, the firm and the family. They demonstrate that human capital theory reformulates citizenship in market terms: rather than a citizen entitled to protections, the individual becomes a self-reliant market subject with the total freedom to invest in herself as she sees fit. The corollary is, of course, the failure to properly invest in herself will result in failure in the market and no social safety net to fall back on. These accounts demonstrate the logic of human capital theory that has gained mainstream traction: health, education, and training are welcomed as investment in the productivity of individuals, but as the benefits of these investments will accrue to individuals, the costs should be borne by individuals and families rather than the public. They signal the role of human capital in the promotion of ideology: rather than just functioning as a conceptual tool, human capital theory has taken on a life of its own with a political momentum that creates real life effects. These critiques illuminate the political effects of economization: in order to be legible as economically valuable, all aspects of life must be available for calculation, speculation, and financialization. The moral poverty of this economistic approach is clear, as is the effect on democratic norms and collective endeavours. As all aspects of life are filtered through the matrix of human capital, public action outside of an economistic calculus of the taxpayer's burden becomes less possible.

What this economization critique misses, however, is what a Foucauldian critique shows us: human capital theory works not only by reducing humans to their productivity, but it also produces a call to instil in humans the appropriate market subjectivities. It justifies not only rollback of certain forms of state provision, but the roll-out of a wider variety of interventions that operate at the level of affect to instil market-compatible behaviors and attitudes. Rational Economic Man is actively made, not born. Although the above works introduce a persuasive critique of human capital theory as providing intellectual cover for roll-back neoliberalism and various forms of privatization/state withdrawal, they dedicate less attention to the way that human capital works as a technology of governance. Moreover, its mode of governance is profoundly gendered in ways that merit closer scrutiny. Human capital theory's embrace in Gender and Development, I argue, hinges on its promise to identify pre-empowerment subjectivities and to prescribe the right interventions to catalyze female forms of entrepreneurship. Foucault's critique of human capital theory provides the starting point for a feminist critique, both because human capital theory has acquired so much power as a governance paradigm in development and because Foucault's analysis of the concept provides broader insights into the operation of neoliberalism. A Foucauldian account of human capital theory has important contributions to make that connect human capital with broader shifts in the operation of neoliberalism at an ideological and governance level.

The opening for Foucauldian engagement on human capital theory is recognized in a growing body of literature that draws out the biopolitical dimensions of human capital theory. Foucauldian scholarship has recognized the implications of human capital's economizing logic as well as its emphasis on self-governance by responsibilized individuals. Human capital theory has been identified by Foucauldians as providing the rationale for biopolitical management of subjects at the level of population, managing the *conduct of conduct* to elicit behaviors rather than repress them (Newheiser 2016; Repo 2015; Oksala 2011; 2013). Although human capital theory purports to provide an account of human freedom – to make one's own decisions about life and work through managing investments in the self – Foucauldians emphasize that this freedom is a façade that hides different forms of governmental intervention. Neoliberal subjects are governed through the logic of personal freedom and the freedom to choose in the marketplace, although they lack the power to shape the options from which they must choose (Oksala 2013). As such, human capital theory has been identified as the policy correlate for Foucault's account of biopolitics that operates through "light touch" governance, manipulating environments and choices rather than directly controlling individuals (Newheiser 2016: 2–3). As yet, human capital theory has not been a major focus of Foucauldian feminist analyses, apart from contributions by Johanna Oksala and Jemima Repo (see also Heyes 2013 for a state of the literature). Oksala (2011; 2013) shows how the self-management dimensions of human capital are filtered through contemporary discourses of empowerment and economic freedom. Repo (2015; 2017) uses Foucault to critique Becker's theories of human capital and fertility, demonstrating the biopolitical tools that govern demographics through fertility decision-making. Human capital theory, she shows, introduced a market logic through which economists could assess populations in terms of quality versus quantity, where fewer children meant higher human capital investments. This work points to fertility as another site of market logic in human capital theory, where reproductive decision making becomes a site of government from a distance: if women make reproductive decisions on a cost-benefit basis, they can be persuaded to have fewer (or "better") children. I expand on their claims in two main ways: first, I use Foucault's critique of human capital to demonstrate the gendered assumptions that underpin the theory itself and second, I demonstrate its deployment in Gender and Development discourse to cultivate new forms of development agency and authority. I demonstrate that the most important governing logic that emerges from human capital theory is the trend towards development interventions that seek to "activate" women's dormant economic power.

Foucault's analysis of human capital presents an essential critique of the theory, first because of the prescience of his engagement with the subject. In his 1979 *Birth of Biopolitics* lectures, Foucault addressed key themes of neoliberalism that would later come to dominate during the 1980s, and far beyond (Flew 2012). Long before its ascendance in development and social policy discourse, Foucault mapped out the conceptual implications of the theory and offered an insightful prediction of its operation today. In the *Birth of Biopolitics* lectures, Foucault provides a historical excavation of neoliberalism, as part of which he identifies human capital as a central innovation that characterizes American neoliberalism. Human capital also presents a site of interest for Foucault because it represents the extension of economic analysis into new areas and sought to provide strictly economic accounts of domains that had been considered "non-economic" (Foucault 2008: 219). It provides a whole new set of tools to understand intimate aspects of human life and behavior through the language of supply/ demand, cost/benefit, rational self-interest. Of course, this is precisely the conceptual innovation Chicago School economists hoped to introduce. In Foucault's analysis, it is the quintessence of neoliberalism: the extension of economic analysis and marketization of all spheres of life brings with it the multiplication of technologies of governance. Under neoliberalism, the market does not serve to restrict government action, but "constitutes the general index" in which government action can occur (Ibid.: 121), because human actions can be modified through market mechanisms and incentives.

An important effect of this economizing logic is apparent in human capital's insistence that humans are an asset in the same way that physical capital is. For Foucault, this signals an important conceptual shift in economic thought because it works to break down some of the most important binaries that structure classical liberal economics. One such foundational separation is between the free laborer and her labor power: human capital theory re-imagines the laborer *as* capital. In classical political economy, the free laborer can exchange her labor power for wages, but there remains a distinction between the laborer and the labor being sold. While the free laborer can sell her labor power as a commodity, the laborer is not a commodity in herself and therefore retains "inalienable" aspects of subjectivity (Feher 2009: 29–30). Part of the neoliberal conceptual innovation of human capital theory is to re-define income as a return on capital, and capital as anything that provides a source of income. By extension, the body is imagined as capital and wages as the return on that capital. As Schultz puts it:

> "Laborers have become capitalists not from the diffusion of the ownership of corporation stocks, as folk law would have it, but from the acquisition of knowledge and skill that have economic value."
>
> (Schultz 1961: 3)

Human capital theory therefore introduces the idea that income is a wage allocated to a particular capital; this capital is inseparable from the human who bears it. This also changes the relationship between laborer and labor power, by eliminating the separation between the two. It means that there is no realm that lies outside of capital: all aspects of the laborer's self and life contribute to either depreciating or appreciating her human capital. Value can be assessed and extracted throughout life, and everything can be re-interpreted in terms of its effect on human capital and therefore on future growth. When human capital theory re-imagines the laborer as being inseparable from her labor power, it re-imagines the worker as an "abilities machine" in the sense that the machine produces an "earning stream" (Foucault 2008: 224). This is because the human capital model understands the machine as "ability and worker individually bound together" (Ibid.: 224–225); human capital is remunerated over the lifespan, rather than selling labor power on the market for certain wages during a limited period of time. Foucault demonstrates that this is a radical move away from the concept of labor power: instead it is a conception of economy and society as comprised of "enterprise units" (Ibid.: 225). In place of a relation of labor and capital, we see a new kind of terrain built by enterprise units consisting of higher and lower values, with greater and lesser earnings streams. In this model, the subject is no longer a laborer who sells her labor power, but an investor who tends her capital and makes strategic choices to increase its value. Foucault captures this dynamic in terms of self-enterprise: when capital is understood as wholly inseparable from the person who possesses it, the worker "appears as a sort of enterprise for himself" (Foucault 2008: 225). This means that each of us is personally responsible for cultivating our capital and increasing its value over time. As such, Foucault theorizes a shift in the subjectivity of humans and their capital that re-configures the relationship between the self, the body, and the capacity for work:

> "*Homo economicus* is an entrepreneur, an entrepreneur of himself… being for himself his own capital, being for himself his own producer, being for himself the source of [his] earnings."
>
> (2008: 226)

The mode of self-governance that Foucault traces here is familiar from his earlier works that introduced governmentality as dominant modes of modern governance. His work conceptualizes neoliberal governance as a form of power that is deployed without individual-level interventions, but through the governance of the general conduct (1984; see also Lemke 2001). This mode of governance operates by adjusting conditions at the macro-level, to which subjects will respond and adjust their behavior. As such, the ideal subject of neoliberal governance is "someone who is eminently governable" (Foucault 2008: 270). Part of his interest in human capital theory therefore stemmed from the observation that this governable subject who responds according to environmental stimulus closely resembles the model of *homo economicus*, the rational economic man, who is the central figure of neoliberal economic thought. The *homo economicus* of human capital theory is one "who can be manoevured, someone who responds systematically to systematic modifications" (Ibid.: 265). The economic agent of human capital is governed from afar, and governs himself, through a spirit of self-entrepreneurship: this distinctly neoliberal *homo economicus* exhibits a distinct form of economic subjectivity and operate according to the logic of market competition, rather than the logic of exchange.

In human capital theory, capital comprises all the "physical and psychological factors" that make a person able to earn a wage (Foucault 2008: 224), meaning labor power is understood as inseparable from the person who possesses it. Human capital theory therefore has the intended effect of economizing all dimensions of life: the crux of its theoretical contribution is to understand all human activities in terms of how they "contribute to the maintenance or deterioration of my human capital" (Feher 2009: 26). This means that beyond calculations about whether to work or spend more time in education/ training, human capital theory interprets all aspects of life in terms of their effect on human capital. The conceptual separation of laborer and labor means a blurring of the domains that have traditionally been used to structure our understanding of capitalist economies. Instead, Foucault uses a different conceptual separation to critique the function of human capital theory as a technology of neoliberal governance. In place of the laborer/labor separation, he argues that the Chicago School's account of human capital theory is premised on the conceptual separation between the innate and acquired elements of human-as-capital. In doing so, he is not advancing an alternative theory of human capital but mapping out how the theory functions as a tool of neoliberal governance. If neoliberal governmentality is concerned with governing at a distance, Foucault sees human capital theory as embodying one such strategy for controlling individuals with responsibility for them (Lemke 2001: 201). Foucault anticipates that this strategy will acquire greater influence in the future: he even predicts that development policy analysis of "the failure of Third World Economies to get going" will come to involve an analysis of human capital resources, and will evaluate these economies in terms of "insufficient investment in human capital" (Foucault 2008: 232). His critique therefore identifies two parts that comprise human capital, in the eyes of neoliberal theorists and policymakers, in order to demonstrate how it works to govern.

Foucault claims that human capital theory operates through the relationship between two categories: "innate elements" and other "acquired elements" (Ibid.: 227). The first half of the human capital model comprises the inborn, hereditary/ genetic predisposition of individuals. These qualities that inhere within the laborer are dormant in that they cannot be fully realized without appropriate investment and promotion by external forces; they are "specific attributes, abilities, and natural endowments" that predispose *homo economicus* to particular kinds of economic behavior (Dilts 2011: 138). The second half of the human capital model, what Foucault refers to as the more "voluntary" aspects that contribute to human capital formation, constitute "acquired elements". These investments include education and training that will cultivate the abilities of the "abilities-machine" (Foucault 2008: 229). It also includes investments made by parents in a child's development: hours spent with a child, affection shown to the child, and cultural stimuli to which the child is exposed. Foucault describes a variety of investments in human capital that essentially correspond to the processes of social reproduction, although he does not use that term. Foucault imagines social reproduction as the "machine of freedom-production and character management" and thereby opens up ways to potentially understand mothering as a strategy of governance. At this point in the lecture, he notes he is running out of time and briefly summarizes some wider implications: beyond children's education and care by parents, he also mentions "all activities concerning the health of individuals", healthcare and public hygiene, as sites that will be re-thought through human capital (Ibid.: 230). As a result, Foucault anticipates that the evaluation of human capital will involve a wide-ranging "environmental analysis" which may involve a whole-scale reconceptualization of social institutions in terms of the extent to which they improve human capital (Foucault 2008: 230; Feher 2009). In this context, investment is not limited to financial resources but covers a wide range of activities that increase the capacity to "earn income or achieve satisfaction" broadly defined (Read 2009: 28). In doing so, it not only translates various elements of social life into market inputs, but also paves the way for interventions to regulate and shape behaviors by altering the environment in which humans make choices about their capital.

Part of the conceptual innovation of Foucault's critique of neoliberalism is the geography of power that he maps: interventions to govern and control the neoliberal subject take place at a distance and enact power on the body through indirect modes of governance. In short, he provides a different way to understand the operation of power today, because he shows us that neoliberal subjects can be governed from a distance, rather than through violent corporeal interventions. The figure of rational economic actor as self-enterprise therefore embodies the range of possibilities for neoliberal governance. If *homo economicus* is an entrepreneurial figure whose existence is determined by continuously making choices to maximize his human capital, then *homo economicus* is also "someone who is eminently governable" (Foucault 2008: 270). The logic of governance that Foucault outlines operates not by repression, but by bringing forth new forms of behavior. It elicits new forms of conduct through incentives and environmental modifications, rather than through violent or coercive interventions. It does, however, create and shape subjects through indirect intervention. The kinds of market subjects who lie at the heart of human capital theory are those who must be "transformed" so that they can "transform themselves" (Brockling 2011: 258; McNay 2009). Human capital theory provides the analytical basis for such interventions, however, because it enables the "environmental analysis" that identifies the kinds of intrinsic qualities a human possesses, and the context in which those qualities can be cultivated through interventions to train, provide skills, and teach behaviors. This is a crucial insight in Foucault's critique: neoliberals propose to promote human freedom by limiting government, but this freedom is in fact shaped and produced.

Here we can see two contrasting visions of markets: neoliberals argue that market rationality is the natural state of humans and that market-based systems allow for the most freedom because they unleash this market rationality, though markets must be protected against the possibilities of monopolies and distortions. The Foucauldian response would suggest that no such market rationality exists, much less as the natural state of all humans, and supposedly free markets are in fact created through particular forms of intervention to shape conduct. This is because the figure of *homo economicus*, who is meant to stand in for a form of pre-existing human rationality, is not in fact a natural figure: it is a form of cultivated subjectivity. The irony of neoliberal governmentality is that the rationale which purports to allow forever increasing human freedom is actually based on ever more invasive interventions. This presents a paradox of "intensification": the form that power takes becomes less obviously interventionist, and less corporeal, but it also becomes more widespread as it filters through all realms of life (Read 2009; Anderson 2012; Lemke 2015). It pulls new spaces into the domain of economic calculation and thereby makes them subject to governance under the logic of cost/benefit. Assuming that rational economic subjects calculate the costs of all their actions, the state can channel these interests by making "desirable" activities inexpensive and "undesirable" activities expensive (Read 2009: 29). Thus when human capital theory extends economic analysis into all realms of life, this is not only an analytical tool, but also a governing technology.

In short, the central relationship that Foucault identifies in his two-part critique of human capital theory is between those qualities that are inborn in the laborer and the use of investment to harness and activate them. As such, he situates human capital theory in the broader context of neoliberalism, as a tool for shaping the economic subjectivity of individuals. It further embeds neoliberalism's expansion of economic analysis into all spheres of life as it blurs the boundaries between the economic (wealth) and the social (humans): human beings are reconfigured as subjects into which investment can be placed to produce an economic result in the future. Foucault took particular interest in neoliberal discourses of human capital and the way they reconfigured everyday practices in terms of the need to be an entrepreneur of one's self. In particular, he used human capital as an example of linkages between the analytical and programmatic axes of neoliberal rationality: he sought to illuminate the extent to which, under the neoliberal lens, the economic is not "firmly outlined and delineated" but comes to include all forms of human action and behavior (Lemke 2001: 197–8). This relationship between analytical and programmatic axes of neoliberal governance has major resonances with prevailing mode of Gender and Development governance.

A feminist critique of human capital theory

Foucault's critique of human capital provides an insightful vision of the relationship between neoliberalism as economic policy and neoliberalism as governmentality that intervenes to shape and influence individuals. His critique of human capital helps to draw out the ways that shifts in macro-economic policy link to governance of individuals at the scale of daily life. Economization of all dimensions of life, as human capital theory proposes, creates space to see how governance of populations might function, as well as how individual neoliberal subjects are molded into self-governing and responsibilized entrepreneurs of the self, in Foucault's terms. His work on this subject has significant implications for a feminist analysis of neoliberalism, both because of the gendered structures that underpin human capital theory, as well as the governing structures that it brings into force. This feminist critique of human capital is essential because of the gendered implications of the human capital theory's challenge to the classical liberal distinction between productive and reproductive spheres. The erosion between these spheres occurred as a result of the shift from focus on the "free laborer" who exchanges her labor for a price, to the human capital model, in which the laborer is the entrepreneur of her own capital. This is the model that constitutes "the target and basis of neoliberal policies" (Feher 2009: 31). Human capital does not presuppose a separation between realms of production and reproduction, but conflates the two by re-imagining all human behaviors and activities in terms of their impact on the value of one's human capital. The work of social reproduction is thus rendered visible to the extent that it impacts human capital:

> "The various things I do, in any existential domain (dietary, erotic, religious, etc.), all contribute to either appreciating or depreciating the human capital that is me, no less than does my diligence as a worker or my ability to trade my professional skills."
>
> (Feher 2009: 30)

This formulation of economic agency as a resource to be generated through social investment – in terms of human capital investment – has accorded particular visibility to girls and women as ideal subjects *in formation*. Returning to the popular understanding of women's labor power as "untapped" or "undiscovered", I suggest that human capital theory structures this conceptualization and proposes mechanisms by which a greater income can be generated from women: in policy terms, this appears as a roadmap for women's empowerment. The dominant discourse on gender in development today promotes the idea that girls and women are "entrepreneurial subjects in waiting" who can power national economies and global sustainable development (Koffman and Gill 2013: 85). Yet, this discourse is underpinned by a series of contradictory narratives in which women represent both vulnerable victims and empowered leaders; altruistic, loving mothers and autonomous rational economic individuals; dormant development power ready to be unleashed and untrained, unskilled and unproductive non-market actors; and risk-averse actors lacking business skills and promising investors who will drive ethical growth. In short, although images of women's and girls' empowerment pervade development discourses the construction of women's empowerment is underpinned by a series of significant tensions that alternately deploy gender essentialisms, neo-classical economic logic, and entrenched development fables to articulate a grammar of neoliberal empowerment. Starting from the categories introduced in Foucault's critique, and mapping these categories on to Gender and Development discourses, helps to reconcile these tensions and uncover the effects of such discourses.

The Smart Economics development agenda accords girls and women visibility and some economic agency, but only to the extent that their "untapped" productive capacities can be harnessed for economic outcomes. Consequently, the focus of Gender and Development governance is located in the identification and cultivation of development subjectivities at the individual level; in this context, the new agents of development are entrepreneurial women who are attributed "cultural propensities to invest widely and look after their families" (Rankin 2001: 20). The human capital theory reconfigures the relations between laborer, capital, and economic power; empowerment-centered development programs similarly shift the focus on economic efforts away from a separation between laborer and capital towards an entrepreneurial system of individual responsibilization aimed at self-sufficiency. Through investment in skills, enhancement of capabilities, and promotion of behaviors, the laborer becomes a form of capital. For example, this framing of female development subjects *in formation* – as both development potential and peril – is embodied in the Nike Foundation's Girl Effect campaign. In 2011, the campaign's website invited visitors to consider the divergent girlhoods that await girls in the global South:

> "A. SHE GETS A CHANCE: she gets educated; she stays healthy; marries when she chooses; raises a family. As a result, she has the opportunity to raise the standard of living for herself and her family.
> B. NONE OF THIS HAPPENS: she is illiterate; married off; is isolated; is pregnant; vulnerable to HIV. As a result, she and her family are stuck in a cycle of poverty."
>
> (quoted in Shain 2013)

When accorded particular visibility in development discourses, women's subjectivity and agency is narrowly circumscribed and mediated by its relation to pre-existing and culturally resonant narratives of femininity, womanhood, and motherhood. In other words, women are highly visible subjects of development, and frequently represented as "untapped" resources not only because of perceptions that they are economically inactive or marginal, but also because of the claim that they possess particular qualities that are more conducive to sustainable growth and poverty eradication. Returning to Foucault's critique of human capital, the two-part structure he proposes for understanding the function of human capital theory serves as a useful guide for feminist re-interpretation. The feminist critique of human capital theory that I propose adopts a parallel structure (adapting the categories of "inborn qualities" and "acquired skills") to conceptualize the representations of women's capital and the biopolitical interventions proposed to harness it.

Inborn qualities

If human capital theory begins from the impulse to identify the "inborn qualities" of a person in relation to her earning capacity, how do Smart Economics discourses represent the supposedly inherent traits of women? Several inborn qualities are frequently attributed to women in the development policy literature and are discursively linked to their construction as uniquely productive subjects: maternal altruism, responsibility, and risk-averseness. The most widespread characterization of women in development discourses is that of women's function as naturally sacrificing, altruistic, and nurturing mothers. Importantly, the ascription of maternal altruism to women propagates an image of the selfless, community-minded woman whose social reproductive labor is a "voluntaristic" product of family love (Brickell and Chant 2010). Discourses valorizing the "good mother" have emerged, not uncoincidentally, since the 1980s alongside policies of economic restructuring and state rollback which re-privatized social reproduction on the assumption that would women re-absorb the care burden. Narratives of the "good mother" are not innocent of their political contexts but perform an important legitimizing function for particular economic agendas (Hart 1997). Representations of women's supposedly "intrinsic" sense of responsibility similarly derive from the collapsing of categories – woman, wife, mother – and the assumption that a woman's decisions in the market are products of her reproductive obligations. The discourses tend to dichotomize the "irresponsible individualist man" and "cooperative, community-minded, caring woman" (Cornwall 2000: 22), evident in the oft-cited (and heavily moralized) images of women's "good" spending on children's needs and men's "bad" spending on sensual pleasures like alcohol and cigarettes (Wilson 2013: 90). Essentialism, albeit flattering, sits at the core of representations of women as development agents.

The image of the caring and self-sacrificing mother is powerful and culturally resonant across contexts, which makes it a salient and effective mode of visibility for women in development discourses. Discourses that valorize motherhood are unassailable and easily gain traction across institutional and policy contexts, where "comfortable and unquestionable" terms and narratives can conceal a range of possible meanings or dissent (Parpart, Rai and Staudt 2003: 3). Essentialist discourses around maternal care that unproblematically equate womanhood with altruistic motherhood, and naturalize a gendered division of labor with reference to innate maternal nature, serve in part to legitimize a policy agenda of privatization of social reproduction. Women's incorporation into development policy in terms of their maternal altruism and voluntaristic performance of social reproduction risks facilitating further exploitation by allowing programs to capitalize on the "altruistic burden" (Brickell and Chant 2010: 146; see also Maclean 2012). Nonetheless, ascriptions of natural, maternal altruism to women are pervasive in dominant development discourses that articulate a case for women's productivity and responsibility as functions of their maternal obligations.

A second common trope, closely related to the altruistic motherhood discourses, reflects an understanding of women as intrinsically and uniquely productive economic agents: doing more work, more often, more quickly, and for less pay. Discussion of the responsible and resourceful agency of poor women "fill the institutional reports" of development agencies, reflecting both increased interest in the poverty experienced by the "Third World Woman" and the articulation of her responsibility to overcome that poverty (Madhok and Rai 2012: 649). Furthermore, there is a significant ambivalence between empowerment and "neoliberal dumping" of responsibility and risk-management in development interventions, where responsibility for care work is offloaded to women and simultaneously valorized in terms of caring, altruistic family relations. Evidence points to a significant slippage between tropes that valorize women's innate "responsibility" and efforts to "responsibilize" women in the Foucauldian sense – to produce self-governing citizens who are empowered, entrepreneurial, and above all else, self-sufficient (Maclean 2013; Rankin 2002). Within the recognition of the "feminization of poverty" and attempts to measure that trend, there has been a significant undercurrent of "feminization of responsibility and obligation" whereupon women's work is diversified and intensified, but this has not been accompanied by a shift in men's contribution to caring labor, an increase in women's negotiating power within the home, or an increase in corresponding rights and rewards (Chant 2008).

When essentialist discourses of female economic agency migrate across discursive domains, development narratives of entrepreneurial and resourceful women in the global South translate into accounts of responsible and prudent women in the global North whose modes of economic agency might serve as a model for post-crash economics. Much of the post-crisis economic discourse on gender and risk positions the moderating figure of the female investor/entrepreneur as the solution to global financial crisis and underdevelopment, through narratives underpinned by similar gendered assumptions and constructions of risk-taking. In the post-crisis political discourse, a binary has been established between "reckless man" and "responsible woman", where women are understood as moral agents able to mediate between the supposedly male desire for profit and the unpredictability of the market (Prügl 2012: 23–4). These same gendered essentialisms are pervasive in post-crisis analysis and prescriptions, where women are attributed a "natural prudence" that makes them well suited to act as agents of economic recovery. The image of feminine subjectivities that emerges from a critical reading of the development literature is characterized by a series of essentialisms that, firstly, conflate women's subjectivities with a range of reproductive activities that are naturalized as the product of feminine altruism. Women are attributed high levels of social capital (in the absence of their access to physical capital) in their communal and inter-personal relationships; these community bonds are understood as potentially productive because they are conducive to alternative forms of economic activity (Rankin 2002). By extension, it reads reproductivity as constitutive of increased responsibility, productivity, and sustainability. These characteristics are imagined, however, as "dormant" (or "untapped" in the current development parlance) and women's potential as yet-to-be-realized by the global economy. As such, representations of natural female altruism and productivity are bound up with claims about which women are most suitable for the empowerment interventions needed to harness their power.

Acquired behaviors

Human capital is, for Foucault, premised on the identification of particular innate qualities and their activation through interventions to bring forth specific skills and qualities that are conducive to economic productivity. Human capital is formed when innate attributes are harnessed in such a way as to transform humans into "abilities-machines" whose abilities will "produce income" (Foucault 2008: 229). These proposed interventions to capitalize on inborn qualities include parental care, education, training, health and hygiene, environmental factors, and mobility. In a feminist reading of the human capital critique, and one that takes into account the current discursive context of "Smart Economics" and the visibility of particular gendered constructions in development, I suggest first, that a narrative of activation underpins the discourse and second, that a range of interventions appear as mechanisms for the activation of dormant potential. Foucault suggests that human capital theory hinges on an analytical link between the inborn capacities of humans and interventions that transform those qualities into productive outputs. In order to develop her human capital, interventions to empower the subject propose to instill the capacity to act "as a certain kind of citizen with certain kinds of aims" (Cruikshank 1999: 4). A feminist re-interpretation of this claim demonstrates that "Smart Economics" development discourses promote a range of development interventions for the activation of the supposedly dormant labor, entrepreneurial, and financial power of the world's poor women; these interventions revolve around the perceived need to limit biological reproduction while instilling women with appropriate skills and aspirations for market success, so that they can operate as more efficient, more productive entrepreneurs.

Political belonging under neoliberalism is increasingly conceived in relation to the ability to live according to the values and norms of the market, focused on individual choices, responsibility, and self-governance. As such, poverty has been re-inscribed as the failure to properly access and participate in markets and the poor as "untrained, unmarketable, and therefore as remediable" (Schild 2000: 286). Women in development discourse occupy a fraught and contested position where they are ascribed a range of qualities – responsibility, efficiency, risk-averseness – associated with market success, but women are nonetheless generally understood as located "outside the purview of capitalist markets" (Rankin 2001: 28). This discourse transforms women's bodies into resources and corporeal sites of development and/ or underdevelopment. As is evident in the dominant tropes of Smart Economics, the bodies of women and girls are imagined to represent capital insofar as they have the potential to generate income and economic growth in the future. The process of empowerment as "unleashing" dormant female entrepreneurship is most commonly imagined in terms of access to credit and financial services in order to "unlock" dormant entrepreneurial potential (Moodie 2013; Roy 2010). Conversely, these bodies represent risky sites of reproduction that require biopolitical intervention to prevent their participation in biological reproduction and, by extension, the reproduction of underdevelopment (Hickel 2014). The relationship between production and reproduction is a key locus of tension in Gender and Development discourses: interventions to minimize reproductivity and incentivize productivity abound.

Activation narratives that propose to integrate women into market cultures and subjectivities start from two interlinked assumptions. First, they presuppose that women are physically distant from markets and market activity because, reflecting the on-going theme of the undervaluation and invisibility of social reproduction, the kind of work that women perform is not considered as such. Development planners have "started to notice" women's role in production, reproduction, and provision, to the extent that they have been identified as ideal target groups for interventions like microcredit, but women are nonetheless generally located outside of the market (Rankin 2001). Second, narratives of women's supposed marginality to market work further promote the idea that women are also external to market cultures and market "rationality", itself a deeply gendered and problematic concept. Women's subordination is imagined, in part, as a result of their lack of "sufficient contact" with modern ideas and markets (Bergeron 2003: 408). Education and training interventions, particularly those specifically targeted at women, have been implicated in efforts to construct a particular form of economic rationality and to instil certain market aptitudes. In order to contest "women's assumed passivity", development interventions aim to expose women to cultures of market responsibility and self-reliance. Among these practices, development policies propose a range of micro-level efforts to instil a particular form of market subjectivity including training in market, administrative, and business culture targeted at ethnically marginalized women (Bedford 2009: 139–40); interventions to teach self-help, personal responsibility and accountability to poor, unemployed groups (Schild 2000: 293); and training to accompany, or as a condition of, credit provision (Rankin 2001; Isserles 2003; Lairap-Fonderson 2002). Education, training, and other interventions therefore function to transform humans into what Foucault calls "abilities-machines", thereby transforming the individual into an entrepreneur of her own human capital.

Conclusion

Human capital theory has widespread influence in development and economic policymaking. A growing body of scholarship has recognized the impact of human capital theory on everything from the structure of government loans for higher education to flexibilization in labor markets. In essence, human capital theory has prompted a conceptual shift to change the way that policymakers see people and their labor power; it has allowed for a blurring of that distinction so that humans and their capabilities come to form a single unit of human capital. This capital can increase in value, through investment, to generate higher returns. It can also depreciate in value, and produce ever-smaller streams of income. We might understand this in term of higher and lower wages, although human capital discourse provides a separate rhetorical register for these matters. It provides an economistic and future-oriented language for rendering our lives and bodies in terms of their ability to produce wealth and the freedom to do so as we wish. In the historical context of its origin, human capital theory was a useful tool for framing Cold War ideological debates in terms of the oppressive determinism of Communism, against the total freedom of the capitalist economic man who was the builder of his own portfolio and the boss of his own personal enterprise (Fleming 2017a). Capitalist man is free to invest in himself as he sees fit, without government interference to tell him how to invest or what to do with his assets. Today, this is a discourse that legitimizes broad changes in labor conditions, including the rise in on-demand work and self-employment. The effect, of course, is the offloading of risk onto individuals who bear the brunt of increased instability in work, and can expect less support from public institutions.

The conceptual power of human capital can be seen in development discourses as well. In fact, it has been a crucial discursive vehicle through which gender had entered development policymaking. It stresses, along the lines of Women in Development frameworks discussed in Chapter 1, the importance of investing in women's human capital by emphasizing the losses that result from their dormant potential. Human capital theory has provided a potent, but risky, conceptual framework for feminist claims in development institutions. It has created new modes of visibility for girls and women, and successfully introduced a language for discussing female economic agency, but it has done so in a way that economizes and responsibilizes girls and women. Its effect has been to give support to pre-existing policy frameworks, rather than ushering in transformative policy shifts. The institutional embrace of human capital theory, in development agencies, governments, and businesses, has given girls and women a newfound visibility as targets of investment whose potential return on investment can be calculated and sold (Murphy 2017). Beyond the implications of this economizing logic introduced by human capital theory, there is a governing logic at work. It is a logic of intervention and activation, as I have demonstrated above. Girls and women, when re-conceptualized a dormant human capital, come under new forms of surveillance and intervention that aim to govern their bodies and behviors in order to produce more market-compatible subjects.

The next chapter turns to examine the role of human capital theory in development institutions; as such it takes up the theoretical insights provided by a feminist critique of human capital and examines these in the empirical context of development governance. Human capital theory has been an essential tool in the current visibility of girls and women in development, and functions as the animating force behind the Smart Economics agenda. This is not a simple product of co-optation of feminism, but the result of complex and contested developments inside institutions, where feminists embraced strategic framings to put gender equality on the agenda. In the World Bank, we can see this process at work: human capital theory entered development policymaking as a strategic tool for addressing development's critics and reforming the modes of economic neoliberalism that had drawn so much criticism. The reformulation of gender equality claims in terms of human capital theory was one component of this, producing a salient rationale for gender in mainstream institutions that might have otherwise been skeptical or dismissive. Human capital theory is the engine of the empowerment agenda.

References

African Development Bank. 2011. "AfDB's Human Capital Development Strategy (2012–2016)." www.afdb.org/fileadmin/uploads/afdb/Documents/Policy-Documents/FINAL%20human%20capital%20development%20strategy%20%282012-2016%29.pdf.

Anderson, Ben. 2012. "Affect and Biopower: Towards a Politics of Life." *Transactions of the Institute of British Geographers* 37(1): 28–43.

Anstey, Caroline. 2013. "Viewpoint: The Price of Violence against Women and Girls." *BBC*. Published March 8 2013. www.bbc.co.uk/news/business-21696469.

Arndt, H.W. 1987. *Economic Development: The History of an Idea*. Chicago, IL: University of Chicago Press.

Asian Development Bank. 2010. "Human Capital Development." ADB Economics Working Paper Series No. 225. www.adb.org/sites/default/files/publication/28427/economics-wp225.pdf.

Babb, Sarah. 2013. "The Washington Consensus as Transnational Policy Paradigm: Its Origins, Trajectory and Likely Successor." *Review of International Political Economy* 20(2): 268–297.

Becker, Gary. 1960. "An Economic Analysis of Fertility." In *Demographic and Economic Change in Developed Countries*, edited by the National Bureau of Economic Research, 209–240. New York: Columbia University Press.

Becker, Gary. 1976. *The Economic Approach to Human Behavior*. Chicago, IL: University of Chicago Press.

Becker, Gary. 1981. *A Treatise on the Family, Enlarged Edition*. Cambridge, MA: Harvard University Press.

Becker, Gary. 1993 [1964]. *Human Capital: A Theoretical and Empirical Analysis*. Chicago, IL: University of Chicago Press.

Bedford, Kate. 2009. *Developing Partnerships: Gender, Sexuality, and the Reformed World Bank*. Minneapolis, MN: University of Minnesota Press.

Bergeron, Suzanne. 2003. "The Post-Washington Consensus and Economic Representations of Women in Development at the World Bank." *International Feminist Journal of Politics* 5(3): 397–419.

Bergmann, Barbara. 1995. "Becker's Theory of the Family: Preposterous Conclusions." *Feminist Economics* 1(1): 141–150.

Boyd, Ginger. 2016. "The Girl Effect: A Neoliberal Instrumentalization of Gender Equality." *Consilience: The Journal of Sustainable Development* 15(1): 146–180.

Brickell, Katherine, and Sylvia Chant. 2010. "'The Unbearable Heaviness of Being': Reflections on Female Altruism in Cambodia, Philippines, The Gambia and Costa Rica." *Progress in Development Studies* 10(2): 145–159.

Brockling, Ulrich. 2011. "Human Economy, Human Capital: A Critique of Biopolitical Economy." In *Governmentality: Current Issues and Future Challenges*, edited by Ulrich Brockling, Susanne Krasmann, and Thomas Lemke, 247–268. Abingdon: Routledge.

Brown, Wendy. 2015. *Undoing the Demos: Neoliberalism's Stealth Revolution*. Cambridge, MA: MIT Press.

Chant, Sylvia. 2008. "The 'feminisation of Poverty' and the 'feminisation' of Anti-Poverty Programmes: Room for Revision?" *The Journal of Development Studies* 44(2): 165–197.

Chant, Sylvia. 2016. "Women, Girls and World Poverty: Empowerment, Equality or Essentialism?" *International Development Planning Review* 38(1): 1–24.

Cooper, Melinda. 2017. *Family Values: Between Neoliberalism and the New Social Conservatism*. Cambridge, MA: MIT Press.

Cornwall, Andrea. 2000. "Missing Men? Reflections on Men, Masculinities and Gender in GAD." *IDS Bulletin* 31(2): 18–27.

Cruikshank, Barbara. 1999. *The Will to Empower: Democratic Citizens and Other Subjects*. Ithaca, NY: Cornell University Press.

Dilts, Andrew. 2011. "From 'entrepreneur of the Self' to 'care of the Self': Neoliberal Governmentality and Foucault's Ethics." *Foucault Studies* 12: 130–146.

Escobar, Arturo. 1995. *Encountering Development: The Making and Unmaking of the Third World*. Princeton, NJ: Princeton University Press.

Feher, Michel. 2009. "Self-Appreciation; Or, The Aspirations of Human Capital." *Public Culture* 21(1): 21–41.

Fine, Ben, and Pauline Rose. 2003. "Education and the Post-Washington Consensus." In *Development Policy in the Twenty-First Century: Beyond the Post-Washington Consensus*, edited by Ben Fine, Costas Lapavitsas, and Jonathan Pincus, 155–181. Abingdon: Routledge.

Fleming, Peter. 2014. "Review Article: When 'life Itself' Goes to Work: Reviewing Shifts in Organizational Life through the Lens of Biopower." *Human Relations* 67(7): 875–901.

Fleming, Peter. 2017a. "The Human Capital Hoax: Work, Debt and Insecurity in the Era of Uberization." *Organization Studies* 38(5): 691–709.

Fleming, Peter. 2017b. *The Death of Homo Economicus: Work, Debt and the Myth of Endless Accumulation*. London: Pluto Press.

Flew, Terry. 2012. "Michel Foucault's The Birth of Biopolitics and Contemporary Neo-Liberalism Debates." *Thesis Eleven* 108(1): 44–65.

Foucault, Michel. 1984. *The Foucault Reader*. Edited by Paul Rabinow. New York: Pantheon Press.

Foucault, Michel .2008. *The Birth of Biopolitics: Lectures at the Collège de France, 1978–1979*. New York: Picador.

Gardiner, Jean. 1998. "Beyond Human Capital: Households in the Macroeconomy." *New Political Economy* 3(2): 209–221.

Goldin, Claudia. 2016. "Human Capital." In *Handbook of Cliometrics*. Heidelberg: Springer Verlag.

Hall, Anthony. 2007. "Social Policies in the World Bank: Paradigms and Challenges." *Global Social Policy* 7(2): 151–175.

Hart, Gillian. 1997. "From 'Rotten Wives' to 'Good Mothers': Household Models and the Limits of Economism." *IDS Bulletin* 28(3): 14–25.

Heyes, Cressida J. 2013. "Foucault Studies Special Issue: Foucault and Feminism, September 2013." *Foucault Studies* 16(0): 3–14.

Heyneman, S. P. 2003. "The History and Problems in the Making of Education Policy at the World Bank 1960–2000." *International Journal of Educational Development* 23(3): 315–337.

Heyneman, S. 2005. "Foreign Aid to Education: Recent U.S. Initiatives- Background, Risks, and Prospects." *Peabody Journal of Education* 80(1): 107–119.

Hickel, Jason. 2014. "The 'girl Effect': Liberalism, Empowerment and the Contradictions of Development." *Third World Quarterly* 35(8): 1355–1373.

Hunt, Diana. 1989. *Economic Theories of Development: An Analysis of Competing Paradigms.* Hemel Hempstead: Harvester Wheatsheaf.

Ilon, Lynn. 1992. "Fitting girls' schooling into existing economic paradigms: Confronting the complexities." *International Journal of Educational Development* 12(2): 147–159.

Ilon, Lynn. 2002. "Agent of Global Markets or Agent of the Poor? The World Bank's Education Sector Strategy Paper." *International Journal of Educational Development* 22(5): 475–482.

Inter-American Development Bank. 2016. "Human Capital Development." www.iadb.org/en/topics/human-development/idb-and-human-development,4258.html.

Isserles, Robin. 2003. "Microcredit: The Rhetoric of Empowerment, the Reality of 'Development As Usual.'" *Women's Studies Quarterly* 31(3/4): 38–57.

Jacobsen, Joyce. 1999. "Human Capital Theory." In *The Elgar Companion to Feminist Economics*, edited by Janice Peterson and Margaret Lewis, 443–449. Cheltenham: Edward Elgar.

Jenson, Jane. 2010. "Diffusing Ideas for After Neoliberalism The Social Investment Perspective in Europe and Latin America." *Global Social Policy* 10(1): 59–84.

Klees, Steven. 2016. "Human Capital and Rates of Return: Brilliant Ideas or Ideological Dead Ends?" *Comparative Education Review* 60(4): 644–672.

Koffman, Ofra, and Rosalind Gill. 2013. "'the Revolution Will Be Led by a 12-Year-Old Girl': Girl Power and Global Biopolitics." *Feminist Review* 105(1): 83–102.

Lairap-Fonderson, Josephine. 2002. "The Disciplinary Power of Micro Credit: Examples from Kenya and Cameroon." In *Rethinking Empowerment: Gender and Development in a Global/Local World*, edited by Shirin Rai, Kathleen Staudt and Jane Parpart, 182–198. Abingdon: Routledge.

Lemke, Thomas. 2001. "'The Birth of Bio-Politics': Michel Foucault's Lecture at the College de France on Neo-Liberal Governmentality." *Economy and Society* 30(2): 190–207.

Lemke, Thomas. 2015. *Foucault, Governmentality, and Critique.* Abingdon: Routledge.

Maclean, Kate. 2012. "Banking on Women's Labour: Responsibility, Risk and Control in Village Banking in Bolivia." *Journal of International Development* 24: (S): 100–111.

Maclean, Kate. 2013. "Gender, Risk and Micro-Financial Subjectivities." *Antipode* 45(2): 455–473.

McNay, Lois. 2009. "Self as Enterprise: Dilemmas of Control and Resistance in Foucault's The Birth of Biopolitics." *Theory, Culture & Society* 26(6): 55–77.

Madhok, Sumi, and Shirin M. Rai. 2012. "Agency, Injury, and Transgressive Politics in Neoliberal Times." *Signs* 37(3): 645–669.

Mahon, Rianne. 2010. "After Neo-Liberalism? The OECD, the World Bank and the Child." *Global Social Policy* 10(2): 172–192.

Mason, Corinne. 2014. "'Cripping' the World Bank." *International Feminist Journal of Politics* 17(3): 435–453.

Moodie, Megan. 2013. "Microfinance and the Gender of Risk: The Case of Kiva. Org." *Signs* 38(2): 279–302.

Murphy, Michelle. 2017. *The Economization of Life*. Durham, NC: Duke University Press.

Newheiser, David. 2016. "Foucault, Gary Becker and the Critique of Neoliberalism." *Theory, Culture & Society* 33(5): 3–21.

Obamba, Milton. 2013. "Uncommon knowledge: World Bank policy and the unmaking of the knowledge economy in Africa." *Higher Education Policy* 26(1): 83–108.

Overseas Development Institute. 2000. *Women, Human Capital and Livelihoods: An Ergonomics Perspective*. London: ODI. www.odi.org/sites/odi.org.uk/files/odi-assets/publications-opinion-files/2855.pdf.

Oksala, Johanna. 2011. "The Neoliberal Subject of Feminism." *Journal of the British Society for Phenomenology* 42(1): 104–120.

Oksala, Johanna. 2013. "Feminism and Neoliberal Governmentality." *Foucault Studies* 16: 32–53.

Parpart, Jane, Shirin Rai, and Kathleen Staudt. 2003. "Rethinking Em(power)ment, Gender, and Development: An Introduction." In *Rethinking Empowerment: Gender and Development in a Global/Local World*, edited by Shirin Rai, Kathleen Staudt and Jane Parpart, 3–21. Abingdon: Routledge.

Prügl, Elisabeth. 2012. "'If Lehman Brothers Had Been Lehman Sisters…': Gender and Myth in the Aftermath of the Financial Crisis." *International Political Sociology* 6(1): 21–35.

Raghavendra, Srinivas, Patrick Carney, Nata Duvvury, and Aoife Callan. 2013. "Intimate Partner Violence: Economic Costs and Implications for Growth and Development." *Women's voice, agency, and participation research series*, no. 3. Washington, DC: World Bank. http://documents.worldbank.org/curated/en/412091468337843649/Intimate-partner-violence-economic-costs-and-implications-for-growth-and-development.

Rankin, Katharine. 2001. "Governing Development: Neoliberalism, Microcredit, and Rational Economic Woman." *Economy and Society* 30(1): 18–37.

Rankin, Katharine. 2002. "Social Capital, Microfinance, and the Politics of Development." *Feminist Economics* 8(1): 1–24.

Read, Jason. 2009. "A Genealogy of Homo-Economicus: Neoliberalism and the Production of Subjectivity." *Foucault Studies* 6: 25–36.

Repo, Jemima. 2015. *The Biopolitics of Gender*. Oxford: Oxford University Press.

Repo, Jemima. 2017. "Sexuality and the Neoliberal Biopolitics of Population: Gary Becker's Economics of Fertility." Presented at the 5th European Conference on Politics and Gender, June 8–10, University of Lausanne, Switzerland.

Roy, Ananya. 2010. *Poverty Capital: Microfinance and the Making of Development*. Abingdon: Routledge.

Schild, Veronica. 2000. "Neo-Liberalism's New Gendered Market Citizens: The 'Civilizing' Dimension of Social Programmes in Chile." *Citizenship Studies* 4(3): 275–305.

Schultz, Theodore. 1961. "Investment in Human Capital." *The American Economic Review* 51(1): 1–17.

Schultz, Theodore. 1981. *Investing in People: The Economics of Population Quality.* Berkeley, CA: University of California Press.

Shain, Farzana. 2013. "'The Girl Effect': Exploring Narratives of Gendered Impacts and Opportunities in Neoliberal Development." *Sociological Research Online* 18(2). www.socresonline.org.uk/18/2/9.html.

Skaperdas, Stergios; Soares, Rodrigo; Willman, Alys; Miller, Stephen C. 2009. *The costs of violence.* Washington, DC: World Bank. http://documents.worldbank.org/curated/en/521481468333266536/The-costs-of-violence.

Surender, Rebecca. 2013. "The Role of Historical Contexts in Shaping Social Policy in the Global South." In *Social Policy in a Developing World,* edited by Rebecca Surender and Robert Walker, 14–36. Cheltenham: Edward Elgar.

Wilson, Kalpana. 2013. "Agency as 'Smart Economics': Neoliberalism, Gender and Development." In *Gender, Agency and Coercion,* edited by Sumi Madhok, Anne Phillips, and Kalpana Wilson, 84–101. Basingstoke: Palgrave Macmillan.

Woolley, Frances. 1996. "Getting the Better of Becker." *Feminist Economics* 2(1): 114–120.

World Economic Forum. 2013. "The Human Capital Report." Geneva: World Economic Forum. http://www3.weforum.org/docs/WEF_HumanCapitalReport_2013.pdf.

World Economic Forum. 2016. "Human Capital Report 2016." Geneva: World Economic Forum. http://reports.weforum.org/human-capital-report-2016/#frame/c36cf.

3 Gender, Development and Smart Economics at the World Bank

Introduction

In 2011, the president of the World Bank Robert Zoellick spoke about the kinds of institutional change that had occurred within the Bank, which had recently sought to bring issues like sustainability, transparency, and corruption to the forefront its work. He also placed gender on this list, acknowledging that: "Eighteen years ago, the World Bank rarely talked about gender. Today we know that gender equality is smart economics" (Zoellick 2011). Zoellick's language here is typical of the Smart Economics agenda and its account of gender equality, because it imagines gender equality as a component of economic growth that has been recently discovered and subsequently made visible to policymakers. Eighteen years ago, gender was *not* on the Bank's agenda; today, it is. His statement raises important questions: how was gender discovered by the Bank? How did the Bank go from being an institution renowned for its technocratic and resolutely economistic approach to poverty (of which gender analysis was not a part) to the institution which today sees itself as the leading source of development knowledge on gender equality?

These questions point us towards the politics of knowledge production in development. The premise here is contested: mainstream development institutions see themselves as scientific (rather than political) institutions, uncovering realities about development and prescribing value-neutral solutions to poverty eradication. Yet, as critical and post-structural development studies literature has demonstrated, the kinds of knowledge claims made about development are the result of contested, politicized, and unequal power relations. In this chapter, I address the politics of development knowledge production that lie behind the Smart Economics agenda, using human capital theory as an entry point. Human capital theory is a central piece of the dominant discourse around gender equality in global development institutions: it has been instrumental in advancing gender issues in developing policymaking, because gender has the noted tendency to appear to economic institutions as a marginal or irrelevant "add-on" to policy. Human capital theory, in fact, underpins the account of gender equality that the World Bank has recently embraced and sought to lead: "Gender Equality as Smart Economics."

This chapter addresses the complex evolution of gender equality issues within the World Bank, with an emphasis on the processes through which knowledge is produced and contested in the institution. Smart Economics is a powerful discourse with roots in many institutions, just as the trends that influence Gender and Development today are not the work of any one institution. However, the World Bank, as I show in this chapter, has been the most powerful producer of Gender and Development knowledge since the 1990s, in part because of explicit efforts to position itself as such. The story of gender in the Bank is bound up with an institutional history of feminists working inside and outside the Bank to effect change; activists critiquing dominant development paradigms and practices; and conceptual and organizational changes within the institution itself. Its efforts to develop and disseminate the Smart Economics agenda have led the field and it has been an influential actor in shaping the kinds of private-public relationships that dominate Gender and Development today. Methodologically, the chapter draws on the analysis of World Bank documents and interviews with World Bank staffers.

Development Bank, "Knowledge Bank"

The World Bank is a pre-eminent producer of development knowledge: today, the Bank and institutions like it "frame the world" with regard to economic policy in global governance (Weaver 2010: 70). Since its foundation in 1944, the World Bank's remit has shifted significantly. It was established as the International Bank for Reconstruction and Development at the Bretton Woods Conference, the post-WWII economic summit at which the International Monetary Fund was also founded, in order to manage the new financial system of fixed exchange rates. Given the post-war context in which the Bank was founded, its original remit was limited to providing funds for reconstruction in post-conflict states. In the following decades, its focus has shifted from post-war reconstruction to development and anti-poverty lending; today it lends in a wide variety of outside sectors, including rural development, education, health and institution building (Weaver 2008; Phillips 2009). The Bank comprises five separate entities under the umbrella of the World Bank Group whose constituent parts are tasked with different kinds of lending and investment activity. The Bank's five related agencies are as follows:

Table 3.1 The World Bank Group

Name	*Function*
International Bank for Reconstruction and Development	Lends to middle income countries to support development and reconstruction
the International Development Agency	Provides interest-free loans and grants to the poorest countries

Name	*Function*
the International Finance Corporation	Lends to and takes private equity in companies
Multilateral Investment Guarantee Agency	Provides a range of services to foreign investment in developing countries, including insurance, technical assistance, and dispute mediation
International Centre for Settlement of Investment Disputes	Provides facilitation for arbitration and mediation of disputes between member states to promote investment in developing countries

Source: Table adapted from Marshall 2008: 9.

As with all global governance institutions that are nominally democratic, geopolitical power relations are at play in the Bank's structure and function. The World Bank has 189 member states, although the United States is far and away the most powerful. The power of the Bank is amplified by its proximity (physical and ideological) to powerful institutions of the American government: the Bank's president is, by tradition, chosen by the US government and as a member state, the US has the largest share of vote and the only veto holder. Political economists have recognized this proximity in terms of the confluence between ideology, policy, and discourse of these institutions (see Wade 2002; Fine et al 2003). For instance, the Washington Consensus policies, around which "everyone in Washington" agreed, understood "everyone" to be the American congress, senior members of the presidential administration, international financial institutions located in Washington, economies agencies of the US government and Federal Reserve, and major think tanks (Williamson 2009: 7–8). Geopolitically, the Bank's proximity to American political power has been both a source of influence and the site of intense criticism. The most recent election of a Bank president, in 2012, marked the first time that a group of states from the global South banded together to challenge the American nominee (although they were ultimately unsuccessful). More broadly, the perception that the Bank is a tool of American power, structurally undemocratic and unable to fundamentally reform its geopolitical alignment has given strength to efforts by other regional groupings to build their own development banks. The nascent BRICS development bank presents the best example of this phenomenon, and signals the broader climate in which the World Bank must compete with other development lenders (see Gray and Murphy 2013; Mawdsley 2012).

Despite the changing development landscape in which rival lenders are increasingly asserting influence and challenging dominant development powers, institutions like the Bank retain their position of power because their resources significantly outstrip all others. In terms of resources, the Bank is the clear leader among global development institutions, lending more than any other: during fiscal year 2016 alone, it committed US$61 billion in loans, grants, investments and guarantees (World Bank 2016b). It also possesses staff and research resources that surpass any academic institution, with over 10,000 employees in 120 mission offices worldwide (World Bank 2016a). The Bank's unparalleled resources – both financial and human – make it a leader in the production and dissemination of knowledge about development. It is not all-powerful, but does enjoy a "monopoly on economic wisdom" around the world (Griffin 2009: 84). Its position in the field is the product of the unparalleled financial and personnel power of the Bank, links with sources of American governmental power, and its reputational position in the development community.

The World Bank, by virtue of its resources, produces publications, reports, and discourses that influence development practice worldwide; it serves as a repository of development knowledge and its staff members are often called upon by developing countries for expertise (Weaver 2008; Griffin 2006; King and McGrath 2004). Indeed, this is not simply a by-product of the Bank's aforementioned resources, but an explicit institutional goal. The Bank has long aspired to a "leadership role in the intellectual realm" of development but, due to institutional and contextual constraints, this goal has been a highly publicized aspect of Bank work only since the mid-1990s under the leadership of James Wolfensohn (Bayliss et al. 2011: 26–27; Mehta 2001). Since this time, the Bank has sought to position itself as a "Knowledge Bank", broadening its mandate from the transfer of capital to the production and transfer of knowledge about and for development. Its mission statement makes clear that knowledge, not financial capital, is the Bank's greatest asset for global development: "We are not a bank in the ordinary sense but a *unique partnership* to reduce poverty and support development" (World Bank 2016a, emphasis added). In the nearly two decades since James Wolfensohn's announcement of the World Bank's transformation from a traditional financial institution to the world's "Knowledge Bank", it has sought to consolidate this position, putting its financial and reputational power behind its knowledge production agenda. It continues to dedicate 25–30% of its total annual budget toward knowledge activities (amounting to US$4 billion dollars annually), is the recipient of knowledge management awards, and scores highly on citation impact measures (Enns 2014: 2; see also Kramarz and Momani 2013). According to a 2014 report, the Bank spent 25% of its 2012 country services budget on knowledge services/ products, an area in which expenditure has steadily increased over the past ten years. Its core knowledge activities are: i) economic and sector work; ii) technical assistance; iii) the World Development Report; iv) external training and capacity development; v) research; vi) impact evaluations; vii) global monitoring; viii) new product development; and ix) internal reports (Doemeland and Trevino 2014: 3). It asserts authoritative knowledge about development and, by virtue of its position as the best funded and most powerful global development institution has significant ability to shape the body of development knowledge.

Knowledge produced by the Bank is the result of contestation within the institution, among its different factions, and is produced for a diverse range of audiences who are differently positioned in the broader power hierarchy of development. This power hierarchy is shaped by a historical legacy and material relationships with their origins in colonial and post-colonial governance projects (see Escobar 1995). The more immediate context, as Jonathan Crush puts it, is the development *machine:*

> "This machine is global in its reach, encompassing departments and bureaucracies in colonial and post-colonial states throughout the world, Western aid agencies, multilateral organizations, the sprawling global network of NGOs, experts and private consultants, private sector organizations such as banks and companies that marshal the rhetoric of development, and the plethora of development studies programs in institutes of learning worldwide."
>
> (Crush 1995: 6)

This "machine" implies a set of relations – social, cultural and geopolitical – from which development discourse emerges (Ibid). While it does generally serve to produce and reproduce a dominant paradigm, there is also room for contestation and resistance within. Despite efforts to establish itself as a Knowledge Bank, the World Bank might be better understood as a "Knowledge Battlefield" where different actors compete for influence around the production of knowledge (Bebbington et al 2004). Just as the Bank is not monolithic, its role as "Knowledge Battlefield" is by no means a clear binary structure pitting internal Bank staff against external activists and campaigners, although this dynamic is not unusual. Knowledge battles are "waged" among Bank staff, external non-Bank actors, other external actors who implement Bank projects, and a variety of sub-communities within the Bank who are linked to external communities (Ibid.: 38). Major shifts in development thinking have altered the interpretation and implementation of the Bank's paradigm; the process by which gender came to occupy a prominent place in the Bank's work provides an instructive example.

The Bank aims to set the agenda for academics, donors, and practitioners in the global North and South. Given the Bank's increasing focus on links with private finance and partnerships with corporations, it has broadened the scope of its audience and shifted aspects of its knowledge production efforts to address the concerns of a private sector audience. The institution brings its influence to bear on the private sector through its Knowledge Bank capacity, by lending expertise and building collaborative cross-sector partnerships. The Bank now presents itself as a uniquely positioned institution with the economic credentials and resources to communicate with the private sector on development issues and to foster partnerships between public and private sectors. For example, this is evident in the publication of the Bank's *Doing Business Report* which ranks countries based on their regulatory environments; the most recent report measures eleven indicators of business regulation including employment regulations, investor protection, credit, taxation, and property laws among others (World Bank 2014a; see Hickel 2014). The *Doing Business* reports address gender in economic development, advancing the argument that women gain more than men from free-market reforms and will be harmed by increased regulation (Bedford 2009b). The Bank's role as a producer of development knowledge requires it to maintain credibility with a variety of audiences, from NGOs to national finance ministers. As such, its staff are well aware that their findings must be couched in particular institutional languages that will appeal to these diverse audiences (Interview WB4).[1] Its gender work has been defined by these tensions inside and outside the organization. The Bank is not static, nor is it monolithic; the history of gender in Bank policy testifies to the institutional complexities and dynamics that shape its policymaking process and amplify its gender equality messaging.

Gender and development in the World Bank

The role of gender in the World Bank's work has shifted dramatically over time, gaining a more prominent role in the institution over the last 30 years. Yet, the progress of gender in the Bank has not followed a linear path of gradual acceptance and integration: it has not been suddenly discovered, but slowly and haltingly integrated into Bank operations via the insertion of gender into broader narratives of economic growth and development models. Its role in the Bank has always been contested and efforts to integrate gender into Bank policymaking have proceeded in cycles of advance, setback, and reformulation. Furthermore, the history of feminist engagement with the Bank has been tied up with feminist debates around the possibility of achieving change within mainstream institutions and strategic debates about efficiency and equality rationales. Conventional wisdom at the Bank has long held that gender equality is a natural by-product of economic growth, and thus an outcome of the Bank's work rather than a relevant area for economic analysis. As a result, gender advocates within the Bank have faced pressure to "sell" their expertise to policymakers and create space for themselves in the policy process. Historically, they have tended to emphasize the efficiency gains of investment in women's productive capacity, rather than stressing the need to address gender equality as a moral issue. This gender-skeptic institutional culture has been noted since the Bank's foundation, and is a powerful force that continues to shape feminist interaction therein.

In its early years as a lender for post-war reconstruction and development, gender was understood within the institution as marginal to the World Bank's work. Its initial focus was limited to providing loans to the governments of post-conflict states and, as such, gender played a minimal role in early policy. For over 30 years, from its founding in 1944 until the appointment of its first Women in Development (WID) advisor in 1977, women as a group and gender as a concept were perceived as largely irrelevant to the Bank's work.

This attitude began to change during the late 1970s and early 1980s though progress remained slow; the Bank's WID unit was founded in 1986 and it introduced statistical indicators for gender in 1988; by 1990 the Bank's WID unit had eight staff members (Kuiper and Barker 2006; Weaver 2010). In the early 1990s, institutional re-organization dissolved the WID office and dispersed WID operations across regional offices, along with a dedicated gender team in the Education and Social Policy sector (Razavi and Miller 1995). Early gender policy in the Bank was heavily influenced by a conceptual association between gender, education, and human capital.

From the earliest days of WID in the Bank, an account of gender equality that stresses equality-as-efficiency has been the most successful at attracting institution by development institutions. As discussed in Chapter 1, early efforts to put gender on the development agenda tended to stress women's role as productive workers and responsible mothers, advancing an account of gender equality as a driver of other economic outcomes. The World Bank was one such institution, where the efficiency rationale proved significantly more attractive to policymakers than equality-based accounts. By its own estimation, the Bank began serious gender work during the 1980s, though this work largely imagined women as mothers confined to the "social" realm of reproduction and therefore uninvolved in economic life. WID work in the Bank from 1975–1985 generally reflected the assumption that women could be targeted in successful projects on health, education, and family planning. However, their relationship to economic development was primarily as beneficiaries of resources, rather than economic agents. Throughout 1980s, the Bank's WID advisers slowly gained more authority, resources, and influence within the institution and regional WID coordinators were appointed (Razavi and Miller 1995; Kabeer 1994). The understanding of women as mothers, instruments of child welfare, and as potential development beneficiaries – still marginal to the development process – characterized the general position of women in Bank discourse until the mid-1990s. Early in the institutionalization of gender in the Bank, its WID team stressed women's human capital as a conceptual framework for integrating gender into economic policy, thereby setting a precedent for reliance on the efficiency rationale (Razavi and Miller 1995: 47). When the Bank did change its position and make concerted efforts to integrate a gender lens into its policies, albeit a conservative one, this shift was prompted by a change in leadership and development climate.

The decade of the 1990s saw important changes in the World Bank's approach to Gender and Development. Although familiar debates about efficiency and equality persisted, gender achieved more substantial recognition within Bank policymaking as an area of broader concern across the institution. The Bank's adoption of a more robust gender and development policy approach during the 1990s was driven by a combination of internal institutional shifts and external pressures of the broader crisis in development. Widespread criticism of development failures stemmed from the apparent growing wealth gap, debt crises across the global South, and anger at the adverse effects of the kinds of structural adjustment policies pursued by development institutions. The resulting paradigmatic crisis challenged the ideas underpinning development, particularly destabilizing assumptions about the roles of the state, civil society, and international institutions in liberalizing reforms. This crisis and reform is best understood in terms of the challenge to the Washington Consensus and emergence of a post-Washington Consensus era. The Washington Consensus was an agreement around a particular neoliberal orthodoxy that united Washington policymakers including the World Bank: proponents of the Washington Consensus held that state intervention posed the greatest risk to economic growth, and that the state should be restrained at all costs. As a corollary, policies to decrease state control over the economy should be implemented, including trade liberalization, privatization, and reduction of state spending, particularly through reducing expenditure on social provision (Öniş and Şenses 2006; Babb 2013). The Washington Consensus policy paradigm was widely translated into development policy, most notably in the form of the notorious Structural Adjustment Programs that offered development loans in exchange for policy reform. Feminist political economy work has shown the gendered harms caused by structural adjustment (whether formally imposed as a loan condition or adopted by governments who are not loan recipients): when market volatility creates financial crises, women tend to bear the brunt of cuts to state spending, as they are felt at the household level (Elson 2003). At the Bank, mounting criticism of the adverse effects of Structural Adjustment – widening inequalities, creating unmanageable debt burdens, reducing state capacity and exposing citizens of debt-burdened states to severe poverty – created a climate of reflection and, to some extent, reform.

Sustained criticism of Washington Consensus policy and challenges to its underlying framework produced an intellectual and political shift; in its place, the so-called post-Washington Consensus appeared. From the Bank's perspective, its post-Washington Consensus outlook moved away from the orthodoxies of economic neoliberalism by acknowledging the role of the state in social provision, the role of institutions in fostering markets, the need to engage with civil society groups, and the importance of anti-poverty action. Most importantly, it marked a shift in the Bank's mission towards poverty eradication. The Post-Washington Consensus emerged partly as a response to critics of earlier structural adjustment and debt conditionality approaches and as an acknowledgement of the adverse impacts of market fundamentalism. In important ways, it has shown the Bank is willing to question its own orthodoxies. World Development Reports in the early 2000s, for instance, highlighted flaws in the trickle-down economics model, foregrounded questions of equality, and advocated anti-poverty measures related to environment, health, and violence (Bedford 2009a). The newfound focus on participation, empowerment, and social capital in Post-Washington Consensus discourse provided space for the consideration of gender, insofar as it allowed the Bank to accord importance to social dimensions, like health and education, that are seen to fall into the realm of women's issues. In the search for development's "silver bullet" that could correct for failures of the state and the market, social capital theories (stressing the value of the bonds of trust and reciprocity in a community) gained prominence and heightened the visibility of economic agents who had been previously overlooked, including women (Rankin 2002; Molyneux 2002).

For the purposes of understanding the role of gender in development in the World Bank, the post-Washington Consensus era does mark an important intellectual turning point where gender acquired more legitimacy under this new paradigm, and where feminist policymakers in the Bank had more opportunity to effect change. Changes in the Bank's institutional climate and economic approach slowly created more conceptual space for the consideration of social aspects of development and the inclusion of non-economists on the Bank's staff (Bergeron 2006). In reaction to critiques of the top-down style of development policymaking, mainstream institutions turned to engage with participatory forms of development and embraced a social capital paradigm that directed greater attention at indigenous peoples, ethnic minorities, and women; similarly, the use of a natural capital framing by advocates of environmental protection was somewhat successful in gaining Bank attention for environmental issues (Bebbington et al 2004). Engagement with social issues traditionally seen as falling outside of the Bank's mandate was partly the result of the Bank's Post-Washington Consensus reforms, as well as growing recognition of activist work on relevant issues (Bergeron 2006; O'Brien et al 2001). Policymaking (and knowledge production) at the Bank has never been fully closed to outside pressure groups, but this time period saw a greater willingness to engage with outsiders who might challenge established wisdom at the institution.

The political climate of the mid-1990s allowed for a similar institutional recognition of feminist activists. Two instances of activist engagement were particularly influential in creating change in the Bank's relationship to gender issues: 1994 saw the anniversary "Fifty Years is Enough" campaign launched protests outside World Bank and IMF annual meetings and sought to pressure donor countries to hold the Bank accountable. In response, the Bank committed itself to further integrating "participatory" and "sustainability" issues into its work (Weaver and Leiteritz 2005). One year later, the 1995 UN Conference on Women in Beijing marked a major moment of recognition for feminist issues on an international stage. The Beijing Platform for Action, ratified by all UN member states, committed signatories to gender mainstreaming. Beijing had a widespread and long-lasting impact on feminist political activism outside of economic development issues, but its effect was especially important at the World Bank, in large part due to the personal influence of World Bank president James Wolfensohn, who had a wider effect at challenging established paradigms in the Bank (Bebbington et al. 2004). In his speech at the Beijing Conference, he acknowledged feminist criticism of the Bank and committed it to increasing funding for girls' primary and secondary education. This speech is frequently acknowledged as a turning point in the Bank's relationship to gender, notable not just for its approach to gender issues but also for its acknowledgment of Bank critics:

> "We [the World Bank] are putting $5 billion annually into projects that involve quite specific issues relating to the advancement of women's rights, to human rights, and to economic opportunity. And if we're doing it wrong, we welcome having a dialogue about it. We want to be partners with the governments that we serve, with the NGOs with whom we work, with the interest groups, and with the civil society, in order to develop in the years to come more effective mechanisms to achieve the objectives for which you're meeting here."
>
> (Wolfensohn 2005 [1995])

The expanded role for feminist advocates at Beijing marked a substantial change for the institution, which had traditionally not regarded external feminist pressure groups as legitimate actors in the policy process (O'Brien et al. 2000). Wolfensohn shifted Bank discourses around women by making them "rhetorically central" to the Bank's claims on inclusive and progressive development, peppering his speeches and statements with images of women and girls (Bedford 2009a: 7). This rhetorical shift created a discursive climate in the Bank in which women could be lauded as key agents of development who had yet to be adequately engaged in the process, laying the rhetorical groundwork for the dominance of the business case for gender that pervades the Bank today. It also contributed to an intellectual climate where Bank economists sought new ways to understand the relationship between gender, development, and inequality: human capital theory provided an essential tool in this endeavour.

Human capital in the post-Washington Consensus Bank

The post-Washington Consensus brought about major intellectual and rhetorical shifts in the Bank's work and therefore opened up policy space for critical staffers to advance feminist (and other) agendas. This period did see the Bank reflect on its legacy and question the paradigm under which it had operated for decades. However, to the typology of roll-back and roll-out neoliberalism discussed in Chapter 1, we can interpret the changes in the Bank as less an abandonment of neoliberalism than a turn to roll-out or reformed neoliberalism, with important gender implications. The Bank's analysis of the failures of structural adjustment reflected an agreement that its reforms had fallen short because of weak states that lacked the institutions to implement them, thus necessitating a turn to good governance reforms. The kinds of Post-Washington Consensus changes undertaken at the Bank moved away from market fundamentalist logic, but advocated for a wide-reaching set of interventions to enable economic development (Winters and Kulkarni 2013). The most concrete manifestation of this shift came in relation to conditions on Bank lending.

During the Washington Consensus period characterized by structural adjustment, countries who borrowed from the World Bank had to meet a set of loan conditionalities that usually revolved around liberalizing reforms and re-structuring of the public sector. Thus the *adjustment* of this relationship was enforced through loan disbursement and monitoring of reforms.

The post-Washington Consensus Bank sought to move away from this model of conditionality, not least because it was at odds with the new ethos of partnership and good governance, but the model persisted in subtle ways. Rather than force borrowers to accept the Bank's conditionalities and undertake the set reforms, Bank lending moved to a more restrictive selection process whereby borrowers made these reforms ahead of time, in order to be eligible to borrow. As such, the good governance agenda has not so much reformed conditionality as attached conditions to a wider range of items, with conditionality linked to governance and democratization issues (Fine et al 2003; Porter and Craig 2004; Babb 2013). Griffin (2006) identifies this as a discursive re-ordering of neoliberalism, where the language of conditions has been replaced with a language of flexibility and benchmarking, but the same mechanisms of discipline remain in place. While the number of conditions attached to Bank loans declined from the ten years between 1995 and 2005, the number of benchmarks increased seven-fold. This mode of benchmark governance requires more interventions in practice, as part of its capacity-building orientation in borrowing countries (2006: 577–579). This amounts to a World Bank which is "less interventionist" but more "starkly coercive," analogous to the model of roll-out neoliberalism (Harrison 2001: 18). The distinction between the conceptual substance of the Post-Washington Consensus and its policy changes raises questions about the extent of reform versus the expansion of existing development paradigms. Critics of the Bank's reformed neoliberalism have argued that it now works to govern through a wider range of social interventions (Larner and Walter 2004); feminist critics have echoed these claims by pointing to increased efforts to govern gender relationships through heterosexual partnerships (Griffin 2009; Bedford 2009a). The Post-Washington Consensus World Bank should therefore be understood in terms of a transformation within the neoliberal paradigm, from roll-back to roll-out neoliberalism, rather than a complete rejection of neoliberalism or adoption of a radical new paradigm.

This critique of the post-Washington Consensus, and the suggestion that it did not radically transform the Bank, does not mean that the institution remains the same as it was in the 1980s. The post-Washington Consensus did mark important departures from previous Bank orthodoxies and did usher in an interest in human development, of which women where central. In line with the emphasis on shifting forms of neoliberalism within the Bank, the effects of the post-Washington Consensus can be mapped through the ascendance of human capital theory. Human capital theory has been fundamental to the changing role of gender in the institution because it has forged a clear conceptual link between gender equality and economic growth for Bank economists.

Starting in the 1960s, human capital theory was a conceptual tool in the Bank's analytical toolbox, when it was used to evaluate the costs of infrastructure projects (as discussed in Chapter 2). In its early remit as a post-war reconstruction institution, the Bank's main lending priority was large-scale infrastructure. Part of lending for such projects was a requirement to consider the borrowing country's ability to engineer and repair such infrastructure in the long-term. To this end, human capital theory was employed by the Bank to calculate the kinds of educational investments needed to train up engineers and technicians to maintain infrastructure (Heyneman 2003: 315–317). Subsequently, the use human capital theory was expanded to include analysis of other forms of non-technical education. Here, the Bank sought to understand the contexts in which education could produce good outcomes for its projects, although it was careful to focus on practical skills (metal and woodworking for boys, domestic skills for girls) and thus avoid the risk of "educated unemployment and political alienation" (Ibid: 318). Even in the early years of the Bank's engagement with human capital theory, gender was present in its analysis, through the clear distinction between the kinds of human capital investments required by girls and boys. Human capital theory as a tool for conceptualizing economic costs and benefits of a range of social phenomena therefore entered the institution through technical education and later gained wider influence.

Human capital theory has subsequently dominated education policy in the institution for years before the advent of the post-Washington Consensus, achieving broader uptake within the institution during its post-Washington Consensus turn to a social investment and human development paradigm (Fine and Rose 2003). It has also been instrumental in the changing role of gender in the institution, because the WID team strategically used this efficiency framing to raise women's visibility among policymakers: they stressed women's "human capital" and "labor productivity" to emphasize the alignment of gender equality with other development goals (Razavi and Miller 1995: 47). The 1990s and post-Washington Consensus era marked the moment in which human capital gained wider traction in the institution and became instrumental in the new visibility of gender equality issues. In particular, human capital theory opened up space for girls and women because human capital's emphasis on calculating rates of return on investment from education mapped onto efficiency-based accounts of gender equality. The efficiency argument (through human capital) worked to advance a feminist cause in the Bank's institutional language. As Larry Summers (former Chief Economist at the World Bank) wrote at the time:

> "In making an argument for investing in female education, I have tried to steer clear of the moral and cultural aspects unavoidably involved in any gender-related question… [it] reflects a conviction that helping women to be better mothers to their children is desirable whatever one's view of the proper role of women in society."
>
> (Summers 1994: 20 quoted in Fine and Rose 2003: 169)

Summers' assertion here is significant in terms of the institutional position that it sets out: he avoids making a moral argument, he explains, because gender equality issues are inevitably bound up with "cultural" questions and various judgments about "the proper role of women in society". This is an institutional position that remains powerful and influential in today's Smart Economics policymaking, in which gender equality advocacy takes place in an economistic register that shies away from normative and rights-based claims.

If human capital provided the Bank with a way to bracket the moral questions of gender equality, it provided a language of investment and return that could be easily applied to bring gender considerations into development sectors in which they were previously absent. From its beginnings in education policy, human capital theory came to inform a broader range of social policy issues in the Bank. When backlash against the structural adjustment programs of the Washington Consensus period prompted a reassessment of development paradigm that had dominated the institution during the 1980s, human capital theory informed its institutional re-orientation. This is not to suggest that the Bank abandoned a market-driven development model, but that it sought to temper its earlier market models with more state involvement and a focus on social investments to produce greater efficiency. Instead, a social investment paradigm was adopted that emphasized the ability for governments and public institutions to facilitate the capabilities of citizens. From the mid-1990s, the World Bank began to develop a human capital framework as a basis for its re-orientation to human development (see World Bank 1995; Psacharopoulos, 1995; World Bank 1999). By 1999, the World Bank justified its use of human capital theory by explaining that the theory had been "thorough[ly] debated," vetted by "Nobel-laureate economists," and therefore accepted (World Bank 1999: 6 quoted in Klees 2016). While its human capital turn allowed for the recognition that gender inequalities could not simply be ameliorated by a focus on equality of opportunity, it also worked to legitimize a view of women as subjects in formation who required intervention to catalyze their human capital. The human capital theory that informed education policy in the World Bank took on a distinct gender dimension that came to influence the institution more broadly because it provided an account of development across the life-course that could encompass other forms of social investment. It identified girls and women as the most overlooked sites of investment, as well as the most potentially productive sites of investment. By the 1990s, human capital theory had been "enthusiastically embraced" by advocates within the World Bank, although feminist critics early on identified its tendency to provide hyperbolic promises of female economic empowerment, while explaining away gender inequalities in terms of maternal altruism (Razavi 1998: 32–33).

Moreover, it is notable that the human capital account of education and gender equality that became influential did not mark a departure from the policies of the Washington Consensus era, but demonstrated important continuities that continue to shape the role of gender in the Bank today. Bank policy documents that responded to critiques of Structural Adjustment

Programs made use of human capital theory to highlight the dangers of underinvestment in human capital, though this theoretical framework produced only "minor changes" in overall policy (Wood 2006: 153). The line of continuity consists in the principle that drives this account of development: efficiency, rather than equality.

> "Investment in people implies striving to reach the point at which human capital investments no longer restrain growth or keep people in absolute poverty. Vital in this is equipping the poor to take advantage of the expanding opportunities that accompany growth through extending better health, nutrition and family planning to the poor."
>
> (World Bank, 1995: 24 quoted in Mahon 2010: 178)

The logic of investment is key here, because of the mode of distribution of resources that it implies. Against the language of universal provision, the language of investment conveys the idea that particular groups (girls and women) can be identified as ideal targets for development intervention. The Bank's social investment paradigm, which rose to prominence during the 1990s, proposed investment specifically in the most disadvantaged groups – girls, indigenous peoples, and the poorest – to allow them to take advantage of economic opportunities. Among these vulnerable groups, women and girls were particularly targeted for human capital-building interventions: women because they were mothers who shaped the quality of future human capital and girls because they constituted "human capital in the making" (Mahon 2010: 178). Social capital frameworks performed a similar function to heighten girls' and women's visibility as development agents, because just as human capital re-conceptualized gendered bodies as development assets, social capital theories framed emotional qualities and inter-personal relationships as resources for development (Rankin 2002). Accordingly, girls and women gained visibility in Bank social policy as ideal targets for interventions to develop their human capital, through a framework that emphasized the social externalities of investment in women's human capital like lower fertility, higher life expectancy, and better nutrition levels. Rhetorically, this placed emphasis on women, "investment," and "activation" over the course of a lifetime (Mahon and McBride 2009: 97). Bank funding for projects with gender-related components increased substantially in the areas of health, population and education (O'Brien et al. 2000: 48). As subsequent years have seen broader uptake of gender across the Bank, the conceptual link between human capital theory and gender equality has continued to be essential to the ability of feminists inside and outside the Bank to "sell" gender to a skeptical institution.

At the level of institutional culture, the Bank is well known for a male-dominated, economistic internal culture that tends to regard "social" issues (like gender equality) as irrelevant to its work (Griffin 2009; Bergeron 2003; O'Brien et al 2000). Among comparable institutions, the Bank is "fairly notorious" for its economistic and functionalist approach to gender, meaning its reluctance to engage with gender issues that are not explicitly linked to achieving existing institutional goals and a tendency to understand gender as a variable for analysis, rather than a set of relational inequalities (Beneria 2012: 175). Gender specialists in the Bank who confront this internal culture have adapted by framing their arguments in familiar institutional narratives that emphasize what gender can do for the Bank, rather than the other way around. They have favoured an incremental approach driven by small changes in line with existing norms, rather than coercive directives and benchmarks: in efforts to prevent hostility and backlash, feminist advocates have sought to "persuade via proof" in line with the prevailing institutional culture (Weaver 2010: 84–86). Strategic integration pursued by gender advocates, combined with institutional change and the reforms undertaken by the Bank in the era of the Post-Washington Consensus created space for new issues to merit consideration in the Bank's work: although the institution remains resolutely economistic, its conception of the economic began to expand during the 1990s. This is evident, for instance, in the changing approach to unpaid household and care work done by women: efforts to engender the Bank's conception of the economy allowed for the recognition of work done within the home and the knock-on effects that unequal care burdens can have on women's work outside the home (Bergeron 2016). Critique and debate from activists, academics, and economists worked to broaden the scope of the Bank's work, in part by demonstrating the economic impact of social and political forces. The newest and most significant iteration of this relationship is evidenced by the "Gender Equality as Smart Economics" agenda that has dominated the Bank's gender agenda since the early 2000s.

Smart Economics and beyond

In the Post-Washington Consensus era at the Bank, gender has taken on a new headlining role. As Robert Zoellick observed, the Bank has made a remarkable transition from an institution that "did not talk about gender" in the mid- 1990s to one that prominently endorses the idea that gender equality is relevant to its objectives (2011). The emergence of gender as a legitimate site of analysis within the Bank can be mapped onto broader trends of the time, in which critiques of the Washington Consensus resulted in a formulation of a post-Washington Consensus approach which accorded a greater role to issues like gender, sexuality, race, ability, and beyond. As argued above, in terms of its policy paradigm, there is some substantive difference between the Washington Consensus and its successor but they cannot be understood as distinct development paradigms because they reflect different orientations within neoliberalism. Nonetheless, for the purposes of tracking the production of Gender and Development knowledge within the Bank, it is necessary to note that the Bank certainly sees itself as a reformed institution whose approach to gender has changed dramatically since the 1990s. The period since 1995 has seen the Bank formulate a new approach to gender in relation to the institution's objectives, dominated by a few trends: as established above, it has been characterized by the rise of human capital in Bank analysis of gender equality beyond education; second, it has created greater space for the private sector to involve itself in gender and development governance; third, and at the convergence of these two trends, it has been dominated by the "Gender Equality as Smart Economics" discourse and its associated policies and projects.

The years between 1995 and 2001 brought about a new attitude towards gender and development in the World Bank, marked by more robust engagement with non-economic aspects and measures of wellbeing and increased emphasis on the relationship between gender equality and economic growth (Tzannatos 2006; Kuiper and Barker 2006). In 1994, the Bank's Board endorsed a policy paper on women's participation in economic development (which included a discussion of the "pay-offs" of investing in women) and the Bank issued an Operational Policy statement establishing the goal of reducing gender disparities and enhancing women's participation in development. Nonetheless, significant gaps existed: this Operational Policy statement on gender did not require all investments to address gender aspects and it did not include Structural Adjustment Policies (Tzannatos 2006). In 2001, the Bank published its first major gender report, *Engendering Development*, which emphasized the social and economic costs of gender inequalities, which would obstruct poverty reduction efforts. It called for women's economic status to be used as a major indicator in the Bank's work. *Engendering Development* took on a landmark status in the Gender and Development field, because it represented a major commitment by the Bank to gender mainstreaming and set out a vision of development in which gender was not a marginal issue or add-on. Yet, the relationship between gender and development that the report sets out is somewhat ambiguous, even acknowledging that while gender inequality is harmful to economic development, "income growth and economic development can be good for gender equality, or bad" (World Bank 2001: 181). Although it represented a major step forward, *Engendering* Development signalled some of the contestation and ambivalence in the Bank's approach to gender issues: while it criticized the Bank's previous failures to recognize women's unpaid work, it also concludes that on balance, gender equality has been aided by periods of structural adjustment.

The importance of human capital theory to the Bank's account of gender and development is evident in *Engendering Development*, where human capital formation (and obstacles therein) is one of the main strategies used to conceptualize gender equality/ inequality. Human capital theory provides *Engendering Development* with framework to theorize the allocation (or misallocation) of resources, particularly as it relates to health and education impacts on girls' and women's labor productivity:

> "By hindering the accumulation of human capital in the home and the labor market, and by systematically excluding women or men from access to resources, public services, or productive activities, gender

> discrimination diminishes an economy's capacity to grow and to raise living standards."
>
> (Ibid.: 3)

Human capital theory plays an important conceptual role here because it provides a framework in which investment in physical capital assets can be compared against investment in health and education. However, the overall effect on policy recommendations remains limited: the account of human capital theory employed in *Engendering Development* fails to challenge Structural Adjustment, and instead becomes another framing device to endorse free-market and free-trade principles (Seguino 2006). Human capital theory allows for greater emphasis on the micro-economic inputs that shape the labor force, but functions more broadly to avoid macro-economic questions around broader inequality and the structures that reproduce it (Wood 2006; Kuiper and Barker 2006). *Engendering Development* endorsed gender mainstreaming as a tool for achieving institutional goals, equated gender equality with growth, and as such constructed a powerful "unilateral instrumentalist approach" to women's empowerment as a development goal (Tinker and Zuckerman 2014). The significance of *Engendering Development* lies in the conceptual and rhetorical frameworks it established, which laid the basis for the Smart Economics agenda today.

In 2006, the World Bank launched its 2007–2010 Gender Action Plan (GAP), which first set out the "Gender Equality as Smart Economics" framework in full and committed the Bank to "advance women's economic empowerment by enhancing women's ability to participate in land, labor, financial and product markets, thus promoting shared growth and accelerating the implementation of the Third Millennium Development Goal on gender equality and women's empowerment" (World Bank, 2006: 9). To this end, it introduced guidelines to "engender" policy-based loans and introduced a discussion of gender mainstreaming in Bank policy operations (Ibid.). Interestingly, the 2007–2010 GAP explicitly sets human capital outside of its purview, because it is temporally framed on interventions that will produce "demonstrable results in a reasonable time frame" (World Bank 2006: 6). The GAP proposes to leave aside "human capital variables (education, health, and labor market experience) and family, social, and cultural factors" that affect labor market participation and empowerment because they are medium to long-term interventions (Ibid.). Nonetheless, it relies on a conception of women's economic empowerment that bears familiar traces of human capital theory, because it sets the main target as "interventions which increase the compatibility between women's productive and reproductive roles" and raise the visibility of women's "contributions to the economy" (Ibid.). Its proposed interventions center on short-term efforts to improve women's market skills in order to produce tangible effects in line with the MDGs timetable (Griffin 2010). Its emphasis on the Smart Economic logic of convergences further structures the conclusions, emphasizing the synergies between equity and prosperity (World Bank 2006: 4).

Importantly, the 2007–2010 GAP also marked a shift towards engaging the private sector in the Bank's gender equality agenda, as it was the first set of Bank gender guidelines which applied to the International Finance Corporation, the Bank's private sector finance arm (previous guidelines were confined to the IBRD and IDA, which provide low and no interest loans to developing countries); the GAP outlined the IFC's role in increasing the numbers of women participants and beneficiaries of private-sector development projects (World Bank 2006). Near the end of the 2007–2010 GAP, the Bank chose to dedicate the 2012 edition of its flagship World Development Report to the issue of gender equality. The report highlighted the GAP message of "Gender Equality as Smart Economics" as its headlining feature and placed greater emphasis on the role of the private sector in providing women access to employment and credit (World Bank 2011; 2012). Since the Bank's 2012 re-organization under its new President, gender has been declared one of four "cross cutting solution areas" and chosen as a special theme for the 2014–2017 replenishment of funds in the International Development Association (Bibler and Zuckerman 2013). Its 2016–2021 Gender Action Plan focuses primarily on gender mainstreaming in risk, resilience, and crisis management (World Bank 2016c).

Criticism of previous Gender Action Plans and lack of progress on gender mainstreaming led the Bank to focus efforts on integrating gender more thoroughly into lending operations from 2010 onwards (Chant 2012). By 2013, the Bank reported that 98% of lending was gender-informed (meaning gender taken into account in at least one stage); in the same year it reported that 54% of operations included gender-informed analysis, actions, and monitoring and evaluation (World Bank 2013). However, the coding system that produces these estimates is problematic. The Bank's tracking system for "gender-sensitivity" allows operations to be declared "gender-informed" if they have taken gender into account at the analysis, action or monitoring stage. By this metric, operations labelled gender-informed could potentially earn that assessment with only a single reference to gender across all stages. Moreover, the coding system provides an example of how gender can evaporate in practice: in 2013, Gender Action reported that the Bank could not give a precise figure on its gender mainstreaming funding, because "the very essence of mainstreaming gender is to make it the job of all Bank staff" and it was therefore not centrally monitored (Lauterbach and Zuckerman 2013). In response to criticism of its gender analysis system, the Bank has taken steps to integrate gender more systematically across the lending process through the introduction of more monitoring systems. The introduction of monitoring mechanisms like this has proven an effective feminist strategy for creating incremental change within the Bank, although their implementation relies on the acquiescence of Bank economists. There are few enforcement mechanisms in place to mandate these kinds of changes, particularly with regard to mainstreaming gender training across the Bank's staff (Bibler and Zuckerman 2013). Gender equality goals have been integrated into the Bank's work to some extent, and gender-mainstreaming efforts have indeed been undertaken in the institution that had a long-standing reputation as a laggard on gender issues. Yet in practice, efforts to mainstream gender have demonstrated the limits of what is possible within that institutional structure. Gender mainstreaming has, in effect, "turned a radical movement idea into strategy of public management" (Prügl and Lustgarten 2006: 55). Feminist critiques of Bank policy have continually been subject to the process of translation and modification that makes them amenable to institutional goals: gender equality issues are permitted to become a part of the Bank's knowledge infrastructure when they are mediated through existing development paradigms.

The adoption of an instrumental rationale for gender equality that leans heavily on the promotion of gender equality as a driver of economic growth has been noted in the World Bank since the earliest days of its engagement with gender (Razavi and Miller 1995; O'Brien et al. 2000; Weaver 2010). The pressure to sell gender to a skeptical institution encouraged feminist advocates to develop strategic framings of gender: women as "untapped" labor resources, women as human capital in need of investment, women as resilient agents for post-crisis growth. These figures have come to animate Bank conversations about poverty, economic growth, and social change, although it is worth noting the Bank's tendency to confuse "gender" with "women" is a fundamental barrier to any transformative work (Griffin 2009: 138). This instrumental approach has proven partially successful, at least to the extent that it has convinced the Bank to invest resources in determining the relationship between gender equality and economic growth. Several decades of World Bank research on this question have yielded mixed results on the question of gender equality as a driver of economic growth – and economic growth as a driver of gender equality – but have prompted its interest in a micro-economic approach to women's human capital and access to productive resources which is evident in its Gender Action Plans since 2007 (Prügl 2017). This is a narrative that has experienced rapid institutional uptake and is now embraced by a variety of institutions both public and private (see Perrons 2015); moreover, the push to make the "Business Case for Gender Equality" has significantly changed the funding landscape for Gender and Development. Feminist advocates in global governance institutions and feminist organizations both argue that there is "currently very little funding space outside of this framework" (Ferguson 2014: 13; Arutyanova and Clark 2013). The equation of gender equality with economic growth has seemingly opened up access to a wider range of funding sources, while closing off space for critical and transformative feminist political action.

The dominant feminist critique of the Bank centers around the contention that the vision of neoliberal capitalism promoted and enforced by the Bank rests upon the devaluation of social reproduction and the degradation of commodified female labor; moreover, the Bank's engagement with gender is limited depending on the extent to which women can be shown to *work for* the institution's priorities. Elisabeth Prügl characterizes it as "neoliberalism with a feminist face": it represents a newer iteration of the Post-Washington Consensus, placing emphasis on social inclusion, the role of institutions in sustaining markets, and the imperative of financial-social balance (2017). This is not an account of co-optation, but reflects some of its key concerns: the World Bank has a noted tendency to "adopt the language of its critics in order to silence them" (Bergeron 2003: 404; see also Griffin 2009, 2006; Bergeron 2006). At the same time, gender equality and the female subject have acquired unprecedented visibility in the Bank's work through its "Gender Equality as Smart Economics" agenda, which represents the epitome of this instrumentalization of gender equality (Calkin 2018). This debate is brought to life within the Bank's policy apparatus, where gender equality is a both a high-profile priority and a source of tension in the institution.

The 2012 World Development Report

The World Bank is a powerful producer of development knowledge, but the institution functions less like the Knowledge Bank than a Knowledge Battlefield: the institution is not a monolith, nor is it indifferent to its critics. As such, gender work in the World Bank is the collective result of different factions and paradigms working together against a broader institutional backdrop that gives priority to particular modes of thinking. Given the size and diversity of the institution, it is difficult (or impossible) to identify a singular position and attribute it to the World Bank as a single entity (see Bebbington et al 2004; Bedford 2009a). As such, it is more instructive to identify concrete sites of World Bank policy discourse and to study the process through which they came to be. The 2012 World Development Report (WDR) provides one such example of the way that the institutional gender skepticism of the Bank's early years has been partly transformed and partly re-incarnated in a new policy agenda, albeit through a contested process. The Bank dedicated the 2012 edition of its flagship report – the World Development Report – to the topic of Gender and Development. It stated goal is to understand the occurrence of "gender gaps in human capital" and suggest policy solutions to allow women to "build their human capital and take up economic opportunities" (World Bank 2012: 6). This report marks an important moment in the Bank's gender agenda, wherein it sought to assert expertise in the field of gender and development and to cement its place as a leading producer of Gender and Development knowledge through the report. The 2012 WDR is also the subject of the following chapter: while that chapter deals in detail with the substance of the report's findings and claims, this chapter addresses the politics of knowledge production behind the report and the institutional dynamics that shaped it.

The Bank's desire to become a leader in the production of Gender and Development knowledge is evidenced by its dedication of substantial resources to the research and publication of the 2012 World Development Report. World Development Reports, like most World Bank publications, are highly influential and debate-shaping contributions that have significant impact; that the Bank chose gender equality and women's empowerment as the subject for this report signals its intention to extend its expertise in this policy area. In line with the Bank's aim to function as a Knowledge Bank as well as financial resource, the World Development Report is one of the Bank's "core knowledge services" (Doemeland and Trevino 2014: 3) and receives the funding to match this status. The yearly WDR represents the most well-resourced and widely disseminated publication in the development field: on the research side, its budget ranges from US$3.5 to US$5 million and it is written over two years by a large team of Bank economists with outside consulting from national development agencies and NGOs. In terms of its publication, over 100,000 copies are produced in eight languages (Wade 2002; Mawdsley and Rigg 2002). However, the full report is not accessible in languages other than English. With regard to the WDR 2012, the report overview and "Key Messages" sections are the only portions that are available in languages other than English. The WDR's publication is accompanied by a global promotional tour by its lead authors and Bank spokespeople.

The WDR has historically played an important role in signalling shifts in the Bank's objectives and public discourse. For example, World Development Reports have played a significant part in establishing and legitimizing the Bank's change of mission to poverty reduction and its transformation into a knowledge bank (Clegg 2010; Mehta 2001; Elson 2009). As the most accessible of the Bank's publications, it acts as the "public face" of the Bank and derives authority from this status, although it does not commit the Bank to any particular policies (Mawdsley and Rigg 2002: 93). The Bank is not formally bound by any of its recommendations, and although they may be implemented in other ways by the institution, the WDR's recommendations are recommended by a research team rather than issued by policymakers in positions of direct power. As a high profile and widely publicized Bank publication, but one whose ambiguous status within the Bank gives it uncertain policy impact, the WDR is often viewed with some suspicion by Bank watchers. Robert Wade summarizes this critical view as such:

> "The WDR is both a research-based document and a political document, in the sense that as the Bank's flagship its message must reflect back the ideological preferences of key constituencies and not offend them too much, but the message must also be backed by empirical evidence and made to look 'technical'."
>
> (2002: 220)

Wade's explanation captures the skepticism that meets WDRs, in part because the research and writing process of past WDRs has been the subject of public scandals at the Bank. Specifically, former Bank staffers have reported pressure to produce findings that supported conclusions endorsed by the Bank's leadership, rather than relying on data to draw their conclusions. Subsequent internal investigations have also found evidence that staff felt pressure to produce

WDRs that endorsed pre-determined conclusions (see Wade 2002; Bayliss et al 2011; Broad 2006). Stylistically, WDRs are well known for reflecting an institutional language of established consensus around development issues, in an effort to set agendas in the broader field. WDRs employ a style that sets out a vision of development knowledge which often fails to acknowledge debate or disagreement, instead advancing an account of "common-sense" development knowledge (Mawdsley and Rigg 2002; 2003). This can be particularly glaring when WDRs discuss the effects of prior World Bank policies without engaged reflection on the institution's role (Bedford 2012; Elson 2012). The World Development Report, as the Bank's flagship report, is therefore notable for its deliberate role in seeking to shape development knowledge without necessarily committing to particular policy changes.

Taking into consideration the status of the Bank, its political position, and the location of the WDR within the Bank's policy machinery, any analysis of the World Development Report requires careful attention to the complexities outlined here: not all parts of the report are created equal. The Bank is an enormous and complex institution whose numerous policies, programs, and sub-divisions cannot be easily assessed through the reading of its publications. Kate Bedford argues that any analysis of Bank documents needs "institutionally sensitive reading practices," by which she means the researcher must pay close attention to the writing codes that are common to the Bank (2009a: xxvi). The reading practices that Bedford advises require the researcher to focus particularly on abstracts, summaries, and conclusions of Bank documents in order to apprehend the prevailing discourses in the Bank; these beginning and ending pieces are frequently the only parts of long documents that Bank staff read, so authors of Bank publications put significant efforts into shaping them. By extension, staff can sometimes manage to include dissenting arguments by hiding them in the middle of large documents. Although the resulting publications can appear contradictory, the location of particular arguments can be indicative of their perceived centrality and the degree to which they are embedded in dominant Bank narratives (2009a: xxvii). Alternately, researchers can track ideological shifts in the Bank by reading its documents against each other to identify competing messages and knowledge claims over time (Prügl 2017). The positioning and framing of various arguments, within a document or across a series of documents, gives some indication of the contestation involved in the drafting process, the diverse audiences of Bank publications and the institutional pressures/ practices employed by staff therein.

Given the power of the WDR to prioritize new policy areas and to shape the direction of funding trends among governments and institutions, the Bank's decision to dedicate its 2012 report solely to gender equality attests to the strategically critical moment for gender in global governance. The Bank announced in April 2011 that its 2012 report would focus on the topic of gender equality and development. The report was researched and written by a core team of thirteen Bank employees; in addition, an extended team of eleven contributed materials and all were supervised by a ten-member advisory board. The core team comprised thirteen members: eight lead researchers (four men, four women) and five research analysts (all women). The report was co-directed by Ana Revenga and Sudhir Shetty, both economists and long-time Bank staffers (in 2012, having served 19 and 25 years respectively). Seventy-five percent of the 2012 WDR team members were economists by training and, although the team consisted mainly of members from Europe, Asia, and Latin America, all had earned graduate degrees from American or European higher education institutions and among the core team, four had earned PhDs from Harvard. The team only included one gender specialist who was a PhD candidate at the time; the other members of the leadership had not previously worked on gender issues (Interview WB2; see also Chant 2013). This is customary with WDRs: the core team members are drawn from a variety of departments and areas of specialty from around the Bank.

The composition of the team matters enormously for a critical analysis of the report, because although the WDR is written in a style of value-neutrality and development knowledge consensus, it is in fact a product of messy the knowledge politics and power structures of development institutions. The team's composition and status is also important in terms of the report's editorial independence: in interviews, team members often stressed the editorial independence of the team and the freedom the Bank gave them to "write whatever we wanted" (Interview WB1). However, as another team member commented, the report's directors and lead economists are long-time Bank employees and are thus shaped by the institution in which they work. Although the Bank did not tell the team what to write, she explained, they didn't need to: the findings were shaped by the team's institutional background (Interview WB3). The dominant features of this institutional culture that emerged from interviews revolved around a preference for quantitative data and metrics and a belief in the team's responsibility to "let the data speak" (Interviews WB1, WB2, WB4). The independence of WDR researchers – freedom from institutional pressure – is one dimension of the intellectual climate that shapes the report; my interviewees' emphasis on being driven purely by their data testifies to this. Yet, the question of the broader institutional climate remains. The resources, profile, and public-orientation of the WDR mean that its team is comprised of specifically selected World Bank economists. As Wade puts it: "You do not get to be a Bank research economist without having demonstrated your commitment to the presumptions of neoliberalism and to the analytical techniques of Anglo-American economics" (2002: 233). Furthermore, the composition of the core team is important as it reflects the internal culture of the Bank that is economistic and somewhat skeptical of "soft" issues like gender; this is an institutional culture that has developed and evolved over decades. This gender skepticism persists in the Bank and is evident in the publicity campaign that surrounded the launch of the report. Perhaps in order to anticipate the reluctance of mainstream economists to engage with issues like gender, much of the launch material for the 2012 WDR framed its findings in terms of surprising, unexpected evidence that challenged the skepticism of its team. To accompany its launch, the report's co-director, Ana Revenga, wrote a blog post on the Bank's development blog called "The Education of a Gender Skeptic":

> "Before I started working on the World Development Report 2012, I often thought of gender equality being at the periphery of my work on development. Like many other World Bank colleagues, I would have told you: 'Yes, gender equality matters and it is a good thing.' But in my mind gender equality was something that happened pretty much automatically with economic development. If asked about policy priorities, I would say: focus on growth, on creating jobs, on reducing poverty and improving equity in opportunities, and gender equality will come right along. But I was wrong. Gender equality is not just something that 'happens' with development. Gender equality is both fundamental to and a means for development. And countries need to work hard at achieving it, because it does not come about on its own with economic growth."
>
> (Revenga 2011)

Similarly, Markus Goldstein, another economist from the WDR 2012 core team, wrote a blog post asking if "we should believe the hype" about adolescent girls. In it, he explains that he was skeptical about the impact of adolescent girls on development until he saw a report that quantified the cost of girls' exclusion from the labor market: its findings forced him to "rethink [his] skepticism" (Goldstein 2012). The report's launch demonstrates a welcome change in the Bank's gender rhetoric, with an emphasis on the role of institutions in producing gender equality, but maintains an insistence on the instrumental case for how gender equality drives development too.

Given the institutional culture of the Bank and its reluctant (and delayed) acceptance of the importance of gender to development, these public-facing materials to accompany the launch of Bank gender publications and programs provide important information about how the Bank continues to see gender and attempts to "sell" it to its audience. To this end, one member of the 2012 WDR team who was involved in the report's publicity tour claimed that the instrumental "Gender Equality as Smart Economics" message that emphasized economic growth was essential to allowing him to tailor the report's message to different audiences (Interview WB4). He especially stressed that national finance ministers, who might otherwise be indifferent to gender equality issues, were a key audience targeted by the "Smart Economics" message and the emphasis on the report's findings being driven by data, not ideology. When asked about its key audience, some members of the WDR team referred to external actors like governments, while others spoke about the role that the 2012 WDR might play in convincing economists within the World Bank of the importance of gender. For either goal, the "Smart Economics" framing was a strategy that was looked upon favourably. One team member suggested that within the institution, World Bank staff would be reluctant to engage with work that was not primarily framed as data-driven economic analysis: they might otherwise perceive it as ideological or biased (Interview WB3). Instrumental rationality continues to drive the Bank's gender work, above all else. On this point, the position of arguments within the WDR 2012 is particularly notable. The "Gender Equality as Smart Economics" message was removed from drafts in the middle of the research process, after consultations with feminist economists and development experts. However, "Smart Economics" language reappeared in the final published version in highly visible places (Chant 2012; 2013). "Smart Economics" appears in the 2012 report as a "headlining term", evident in its frequent appearance on the report's cover, foreword, and main messages (Ibid.: 109). The positioning of "Smart Economics" language in the report is particularly important in light of its limited translation into languages other than English. The only parts of the report that were translated were the "report overview" and "key messages" where "Smart Economics" messages were prominently featured.

Despite its resources and prestige, the WDR occupies a somewhat strange institutional position: it is the flagship report of the Bank, well-funded and highly publicized, but is not underpinned by direct policy commitments. It is produced by the Bank and its content approved at multiple levels, yet, as one team member stressed, the fact that WDR core team members are selected from a variety of departments and re-assigned for two years to work full-time on the WDR team means that they are simultaneously "inside and outside" of the Bank (Interview WB1). Issues around editorial independence are highly contested and there is significant tension in the relationship between the WDR and the Bank, especially given the revelations in the 2006 Deaton report which cited Bank staffers discussing interference into their research process and pressure to conform to Bank message. The World Development Report in particular has been cited as a prime example of research in which conclusions were "either predetermined or negotiated in advance" (van Waeyenberge and Fine 2011: 38; Deaton 2006).

Indeed, evidence from Sylvia Chant and my own interviews with staff suggests that much of the report's content was pre-agreed before the research and consulting process had finished. The report had already been drafted by the time consultation with gender and development experts began in autumn 2010, and before the results of its multi-country qualitative survey had finished (Chant 2013: 103). The qualitative multi-country survey commissioned for the 2012 WDR was eventually published in 2013, with a focus on the way gender norms shape agency and decision-making processes (see Munoz Boudet et al 2013). One junior member of the team explained that the report's framework and main areas of focus were pre-determined in initial meetings of the senior staff and were not closely related to the results of the qualitative study. The difficulty dealing with the report's pre-determined structure was evident, the interviewee suggested, in the cursory way the results from that study were used to provide first-person anecdotes and quotes throughout the text but not integrated into the body of the report (Interview WB3). Geopolitical considerations were also taken into account when writing the report: forced marriage and arranged marriage were topics that some researchers suggested for inclusion, but more senior staff rejected this topic for being too politically sensitive (Interview WB3). Although the report's research and writing process were firmly situated within institutional cultures and circumscribed by the need for higher-level approval, the report's team included dissenting voices who raised alternatives.

Its institutional position means that the 2012 WDR cannot be interpreted as the last word on gender policy in the World Bank. However, it provides an important window into the way that knowledge is produced there. It is not made by top down directive alone, although there are substantial pressures that drive the kinds of gender equality messages that are publicized by the Bank. The 2012 WDR represents a major step forward for the World Bank, which had not previously given space to intrinsic arguments about gender equality, and had tended to rely on a modernization development-as-equality framing. Yet with the 2012 WDR, the institution acknowledged the intrinsic value of gender equality and the complex relationship between gender equality and growth. These messages are within the 2012 WDR, and are available for the careful reader. However, the kinds of headline messages and promotional narratives that are highlighted in the report's most visible and circulated materials reflect established tropes of instrumentalization of gender and economization of equality issues. In essence, it shifts the Bank's language slightly but leaves its underlying development paradigm in place.

Conclusion

A critical, post-structural approach to development ask us to focus our attention on the process by which development knowledge is created and sustained. It demands an analysis that acknowledges the contested nature of any development knowledge, no matter how supposedly authoritative or value-neutral its presentation. The image of development as a complex machine, to return to Jonathan Crush's metaphor, clarifies this understanding of development as a complex and multi-faceted enterprise. Development, as a deliberately process driven by a set of institutions around a shared paradigm, undoubtedly takes place in a broader context of colonial power relations and stark economic inequalities. But the parts of the development machine are not working together in perfect harmony in service of a singular end-goal. The knowledge produced and acted upon by development institutions is always constructed and contested by a variety of forces. As the above discussion of gender work in the World Bank shows, gender has been integrated into the Bank's work through a long and halting process of which many feminist advocates were a deliberate part. Their efforts have not succeeded in radically transforming a conservative economic institution, but they have undoubtedly raised the profile of gender issues on its agenda and contested its long-held skepticism of gender.

As such, feminist engagement with development cannot be simply written off as co-optation or appropriation. Feminist work in mainstream development institutions does shift discourses and paradigms, although it sometimes has unintended consequences. The evolution of gender in the World Bank's policymaking goes to evidence this dynamic. The recognition of gender as an important component of development in the institution has not proceeded smoothly, nor has it been wholly resisted and rejected. Gender has acquired increased influence in the institution, albeit through its inclusion in particular economistic narratives that showed Bank policymakers what gender could do for development, or how it might speed the achievement of institutional goals. The integration of gender in institutional policymaking has been characterized by successes and setbacks, where gender equality has acquired currency in Bank discourse as a driver of growth, but the reliance on an instrumental account of equality puts up barriers to robust engagement with feminist economists. At the same time, the instrumental account of Smart Economics introduced at the Bank has taken on a life of its own. It now animates a popular cross-sectoral discourse that is adopted by ever-more NGOs, businesses, and elite political figures.

Human capital theory has played an important role in the World Bank's orientation to gender, in part because it created a conceptual framework within which gender equality could be understood as enhancing women's capital and thus contributing to achieving broader development goals. This began with an account of female education as building human capital, and translated into a broader set of human capital investments in girls and women. This chapter traced the ascendance of dominant gender discourses in the Bank through the institution's history, highlighting the influence of human capital theory in policy shifts. The following chapter addresses the specifics of this agenda and subjects the Bank's gender agenda to a feminist critique of human capital theory. While the policymaking process of the Bank cannot be understood in blanket narratives of co-optation or malicious appropriation of feminism, the material effects of its discourses deserve scrutiny because of the power relationships they produce and legitimize.

Note

1 During the summer of 2013 I conducted phone interviews with four members of the 2012 World Development Report team, including one director, two lead researchers, and one research analyst. Those interviews are referenced in-text as WB1, WB2, WB3 and WB4.

References

Arutyunova, Angelika, and Cindy Clark. 2013. *Watering the Leaves, Starving the Roots: The Status of Financing for Women's Rights Organizing and Gender Equality.* Toronto: Association for Women in Development AWID. www.bridge.ids.ac.uk/global-resources/resource/A66844.

Babb, Sarah. 2013. "The Washington Consensus as Transnational Policy Paradigm: Its Origins, Trajectory and Likely Successor." *Review of International Political Economy* 20(2): 268–297.

Bayliss, Kate, Ben Fine, and Elisa Van Waeyenberge, eds. 2011. *The Political Economy of Development: The World Bank, Neoliberalism and Development Research.* London: Pluto Press.

Bebbington, Anthony, Scott Guggenheim, Elizabeth Olson, and Michael Woolcock. 2004. "Exploring Social Capital Debates at the World Bank." *The Journal of Development Studies* 40(5): 33–64.

Bedford, Kate. 2009a. *Developing Partnerships: Gender, Sexuality, and the Reformed World Bank*. Minneapolis, MN: University of Minnesota Press.

Bedford, Kate. 2009b. "Doing Business with the Ladies: Gender, Legal Reform, and Entrepreneurship in the International Finance Corporation." *Labour, Capital and Society* 42 (1&2): 170–194.

Bedford, Kate. 2012. "Gender WDR: Limits, Gaps, and Fudges." *Bretton Woods Project*. Published 8 February 2012. www.brettonwoodsproject.org/2012/02/art-569646/.

Benería, Lourdes. 2012. "The World Bank and Gender Inequality." *Global Social Policy* 12(2): 175–178.

Bergeron, Suzanne. 2003. "The Post-Washington Consensus and Economic Representations of Women in Development at the World Bank." *International Feminist Journal of Politics* 5(3): 397–419.

Bergeron, Suzanne. 2006. "Colonizing Knowledge: Economics and Interdisciplinarity in Engendering Development." In *Feminist Economics and the World Bank: History, Theory, and Policy*, edited by Edith Kuiper and Drucilla Barker, 127–141. Abingdon: Routledge.

Bergeron, Suzanne. 2016. "Transgressing Gender and Development: Rethinking Economy Beyond 'Smart Economics.'" In *Social Sciences for an Other Politics*, edited by Ana Cecilia Dinerstein, 65–77. New York: Springer.

Bibler, Sarah, and Elaine Zuckerman. 2013. "How Do IFI Gender Policies Stack Up?" Washington, DC: Gender Action. www.genderaction.org/publications/ifigenderpolicies.pdf.

Broad, Robin. 2006. "Research, Knowledge, and the Art of 'paradigm Maintenance': The World Bank's Development Economics Vice-Presidency." *Review of International Political Economy* 13(3): 387–419.

Calkin, Sydney. 2018, forthcoming. "The World Bank and the Challenge of Gender Mainstreaming for Feminist IPE." In *Handbook on the International Political Economy of Gender*, edited by Juanita Elias and Adrienne Roberts. Cheltenham: Edward Elgar. Ahead of print.

Chant, Sylvia. 2012. "The Disappearing of 'smart Economics'? The World Development Report 2012 on Gender Equality: Some Concerns about the Preparatory Process and the Prospects for Paradigm Change." *Global Social Policy* 12(2): 198–218.

Chant, Sylvia. 2013. "The Long Shadow of 'smart Economics': The Making, Methodologies and Messages of the World Development Report 2012." In *The International Handbook on Gender, Migration and Transnationalism*, edited by Laura Oso and Natalia Ribas-Mateos, 97–126. Cheltenham: Edward Elgar.

Clegg, Liam. 2010. "Our Dream Is a World Full of Poverty Indicators: The US, the World Bank, and the Power of Numbers." *New Political Economy* 15(4): 473–492.

Crush, Jonathan. 1995. "Introduction: Imagining Development." In *Power of Development*, edited by Jonathan Crush, 1–26. Abingdon: Routledge.

Deaton, A., A. Banerjee, N. Lustig, and K. Rogoff. 2006. "An Evaluation of World Bank Research, 1998–2005." Washington, DC: World Bank. http://siteresources.worldbank.org/DEC/Resources/84797-1109362238001/726454-1164121166494/RESEARCH-EVALUATION-2006-Main-Report.pdf.

Doemeland, Doerte; Trevino, James. 2014. *Which World Bank reports are widely read?* Policy Research working paper no. WPS 6851. Washington, DC: World Bank. http://documents.worldbank.org/curated/en/387501468322733597/Which-World-Bank-reports-are-widely-read.

Elson, Diane. 2003. "Gender Justice, Human Rights, and Neo-Liberal Economic Policies." In *Gender Justice, Development, and Rights*, edited by M. Molyneux and S. Razavi, 78–114. Oxford: Oxford University Press.

Elson, Diane. 2009. "Gender Equality and Economic Growth in the World Bank World Development Report 2006." *Feminist Economics* 15(3): 35–59.

Elson, Diane. 2012. "Review of World Development Report 2012: Gender Equality and Development." *Global Social Policy* 12(2): 178–183.

Enns, Charis. 2014. "Knowledges in Competition: Knowledge Discourse at the World Bank during the Knowledge for Development Era." *Global Social Policy* 15(1): 61–80.

Escobar, Arturo. 1995. *Encountering Development: The Making and Unmaking of the Third World*. Princeton, NJ: Princeton University Press.

Ferguson, Lucy. 2014. "This Is Our Gender Person." *International Feminist Journal of Politics* 17(3): 380–397.

Fine, Ben, Costas Lapavitsas, and Jonathan Pincus. 2003. *Development Policy in the Twenty-First Century: Beyond the Post-Washington Consensus*. Abingdon: Routledge.

Fine, Ben, and Pauline Rose. 2003. "Education and the Post-Washington Consensus." In *Development Policy in the Twenty-First Century: Beyond the Post-Washington Consensus*, edited by Ben Fine, Costas Lapavitsas, and Jonathan Pincus, 155–181. Abingdon: Routledge.

Goldstein, Markus. 2012. "Should We Believe the Hype about Adolescent Girls?" World Bank *Development Impact Blog*. Published 20 November 2012. http://blogs.worldbank.org/impactevaluations/should-we-believe-the-hype-about-adolescent-girls.

Gray, Kevin, and Craig Murphy. 2013. "Rising Powers and the Future of Global Governance." *Third World Quarterly* 34(2): 183–193.

Griffin, Penny. 2006. "The World Bank." *New Political Economy* 11(4): 571–581.

Griffin, Penny. 2009. *Gendering the World Bank: Neoliberalism and the Gendered Foundations of Global Governance*. Basingstoke: Palgrave Macmillan.

Griffin, Penny. 2010. "Gender, governance and the global political economy." *Australian Journal of International Affairs* 64(1): 86–104.

Harrison, Graham. 2001. "Post-Conditionality Politics and Administrative Reform: Reflections on the Cases of Uganda and Tanzania." *Development and Change* 32(4): 657–679.

Heyneman, Stephen. 2003. "The History and Problems in the Making of Education Policy at the World Bank 1960–2000." *International Journal of Educational Development* 23(3): 315–337.

Hickel, Jason. 2014. "The New Shock Doctrine: 'Doing Business' with the World Bank." *Al Jazeera English*. Published 4 April 2014. www.aljazeera.com/indepth/opinion/2014/04/new-shock-doctrine-doing-busines-20144473715915842.html.

Kabeer, Naila. 1994. *Reversed Realities: Gender Hierarchies in Development Thought*. London: Verso.

King, Kenneth, and Simon McGrath. 2004. *Knowledge for Development? Comparing British, Japanese, Swedish and World Bank Aid*. London: Zed Books.

Klees, Steven. 2016. "Human Capital and Rates of Return: Brilliant Ideas or Ideological Dead Ends?" *Comparative Education Review* 60(4): 644–672.

Kramarz, Teresa, and Bessma Momani. 2013. "The World Bank as Knowledge Bank: Analyzing the Limits of a Legitimate Global Knowledge Actor." *Review of Policy Research* 30(4): 409–431.

Kuiper, Edith, and Drucilla Barker. 2006. *Feminist Economics and the World Bank: History, Theory and Policy*. Abingdon: Routledge.

Larner, Wendy, and William Walters. 2004. *Global Governmentality: Governing International Spaces*. Routledge.

Lauterbach, Claire, and Elaine Zuckerman. 2013. "Assessing the Effectiveness of World Bank Investments: The Gender Dimension." WINDER Working Paper no. 2013/017. United Nation University, World Institute for Development Economics Research. www.genderaction.org/publications/assessingeffectiveness.pdf.

Mahon, Rianne. 2010. "After Neo-Liberalism? The OECD, the World Bank and the Child." *Global Social Policy* 10(2): 172–192.

Mahon, Rianne, and Stephen McBride. 2009. "Standardizing and Disseminating Knowledge: The Role of the OECD in Global Governance." *European Political Science Review* 1(1): 83–101.

Marshall, Katherine. 2008. *The World Bank: From Reconstruction to Development to Equity*. Abingdon: Routledge.

Mawdsley, Emma. 2012. *From Recipients to Donors: Emerging Powers and the Changing Development Landscape*. London: Zed Books.

Mawdsley, Emma, and Jonathan Rigg. 2002. "A Survey of the World Development Reports I: Discursive Strategies." *Progress in Development Studies* 2(2): 93–111.

Mawdsley, Emma, and Jonathan Rigg. 2003. "The World Development Report II: Continuity and Change in Development Orthodoxies." *Progress in Development Studies* 3(4): 271–286.

Mehta, Lyla. 2001. "The World Bank and Its Emerging Knowledge Empire." *Human Organization* 60(2): 169–196.

Molyneux, Maxine. 2002. "Gender and the silences of social capital: Lessons from Latin America." *Development and Change* 33(2): 167–188.

Muñoz Boudet, Ana María, Patti Petesch, and Carolyn Turk. 2013. *On Norms and Agency: Conversations about Gender Equality with Women and Men in 20 Countries*. Washington, DC: World Bank. https://openknowledge.worldbank.org/handle/10986/13818.

O'Brien, Robert, Anne Marie Goetz, Jan Aart Scholte, and Marc Williams. 2000. *Contesting Global Governance: Multilateral Economic Institutions and Global Social Movements*. Cambridge: Cambridge University Press.

Öniş, Ziya, and Fikret Şenses. 2005. "Rethinking the Emerging Post-Washington Consensus." *Development and Change* 36(2): 263–290.

Perrons, Diane. 2015. "Gendering the Inequality Debate." *Gender & Development* 23(2): 207–222.

Phillips, David. 2009. *Reforming the World Bank: Twenty Years of Trial – and Error*. Cambridge: Cambridge University Press.

Porter, Doug, and David Craig. 2004. "The Third Way and the Third World: Poverty Reduction and Social Inclusion in the Rise of 'inclusive' Liberalism." *Review of International Political Economy* 11(2): 387–423.

Prügl, Elisabeth. 2017. "Neoliberalism with a Feminist Face: Crafting a New Hegemony at the World Bank." *Feminist Economics* 23(1): 30–53.

Prügl, Elisabeth, and Audrey Lustgarten. 2006. "Mainstreaming Gender in International Organizations." In *Women and Gender Equity in Development Theory and Practice: Institutions, Resources, and Mobilization*, edited by Jane Jaquette and Gale Summerfield, 53–71. Durham, NC: Duke University Press.

Psacharopoulos, G. 1995. *Building Human Capital for Better Lives.* Washington, DC: The World Bank. http://documents.worldbank.org/curated/en/617741468765916089/Building-human-capital-for-better-lives.

Rankin, Katherine. 2002. "Social Capital, Microfinance, and the Politics of Development." *Feminist Economics* 8(1): 1–24.

Razavi, Shahra. 1998. "Becoming multilingual: the challenges of feminist policy advocacy." In *Missionaries and Mandarins: Feminist Engagements with Development Institutions*, edited by Carol Miller and Shahra Razavi, 20–42. London: UNRISD.

Razavi, Shahras, and Carol Miller. 1995. "From WID to GAD: Conceptual Shifts in the Women and Development Discourse." UNRISD's Contribution to the Fourth World Conference on Women. United Nations Research Institute for Social Development Geneva. www.unrisd.org/80256B3C005BCCF9/(httpPublications)/D9C3FCA78D3DB32E80256B67005B6AB5?OpenDocument.

Revenga, Ana. 2011. "The Education of a Gender Skeptic: What I Learnt from the WDR 2012." World Bank '*Let's Talk Development*' Blog. Published 18 September 2011. http://blogs.worldbank.org/developmenttalk/the-education-of-a-gender-skeptic-what-i-learnt-from-the-wdr-2012.

Seguino, Stephanie. 2006. "Taking gender differences in bargaining power seriously: equity labor standards, and living wages." In *Feminist Economics and the World Bank: History, Theory, and Policy*, edited by Edith Kuiper and Drucilla Barker, 94–116. Abingdon: Routledge.

Summers, Lawrence. 1994. "Investing in All the People." World Bank Institute Resources. Washington, DC: The World Bank. http://elibrary.worldbank.org/doi/abs/10.1596/0-8213-2323-7.

Tinker, Irene, and Elaine Zuckerman. 2014. "Women's Economic Roles and The Development Paradigm." In *International Development*, edited by Bruce Currie-Alder, Ravi Kanbur, David M. Malone, and Rohinton Medhora, 116–132. Oxford: Oxford University Press.

Tzannatos, Zafiris. 2006. "The World Bank, Development, and Gender Equality." In *Feminist Economics and the World Bank: History, Theory and Policy*, edited by Edith Kuiper and Drucilla Barker, 13–39. Abingdon: Routledge.

Van Waeyenberge, Elisa, and Ben Fine. 2011. "A Knowledge Bank?" In *The Political Economy of Development: The World Bank, Neoliberalism and Development Research*, edited by Kate Bayliss, Ben Fine, and Elisa Van Waeyenberge, 26–48. London: Pluto Press.

Wade, Robert Hunter. 2002. "US Hegemony and the World Bank: The Fight over People and Ideas." *Review of International Political Economy* 9(2): 215–243.

Weaver, Catherine. 2008. *Hypocrisy Trap: The World Bank and the Poverty of Reform.* Princeton, NJ: Princeton University Press.

Weaver, Catherine. 2010. "The Strategic Social Construction of the World Bank's Gender and Development Policy Norm." In *Owning Development: Creating Global Policy Norms in the IMF and World Bank*, edited by Susan Park and Antje Vetterlein, 70–90. Cambridge: Cambridge University Press.

Weaver, Catherine, and Ralf Leiteritz. 2005. "'Our Poverty Is a World Full of Dreams:' Reforming the World Bank." *Global Governance: A Review of Multilateralism and International Organizations* 11(3): 369–388.

Williamson, J. 2009. "A Short History of the Washington Consensus." *Law and Business Review of America* 15(7): 7–18.

Winters, Matthew, and Shyam Kulkarni. 2014. "The World Bank in the Post-Structural Adjustment Era." In *Handbook of Global Economic Governance: Players, Power and Paradigms*, edited by Manuela Moschella and Catherine Weaver, 251–266. Abingdon: Routledge.

Wolfensohn, James D. 2005. *Voice for the World's Poor: Selected Speeches and Writings of World Bank President James D. Wolfensohn, 1995–2005*. Washington, DC: World Bank.

Wood, Cynthia. 2006. "Adjustment with a woman's face: gender and macroeconomic policy at the World Bank." In *Feminist Economics and the World Bank: History, Theory, and Policy*, edited by Edith Kuiper and Drucilla Barker, 142–161. Abingdon: Routledge.

World Bank. 1995. *Investing in People*. Washington DC: World Bank. http://documents.worldbank.org/curated/en/1995/02/697661/investing-people-world-bank-action.

World Bank. 1999. *Education Sector Strategy*. Washington, DC: World Bank. http://documents.worldbank.org/curated/en/406991468178765170/Education-sector-strategy.

World Bank. 2001. *Engendering development through gender equality in rights, resources, and voice*. A World Bank policy research report. Washington, DC: World Bank. http://documents.worldbank.org/curated/en/512911468327401785/Engendering-development-through-gender-equality-in-rights-resources-and-voice.

World Bank. 2006. "Gender Equality as Smart Economics: A World Bank Group Gender Action Plan (Fiscal Years 2007–2010)." *Gender Action Plan*. Washington, DC: World Bank. http://siteresources.worldbank.org/INTGENDER/Resources/GAPNov2.pdf.

World Bank2011. *Gender equality as smart economics: World Bank Group gender action plan – four-year progress report (January 2007-December 2010)*. Washington, DC: World Bank. http://documents.worldbank.org/curated/en/519961468325777020/Gender-equality-as-smart-economics-World-Bank-Group-gender-action-plan-four-year-progress-report-January-2007-December-2010.

World Bank. 2012. *World Development Report 2012: Gender Equality and Development*. Washington, DC: World Bank. https://openknowledge.worldbank.org/handle/10986/4391.

World Bank. 2013. "World Bank Group Gender Equality Highlights." Washington, DC. www.worldbank.org/content/dam/Worldbank/document/Gender/Gender%20Board%20Update%202013%20Glossy%20summary.pdf.

World Bank. 2014. "Doing Business 2014." Doing Business. Washington, DC: World Bank. www.doingbusiness.org/.

World Bank. 2015. "World Bank Group Gender Strategy (FY16–23): Gender Equality, Poverty Reduction and Inclusive Growth." Washington, DC. https://openknowledge.worldbank.org/handle/10986/23425.

World Bank. 2016a. "What We Do." www.worldbank.org/en/about/what-we-do.

World Bank. 2016b. "World Bank Group Support Tops $61 Billion in Fiscal Year 2016." Text/HTML. *World Bank*. www.worldbank.org/en/news/press-release/2016/07/12/world-bank-group-support-tops-61-billion-in-fiscal-year-2016.

World Bank. 2016c. "Gender action plan: 2016–2021." Washington, DC: World Bank. http://documents.worldbank.org/curated/en/243921492664887890/pdf/114422-WP-PUBLIC-gender-action-plan-2016-2021.pdf.

Zoellick, Robert. 2011. "World Bank Group Speech to Morocco Industry Summit, Casablanca, Morocco." presented at the Morocco Industry Summit, Casablanca, Morocco, 5 May. http://go.worldbank.org/JYSTLL99I0.

4 Unlocking Female Resources

Introduction

Girls and women have acquired increased policy visibility as they have been fitted into broader narratives of economic growth. In many cases, this means representing girls and women as literal wealth to be accumulated. Gender and Development discourse today is replete with imagery of natural resource extraction, imagining women as resources whose potential should be "unlocked", "unleashed", "tapped" or "harnessed". The "energy, talent and strength" of girls and women is lauded as "humankind's most valuable untapped natural resource" (Ban Ki Moon quoted in United Nations 2012). This language provides a popular rhetorical framework for endorsing a business case for gender equality, in part because it conceptualizes gender equality as a booster to speed existing growth. This discourse therefore presents a seemingly feminist-friendly call to include women, while reproducing a definition of economic life that wholly erases social reproductive labor. And yet, it also reproduces the mistaken assumption that women have been *left out* of the economy, or that they have so far been unable to contribute economically. Assertions about the discovery of women's economic agency and the value that can be extracted from them dominates a cross-sectoral discourse that unites national governments, international development institutions, and global brands. This economic agency has been discovered and legitimated as a site of urgent intervention, I argue, through the use of a human capital logic that conceptualizes women as potentially productive and entrepreneurial, but unskilled and inactive development subjects. Women's newfound development visibility is underpinned by this paradoxical representation: women are attributed a unique and intrinsic mode of feminized economic agency, while they are also understood as dormant resources whose capabilities must be harnessed. This relationship hinges on the call to intervene in, and activate the potential of, women across the global South. This chapter addresses these themes through the 2012 World Development Report on gender equality and development, which articulates the most detailed account of the Smart Economics agenda as it relates to development policy. The chapter argues that in the 2012 WDR, women's economic agency is primarily configured as a feature of their reproductive capacities, which must be managed and harnessed through a series of interventions to instil market mentalities into women. Because women appear in the report as unique drivers of post-crisis growth who are marginal to markets, the report advocates for interventions to train and shape their skills and aspirations for economic participation.

This chapter employs the conceptual categories introduced in the feminist critique of human capital to analyze the 2012 World Development Report. It analyzes human capital theory by drawing on some of the conceptual categories introduced by Foucault; although he critiqued human capital theory at a different point in its history, and the figure I analyze here is not precisely the same manifestation of human capital as the one that Foucault identified. The figure that is the focus of this chapter is the adaptable, resourceful woman who animates development discourses. I show that a feminist critique of human capital theory can draw our attention to a few unexamined dimensions of the "Gender Equality as Smart Economics" frameworks: 1) it highlights the essentialist terms upon which women's economic agency is identified and constructed, through tropes about maternal responsibility and productivity; 2) it demonstrates the relationship between the kinds of intrinsic qualities ascribed to women and the interventions prescribed to activate their economic agency, showing the inclusions and exclusions within the Smart Economics discourse that constrain the kinds of female agency that are valued; and 3) it demonstrates the gendered dimensions of the entrepreneurship-building interventions advocated therein. The chapter explores the role of human capital in the report's theoretical framework before examining each of the above topics in turn. While the 2012 World Development Report and the politics of its production were covered in the previous chapter, this chapter engages in a close reading of the text. It quotes extensively from the report: quotations from the 2012 WDR are cited in square brackets throughout, while secondary sources are given in the usual author-date style.

Core concepts: Gender, markets and equality

The 2012 World Development Report, sub-titled "Gender Equality and Development" presents the Bank's efforts to analyze the factors that have contributed to changes in gender relations and obstacles that have slowed progress, identify priority areas for change, and make recommendations for policy change at the domestic and international level. To this end, the report explores differences in health, education, agency, and access to opportunities; it identifies households, markets, and institutions as interlocking structures that aide or impede progress. In brief, its conclusions are as follows:

Table 4.1 The 2012 World Development Report: key findings and policy recommendations

The 2012 World Development Report:
1. Gender equality produces productivity gains, enhances intergenerational outcomes, and increases the representativeness of institutions.
2. Gender gaps are closing in educational enrollment, life expectancy, and labour force participation.
3. Gender gaps persist in mortality rates, schooling disparities, access to economic opportunities, and decision-making power.
4. Gender gaps persist because: • income growth alone does not drive gender equality; • gender and other forms of disadvantage cluster together; • formal and informal institutions work together to reinforce inequalities; • insufficient public action to make globalization work for women
5. Policy makers at the domestic level should take action to lower female morality rates, to shrink educational gaps, narrow gender productivity gaps, diminish gender gaps in decision making power, and limit the reproduction of inter-generational inequality.
6. The international community can assist through collecting better data, continued funding commitments for development work, and cross-sector partnerships.

Source: Table adapted from World Bank 2012: xx –xxiii.

The previous chapter presented the 2012 WDR as an illustrative space to view thc politics of knowledge production at the World Bank. The annual World Development Report, as the Bank's flagship report, plays a broader role in shaping the intellectual landscape of the Bank's work, which can involve forcing engagement with economic paradigms that have previously fallen outside of the Bank's view. The linguistic and conceptual shifts that appear in the WDR are in fact essential for understanding the policy direction of the Bank: discursive shifts in World Development Reports can be indicative of broader ideational changes in the Bank and can help to open space for debate within the institution (Elson 2009; Clegg 2010). In this vein, the previous chapter argued that multiple constituencies worked to shape the report's findings and messages, although the broader gender politics of the institution succeeded in directing a narrative of gender skepticism/female efficiency that dominated the report's headline messages and its wider promotion in the development field. For instance, despite internal contestation over the issue during its drafting stage, the "Gender Equality as Smart Economics" messages frame the report's most visible pieces and have dominated its publicity process (see Chant 2013). The 2012 WDR plays an important role in promoting the wider "Gender Equality as Smart Economics" agenda within the Bank and outside it, particularly in relation to its private sector partners, reflected in the widespread uptake of its core messages. Nonetheless, it would be too simplistic to understand the 2012 WDR as just another example of the

Bank's institutional resistance to critical gender work. In several important ways, the 2012 WDR represents progress in the World Bank's engagement with feminist scholarship and critical voices.

Given the troubled history between feminist economists, development NGOs, and the World Bank, the 2012 WDR on gender equality was received with a mix of surprise at the progress made, and fatigue with the persistence of longstanding gender tropes (see Elson 2012; Razavi 2012; Benería 2012). In several regards, the 2012 WDR testifies to successes of gender mainstreaming within the Bank, as it reflects effort to engage with feminist critique of Bank policy. First, although it focuses primarily on making the instrumental case, the 2012 WDR explicitly acknowledges the intrinsic value of gender equality and used human rights frameworks to do so. Although the report dedicates the bulk of its text to promoting the instrumental returns on equality, the emphasis on equality's intrinsic value and use of a human rights framework marks an evolution for the Bank (Harcourt 2012). Second, the report acknowledges that economic growth and/or increased incomes do not automatically improve the position of women in society. It shows, for example, that violence against women persists in countries with high incomes; this marks a departure from the general tendency for the Bank to imagine gender equality as an issue of economic modernization (that is, gender inequality falls when incomes rise). Recent Bank publications on gender including the 2012 WDR have acknowledged some ambiguity in the relationship between gender equality and macroeconomic growth, prompting a shift in focus to gender in micro-economics at the level of the household (see Prügl 2017). This caveat to the Smart Economics message tempers its conclusions, though it is a point of ambiguity that is smoothed over in summaries and promotional material. Third, and related to growing interest in gender at the household level, the 2012 WDR signals the Bank's recognition of unpaid care work and the gendered nature of this work as it relates to women's time use. While earlier Bank reports advocated paid employment as the key to gender equality, the 2012 WDR also shows awareness of unpaid care work as it relates to women's equal status in the workplace and the family (see also Elson 2012; Razavi 2012; Benería 2012; Evans 2012). These gains have been recognized by feminist political economists as important conceptual advances for the Bank's gender work, albeit operating within a familiar WID paradigm.

Despite limited engagement with feminist critiques, the 2012 WDR still evidences a conceptual framework that imagines markets as the most efficient promoters of gender equality. It continues to presume that markets are socially dis-embedded and can therefore address gendered inequalities through market mechanisms. This conceptual framework might appear unremarkable for a mainstream economic institution, but it has larger significance because of the World Development Report's position in the field and status as a standard-bearer for development knowledge. By continuing to imagine gender as an input *into markets*, rather than a constitutive component *of the market,* the analysis presents an understanding of gender as an identity characteristic of certain economic actors rather than gender as a power relationship (see Razavi 2012; Elson 2012). The overall effect is to de-politicize the issue through is the recourse to an economic discourse of value neutrality and scientific objectivity. This is significant at a conceptual and rhetorical level. World Development Reports tend to suggest consensus around hotly contested issues by referring to "standard" economic theory or "broad opinion" of experts: WDRs employ rhetorical methods to frame their conclusions as reflective either of broad consensus or as the sole acceptable option between two extreme options (Mawdsley and Rigg 2002: 98–99).

Feminist appraisal of the report has been critical of its persistent use of an instrumental approach to women, proposing to identify the most effective ways to "unlock" women's potential and maintaining its insistence that women can benefit from a de-regulatory and pro-globalization agenda This process of "unlocking" women's potential that features prominently in the 2012 WDR has been criticized in the feminist literature as evidence of reliance on a modernization narrative that uncritically equates growth with equality, in service of the same policy solutions. (Razavi 2012; Elson 2012; Chant 2012; Evans 2012). Feminist critics, particularly Marxian-influenced feminists, identified the 2012 WDR as a clear attempt to legitimize and depoliticize inequality, by blaming poverty on cultural norms and gender inequalities, and thereby open up space for capital accumulation by private firms (Roberts and Soederberg 2012). As yet, in the feminist literature on the 2012 WDR there has been little engagement with the role of human capital theory in the report or its role in the larger project of Gender and Development governance.

A critical reading of this human capital account of gender equality provokes a different set of questions than those addressed in current analysis of the 2012 WDR (and broader Smart Economics agenda). While the report instrumentalizes human capital theory to conceptualize various dimensions of women's bodies, lives and relationships in terms of their relationship to economic activity, a feminist Foucauldian approach invites an alternative view. It alerts us to the relationship between the way that subjects are identified as suitable for development, and the kinds of interventions then designed to shape their economic and political subjectivity; in Foucault's terms, human capital theory operates through the two categories of inborn qualities and acquired behaviors to understand humans as productive capital. This duality maps on to analytical and programmatic components of development interventions, identifying pre-empowerment subjects and prescribing appropriate interventions to catalyse economic productivity. Human capital theory in the 2012 WDR does provide new modes of visibility for women as actors in development, but it does so by narrowly circumscribing their agency in relation to pre-existing and culturally resonant narratives of femininity, womanhood and motherhood. Women are highly visible subjects of development in the report not only because of perceptions that they are economically inactive or marginal, but also because of the claim that they possess particular qualities that are more conducive to sustainable growth and poverty eradication. I make the case in this chapter for a critical appraisal of "Gender Equality Smart Economics" as a neoliberal project that aims to intervene and instrumentalize *certain* kinds of women for *certain* kinds of economic activity, but is premised on the identification of idealized pre-empowerment subjects whose entrepreneurial creativity can be cultivated and harnessed by markets. The starting point for this argument lies in the report's conceptual framework and its vision of gender and the market.

The 2012 WDR has multiple functions and audiences, all of which shape its key messages. It is aimed at contributing to the goal of collecting better data on gender, because it identifies a lack of gender-disaggregated data as an obstacle to institutional action on gender inequality. It also functions as a piece of research written by the World Bank, for the World Bank, with the mission of continuing to shift internal institutional culture and push the Bank's engagement with gender work. Externally, the WDR functions as a key piece of the Bank's knowledge-building mission in which it stakes a claim to set development agendas across the landscape of international and national development institutions. As such, the 2012 WDR is driven by a core narrative, rather than simply by data analysis. It is driven by the recognition of mainstream economists' gender skepticism, the partial validation of that skepticism, and the central message that prudent, cautious, gender-skeptic development professionals should recognize the economic benefits of gender equality. Much of its analysis therefore starts from a rhetorical position of acknowledging social realities and presenting these in a new way that demonstrates economic benefits of gender equality, or articulates new ways to intervene in and capitalize on pre-existing social roles and institutions.

Gender equality issues in the report are situated within a market fundamentalist framework, in which gender inequality results from flawed markets and gender equality from free market mechanisms. To this end, the report uses human capital theory to understand the persistence of gender inequalities, which it frames as "gender gaps in human capital" [xiii], by arguing that investment in human capital can produce positive effects on economic growth and gender equality. By extension, the lack of investment in women's human capital is understood as a key driver of gender inequality. The human capital framework provides an explanation for gender inequalities in the language of investment, where the intrinsic value of gender equality is secondary to potential return on investment in girls and women. The human capital framework in the report also provides a way to understand female agency. The report argues that women can "build their human capital and take up economic opportunities" when they have greater decision-making power [6]. Human capital theory is therefore central to the report's conceptual framework, providing a basis for the report's analysis of gender in relation to economic participation (either possessing or lacking the requisite human capital to compete for opportunities) and the process of empowerment itself (allowing women to cultivate their own human capital). With human capital theory, the report articulates the link between those subjects who are *not yet market subjects* and the kinds of interventions necessary to connect them with market cultures and market structures. Much of its vision of gender equality rests on the notion that changing the relationship between women and markets will create equality: it sees gender equality (and inequality) as functions of the market, and represents women's marginality from the market as a major factor that inhibits their empowerment.

The report's framework is evident in three assumptions it makes about the relationship between gender and markets: that they eliminate employment discrimination, that they equally compensate work of equal value regardless of gender, and that they shift gender norms by demonstrating the economic contribution made by women. On employment discrimination, the report's conceptual framework holds that "greater competition in product markets should reduce discrimination in factor markets" and that "stronger competitive pressures from greater economic integration should force employers to reduce costly gender (and other) discrimination" [264]. Discrimination against women is primarily imagined in terms of a market failure that produces "information problems" wherein employers do not have adequate information about women's skills and talents:

> "If labor markets work well, educated women will enter the labor force and contribute their talents and skills."
>
> [100]

> "Reducing barriers to more efficient allocation of women's skills and talents can generate large (and growing) productivity gains."
>
> [47]

Asserting that markets are the most natural and efficient allocator of resources, the report presumes rationality on the part of employers who exclude women from employment and assumes that these women have *not yet* had the chance to prove their value in the marketplace. It explains gender discrimination in markets through disparities in human capital and thus through the argument that when women do face employment discrimination, it may be a result of an employer's rational calculation about the relative skills presented by men and women [215, 239, 300]. This skill disparity may not itself be natural (and the report suggests that better education can close the "skill gap") but it argues that discrimination nonetheless occurs on the basis of an economic calculation. Similarly, this economic framework is unable to account for the persistence of gender inequality because it cannot account for gender as a constitutive dimension of markets themselves. For instance, the report explains that female-dominated jobs pay lower wages than male-dominated ones "largely because of their (unmeasurable) skill-related characteristics and tastes" and because these jobs are more flexible, requiring fewer skills [206]. By assuming that markets efficiently ascribe market value to skill, it hides the way that women's work is devalued *because* it is done by women; it conflates low pay with low productivity, compounding the undervaluation of care work. Its reliance on a market fundamentalist conceptual framework is apparent in the relationship posed between markets and gender norms or, more specifically, the mutually reinforcing nature posited between properly functioning markets and gender equality.

Shifts to gender norms are imagined here primarily in terms of rational economic actors responding to the market. To this end, the report frequently refers to the power of "market signals" [12, 14, 21, 289], the "functioning of markets" [7, 21, 27, 5, 238], market-based "incentives" to shift gender norms [8, 62, 99, 100, 174, 181, 198, 200, 215, 238, 299, 301], and the power of the market to "reshape attitudes and norms" [xxi]. As such, market logic is positioned as an enlightening force with the power to reshape gender relations; however, when "market signals are muted", barriers will remain to the empowerment of women within severely disadvantaged groups [13, 21, 215]. The report thus imagines individuals and institutions as rational economic actors responding to incentives and promoting gender equality on the basis of self-interest, situated within the broader narrative of "Gender Equality as Smart Economics" which claims that once the economic advantages of gender equality are "discovered", market forces will speed its arrival. This market orientation is essential for understanding the report's vision of equality: because it imagines inequality as a function of the market, its prescriptions for women's empowerment revolve around activating women's intrinsic qualities and shaping them in order to better participate in markets and gain equal status.

Motherhood and reproduction

Rhetorically, much of the Bank's Smart Economics agenda must be justified in a language of gender-skepticism: why women? Why gender? As such, the 2012 WDR is faced with the task of justifying its focus on girls and women in terms of their added contribution to economic productivity. This is accomplished with reference to a few tropes of women as engines of development: more productive, more efficient, and unrecognized resources for growth. Motherhood is perhaps the most important site of this narrative move: reproductivity (and its relationship to productivity) structures much of the report and its interpretation of women's position in relation to markets. The kind of female figure who animates the 2012 WDR is a married, heterosexual mother. At a textual level, this is indicated by the rhetorical collapse of woman/wife/mother throughout the document. Mothers are the norm in the report, throughout which women are unproblematically assumed to have children and a special inclination to care for children. Throughout the entire report, "childless women" receive one mention [205], while "women without children" are mentioned seven times in three consecutive pages [221–223], in relation to the impact of "family formation" (marriage and childbearing) on women's formal and informal employment. These few exceptions aside, throughout the report the categories of women and mothers are collapsed. Benevolent, maternal sentiment is one of the dominant characteristics that the report attributes to women, and motherhood is seen to prescribe particular female behaviors (both productive and reproductive).

The life course is further mapped out along a pathway of heterosexual couplehood and reproduction from which there is little recognition of the possibility of alternatives. For example, a discussion of women and men's different time allocations to productive and reproductive work appears under the sub-section title: "First comes love, then comes marriage, then comes a baby sitting in a carriage" [218]. Explaining the reproduction of gender inequality, the report claims that "by the time girls and boys become adults and form households, women typically have fewer years of education than men …" [46]. The conflation of motherhood and womanhood is further evident in the graphics used to represent women in different age groups, where the figure representative of women 15–49 is represented as a pregnant woman (Figures 4.1 and 4.2). Female bodies here are starkly reduced to their reproductive capacities. This graphic is used throughout, as are the phrases "reproductive years" and "reproductive ages" to designate women ages 15–49. The pregnant "stick figure" in a dress provides a striking representation of the deeply essentialist representations of women that persist: while the report purports to expand women's economic agency, it instead relies on entrenched gender hierarchies and reductive essentialisms in order to understand womanhood and motherhood.

Figure 4.1 Image from World Bank 2012: 15
Source: Permission granted under Creative Commons license.

Figure 4.2 Portion of Figure 4.1
Source: Permission granted under Creative Commons license.

Beyond linguistic and visual choices that collapse gender/sex/sexuality/marital status/children into "woman", this signals a deeper conceptual conflation that has implications for the economic analysis of the report. A post-structural feminist analysis of neoliberalism can show us how particular bodies become visible as productive and economically viable, while others are marginal. The lens of heteronormativity points to the reliance of neoliberalism on the conceptualization of gender as two complementary bodies – female/feminine and male/masculine – which perform different functions. Heteronormativity is a fundamental premise for the World Bank's neoliberalism, Penny Griffin has demonstrated, because neoliberal thought associates successful economic behavior with heterosexual masculinities and therefore renders "non-men and non-masculine bodies" unproductive (Griffin 2009: 153; see also Bedford 2009). However, accounting for the newfound emphasis on female economic agency as an ideal development resource, the Bank's economic discourses work to re-imagine women's productive capacity "as part of their reproductivity" and duty to the family (Ibid.: 154–155). Using heteronormativity to study neoliberalism demonstrates that reproductive heterosexuality constitutes the basis for economic life in World Bank discourse, where men and women perform complementary economic roles. This is a gender binary upon which with 2012 WDR relies: a maternal, caring nature is attributed to women as a natural feature of womanhood and further employed as an implicit marker of female difference. The report finds that women's control of income "changes spending in ways that benefit children" [5, 48] and argues that increases in women's incomes will therefore result in greater expenditure on child wellbeing. Reproduction is assumed to be both the defining feature of a woman's life and the dominant force on shaping her subjectivity:

> "For example, many conditional cash transfer programs initially targeted women because – cognizant of how women were likely to spend money differently from men – it seemed a way to get more of the transfer spent on children's endowments."
>
> [34]

> "Women's exercise of agency improves their children's welfare. Gender differences in preferences are reflected in different patterns of expenditure and consumption within the household, with women more strongly favoring investments in children's human capital."
>
> [151]

> "In a world where women care about different things from men (and women do appear to care for children more than men do), it may be that when women have more voice, they can drive institutional investments in a way that favors children."
>
> [68]

The report's repeated assertions of difference between men and women's preferences and spending habits work to normalize gendered differences as a product of nature. It is reflective of the broad drive in Smart Economics discourses to isolate and identify the most efficient investments: in this case, mothers who present the opportunity to affect present-day and future outcomes by shaping future human capital. Claims about supposedly natural female difference which often appear in this discourse do provide an essentialized picture of a universal female subject, although they tend to do so in ways that emphasize the natural goodness of women as mothers or caregivers. Furthermore, these essentialisms support assertions that improving women's economic power will allow them to direct spending and therefore benefit children. This points to a tension that bubbles beneath the surface of the report: despite its discussion of socially constructed gender norms and advocacy of shifts to gender norms that confine women to reproductive care work, the report continually reinforces the notion that women are natural carers and that the performance of care work is attributable, at least in part, to a "natural" feminine altruism. This has the effect of collapsing the report's earlier distinctions between sex and gender, instead promoting an unproblematic binary narrative in which female bodies express feminine (reproductive) behaviors and male bodies express masculine (productive) behaviors. Further, the representation of maternal care as both natural and intrinsic to femininity serves to normalize unpaid care work as a natural product of maternal sentiment or altruism. The valorization of motivations like care and cooperation marks a departure for the Bank: while Bergeron (2016) argues that this holds the potential to re-orient economic analysis away from an exclusive focus on the market, a reading of the report through human capital shows that it merely represents the extension of market logic to encompass new areas. That the report attributes these motivations to women, and suggests they are relevant to its economic analysis, is notable: yet, it routinely introduces essentialist ideas of female cooperation or altruism in order to emphasize an under-recognized productive capacity. This idea of intrinsic female altruism is often used to justify women's inclusion in anti-poverty policy, albeit in a way that aims to "capitalize on this altruistic burden" (Brickell and Chant 2010: 146). Moral valorization of female altruism carries with it the risk that policy tools will instrumentalize and increase this altruistic burden (Ibid.). Official recognition of the double burden is a complicated feminist victory, because this recognition has been institutionalized in Smart Economics discourse less as critique than as valorization of the idea that good mothers do more work, more efficiently.

Motherhood therefore occupies a central role in the report because of the emphasis Smart Economics narratives place on women's instrumental role in the achievement of development outcomes. The report acknowledges the intrinsic value of gender equality, but this case is outweighed by the extensive discussion of the instrumental importance of gender equality and the potential for women's empowerment to achieve secondary outcomes. This instrumental case is built on two related claims: firstly, that because women allocate a greater share of their resources to children than men do, women's control of income will result in increased investments in children's human capital and better outcomes overall. Secondly, because women's labor is currently "misallocated" [4, 47] in low paying or unpaid jobs (read: reproductive work), their employment in high quality, higher wage jobs will raise family incomes and by extension, national economic growth. Indeed, the harnessing of the double burden to extract productive and reproductive labor from empowered women rests on the premise that productivity and efficiency are natural manifestations of their responsible, family-oriented feminine nature.

At one level, it comes as no surprise that women's human capital is primarily understood in terms of her reproductive capacity. The overall Smart Economics paradigm is concerned with long-term intergenerational outcomes, for which women's human capital is represented as a powerful point of intervention and investment in order to achieve better outcomes for children and the transmission of different (empowered) norms. Part of the current visibility of girls and women in development is the product of human capital theory's emphasis on futurity, and by extension the role of girls and women in reproducing future generations of human capital. Gender's ascendance to the centre of human capital theory was driven by the recognition that women were key actors in the kinds of calculations that increased or decreased human capital, and thus were central to understanding inter-generational changes. However, the valorization of motherhood exists in tension with a competing discourse around fertility and the potential for childbearing to negatively impact a woman's productivity. Because the Bank's neoliberalism rests on a binary opposition between men/masculinity/productivity and women/femininity/reproductivity, women are understood as participating in economic life on fundamentally different terms. As such, Penny Griffin argues that women's productivity is understood in Bank discourses as an extension of their "natural" caregiving role (Griffin 2009: 153–155). The conceptual binaries that she highlights are clearly present in the 2012 WDR, and the equation of female bodies with maternal altruistic subjectivities and natural caregiving roles is also present. Yet, the role of reproductivity in the 2012 WDR is complicated by its insistence that women's reproductivity is at once central to their importance as development agents and yet is the primary obstacle to their full empowerment in the market. In other words, the 2012 WDR presents a contradictory picture of the mother-as-development agent: while her maternal caring nature makes woman an efficient and altruistic economic agent, her reproductivity also presents a threat to her productive capacities.

The dominant narrative of altruistic and economically empowered motherhood is simultaneously undermined by a secondary narrative running throughout the report that positions childbearing as an obstacle to economic empowerment. The report frequently asserts that economic empowerment is dependent on lowering fertility and delaying childbearing. In doing so, it reinforces the productive/reproductive labor distinction and represents the two as existing in tension; for instance, discussions of female employment consider women's efforts to "reconcile work and home responsibilities" [341] or gender differences in the ability to "substitute market inputs for home time" [221]. Reproductive labor obligations (whether a manifestation of preference or a social obligation) are presented as major obstacles to women's economic participation and, by extension, overall economic growth, while at the same time representing one of the primary characteristics of women that make them better investments for development funds. At numerous points in the report, childbearing is represented in terms of its potential to constrain or prevent women from full economic participation [66, 151, 158, 159, 288, 314, 367]. Accordingly, delayed childbirth is equated with women's greater ability to exercise agency and acquire skills necessary for economic success.

> "The decline in fertility that has come with higher incomes has helped lower the number of deaths associated with maternal morality. And bearing fewer children has given women more time to invest in acquiring human capital and to participate in the economy."
>
> [11, 62]

The language used to discuss reproduction, particularly in considering how best to delay reproduction, imagines that child-bearing is an inevitable and fundamental part of womanhood. For example, the report repeatedly stresses that one of the main benefits of job training is its potential to delay pregnancy and reduce the number of early pregnancies [33, 289, 314]. Similarly, labor force participation and decreased fertility are frequently paired as evidence for the positive outcomes of development policies [55, 66, 265]: "For example, a land titling program in Peru increased joint ownership rates by including provisions to lift constraints women faced. It also increased mothers' participation in the labor market and decreased fertility" [345]. In this way, fertility and productivity form a pair of complementary opposites which together fuel the economic empowerment envisioned by the report. Many of the interventions promoted by the report therefore work to facilitate reproduction while minimizing its negative impact on productivity: fewer children [12, 33, 55, 62, 317], child care provision [26, 32, 214, 222, 297, 299], redistributed care within the family unit [173, 338], and flexible work arrangements [181, 198, 220, 222, 236, 263] aim to allow for social reproductive work to take place without displacing productive work.

> "Enjoying ever higher education, women have greater control over their life choices. They use those choices to participate more in the labor force; have fewer children; diversify their time beyond housework and childcare; and shape their communities, economies, and societies."
>
> [55]

The report presents feminine subjectivities as intrinsically maternal and altruistic; at its core, the Smart Economics narrative relies on this narrative to align a particular construction of femininity with existing models and to "add" women in a manner within the bound of acceptable practice. This is a familiar feature of the Bank's gender work: "cultural" factors have been welcomed into its analysis when they align with existing models of economic participation (Bergeron 2006). Simultaneously, the report imagines fertility as a potential obstacle and imagines women unencumbered by family obligation to be better economic actors. The economically empowered woman is undoubtedly maternal, family, and community oriented, but her empowerment corresponds to the ability to replace care work with productive work. The above excerpt clearly lays out a vision of the empowered woman and her priorities: given increased agency, she redistributes her time between productive and reproductive obligations, minimizing time spent on housework and care by having fewer children and dedicating more time to the labor force, community, and economy. She is situated in the broader structures of neoliberal governance as a responsible and self-managing subject who is "actively engaged in making re/productive life decisions in the marketplace of choice" (Repo 2015: 155). The report's valorization of motherhood is thus linked to a particular kind of self-managing subject that allocates time to productive and reproductive activities in order to maximize income. As such, the links between the ascription of a natural female altruism and offloading of a development burden onto women are clear.

The above analysis of the 2012 WDR unpacks the kind of essentialisms and discursive constructions that underpin women's development visibility. The ascription of intrinsic qualities to girls and women projects an image of idealized development agency that amounts to a fiction: it associates girls and women with a range of supposedly essential female qualities that equate to development productivity, altruism, and efficiency. At the same time as these tropes are used to identify women as ideal development subjects, they work to exclude others from development discourses. If human capital theory provides institutions like the Bank with a rubric for assessing women's potential as empowered economic subjects, it also uses these categories to circumscribe the boundaries of economic agency. In essence, women come to be understood as promising but pre-empowerment subjects when they conform to a series of characteristics outlined in the human capital critique: altruistic, maternal, and responsible. Age and sexuality are the two main categories through which the 2012 WDR distinguishes ideal, pre-development female subjects from disempowered subjects whose human capital characteristics do not promise productivity.

Sexuality is equated with vulnerability and excluded from the report's conception of productivity. Not only is productivity circumscribed by its relationship to heterosexual couplehood and childbearing, but it is also contingent on the social position of homosexuality. Sexual orientation as a category or concept appears only three times in the report, each time listed among other "factors of exclusion" that contribute to gender inequality, like ethnicity or disability [13, 55, 76]. This is borne out in the 2012 WDR: the word "heterosexual" only appears once in the report, in the context of HIV/AIDS transmission [135]; the word "homosexual" never appears. The concept of sexuality thus appears here only in terms of its proximity to risk taking behaviors and the transmission of disease. The confluence of bodies, sexuality, risk behavior, and vulnerability is an important and recurring theme in the report, particularly in the way it conceptualizes male bodies and masculine subjectivities. Age represents another critical point of divergence in the report's identification of development agency. Young women and adolescent girls are a primary focus of the report in their representation as future human capital. Women of what the report calls "reproductive age" (15–49) are made visible in terms of their status as mothers, wives, and workers. Women who fall outside of the "reproductive age" bracket (over 49) feature in the report only in terms of their vulnerability and unproductivity. As evidenced in Figures 4.1–4.2, women over the age of 60 are not represented as an important or visible category in the report. Older women appear primarily as vulnerable widows [163, 154, 156], family members who require burdensome care [47, 328], or as conservative elders who perpetuate oppressive norms [354, 170]. Empowerment is circumscribed to exclude women in this category, who fall outside of the models of productivity employed in the report. Similarly, disability appears in the report only as a marker of vulnerability and as a factor that compounds inequalities [xxi, 12, 13, 26, 55]. The report's conception of empowerment, which is reduced to a crude measure of economic productivity, subsequently excludes those bodies or subjectivities that are not understood to contribute productively in the economy. In other words, women gain visibility as agents of development when they conform to expectations about the qualities and behaviors of good mothers, wives, and caregivers. Others become invisible or written off as unproductive, non-market subjects.

Pliant and resilient subjects

One of the longstanding critiques of earlier development frameworks like Women in Development revolves around the way these models attempted to integrate women into pre-existing frameworks – to "add women and stir" (see Chapter 1). The WID model advocated that women could act in an economic capacity, like men, if they were given suitable opportunities to interact in market life. It advocated for an understanding of women as able to function according to the male model. The Smart Economics discourse contains major resonances with this trope, as I will discuss below, wherein interventions are proposed to train women in market cultures and skills so that they can interact in the market. But Smart Economics too marks an important change, because it proposes a new understanding of gender and economy: women increasingly appear as ideal subjects of economic agency and post-crisis growth because of assertions about their flexibility and resilience (Calkin 2015). Rather than marginal actors who might act *like men* given sufficient training, women increasingly function as the referent subject of economic agency. They are attributed a flexible and resourceful form of economic agency that is best suited to ensuring post-crisis growth. In the 2012 WDR, the economically empowered woman in the report is characterized by her pliant and flexible subjectivity that is closely related to the assumption that women possess innate maternal and familial altruism. The figure of the productive woman animates wider Gender and Development discourse today: she is "active, productive, flexible, docile, a source of cheap labor and a good investment" (Harcourt 2009: 69). The stress on women's resilience, responsibility, and sustainable model of economic participation is especially prevalent in financial and development discourses that position women as antidotes to macho, crisis-prone economic models. In the 2012 WDR, this is manifest in the assertions that women are more easily adapted to new norms and shifting social patterns, including shifting patterns of productive/ reproductive work, and that they are more resourceful and therefore better able to "cope" with instability. In this way, empowered women are positioned in opposition to men as the ideal leadership figures in sustainable development, securing a future for the family through resourcefulness and entrepreneurship.

The female subject envisioned in the report is a pliant subject who is easily incentivized to take on new responsibilities or behaviors. Young women are represented in the report as more easily adapted to new social and gender norms, adapting to change faster than men do [194]; they value flexibility in work arrangements and move between unpaid, informal, and formal employment [220–222]; and they are easily incentivized to adopt new behaviors or skills, evidenced in the report's repeated citations of the positive impact of conditional cash transfer programmes. Conditional Cash Transfers and similar mechanisms are encouraged and their impact, particularly on women, is stressed: "many conditional cash transfer programs targeted women, in part because women were likely to spend more of the transfer on children's endowments" [320, 34, 113, 315]. Much of the report's narrative of empowerment is premised on the notion that women are more likely to adapt to changing economic, political, and social contexts, and to pass on these new norms to the next generation [172]. In contrast to men, who are represented as less easily adaptable and thus less suitable development subjects, women are understood to possess natural characteristics that enable them to cope in precarious conditions and to exercise responsibility and secure the needs of their families. This trope is particularly evident in a short section on changing gender roles in Georgia shortly after the collapse of the USSR. Drawn from an internal Bank case study, this text appears in a chapter that is dedicated to promoting a shift in gender roles that enables women to participate in formal economic life more fully, so we can interpret this case study as one introduced to provide positive examples and/ or guidance through the valorization of a certain kind of female subjectivity.

> "[Georgian women] realized long before men that there was no return to secure state employment, and they proved more flexible in adjusting to

> occupational change. They often took jobs below their qualifications, opting to be unskilled workers in informal activities such as street vendors, running shuttle services to Turkey, sitting babies, or cleaning houses. Petty trade remains the largest arena of self-employment for women, who were ready to "downgrade" their work to provide for their families, while their husbands and other men remained at home and refused to take jobs that did not match their status and educational training."
>
> [332]

The construction of womanhood in this passage reveals some of the core assumptions that underpin the report's representation of women's engagement and their economic potential. Firstly, the text affirms women's willingness to "downgrade" their work and accept precarious, low paying jobs; women were willing to do this, the text suggests, in order to meet their reproductive obligations and provide for their families. It draws on tropes of self-sacrifice and subordination of one's own needs for the family (a familiar narrative theme of female altruism). This valorization of women's willingness to take up informal work sits uncomfortably with the report's human capital framework that advocates investment in women's skills and alternative care arrangements to enable them to compete with men for highly skilled and paid jobs in the formal labor market. Secondly, the text sets up an implicit comparison between men and women, finding flexible feminine subjectivities are better suited to succeed in this economic context. While men stayed at home and "refused" to take jobs that they didn't feel matched their status, women "realized" the constraints of the economic context and expressed willingness to forfeit concerns of status by demonstrating flexibility and resilience. Male and female subjectivities thus exist in opposition in this passage, where male subjectivities are characterized by stubbornness, pride, and a refusal to sacrifice in order to provide for the family. Female subjectivity, by contrast, is primarily understood with reference to reproductive obligations and willingness to sacrifice anything in order to fulfil those obligations and the relative ease with which women can be trained in new economic skills and forms of income generation.

The tropes of female flexibility and adaptability in the context of economic precarity are familiar from other Bank publications that cultivated a similar notion of female subjectivity. The World Bank's 2000 *Voices of the Poor* report provides an early example of the narrative tropes of the "dysfunctional" male subject and resilient female subject who is better able to cope with insecurity and provide for the family:

> "Many men are collapsing, falling into domestic abuse and violence [...] Women, on the other hand, seem to swallow their pride and hit the streets to do demeaning jobs to bring food to the family table."
>
> (Narayan et al. 2000: 219 quoted in Pupavac 2005: 176)

In the *Voices of the Poor* report, men are characterized by aggression and instability, and women by flexibility and resourcefulness. It advocates policy to empower women, on the assumption that they represent "a more appropriate personality to secure sustainable household and communities" (Pupavac 2005: 175). As in the 2012 WDR, the valorization of certain personalities and subjectivities is overlaid by a concern to empower those best suited to securing families and communities in the face of precarious economic circumstances. The WDR 2012 similarly employs affirmative essentialisms to valorize assumptions about women's self-sacrificing and adaptable nature in order to position women at the centre of a sustainable development agenda. It does not so much challenge gender binaries as re-signify and invert them by positioning women and an idealized feminine nature as the ideal neoliberal economic subjectivity. It operates through these affirmative essentialisms and thus subverts, to some extent, the tendency to relegate women to private/non-productive spheres while embracing deeply problematic assumptions about women's affinity to care, their altruism, and their superior ability to cope in precarious contexts. Within the 2012 WDR and Smart Economics discourses more broadly, the supposedly innate feminine characteristics of altruism, resourcefulness, and duty to family are unproblematically ascribed to women and mapped on to discourses of crisis and precarity in order to signify women's position as the ideal subject of neoliberal governance.

The claims that women are more resourceful, resilient, and reliable under pressure are significant in the broader politico-economic context because they resonate so closely with dominant narratives of gender and financial crisis. Clearly, these are the kinds of essentialist tropes that feminist scholarship rejects because of the tendency for seemingly positive claims about benevolent mothers to naturalize the double burden or re-write inequalities as maternal self-sacrifice. Leaving this aside, attributions of distinctively feminine resilience and resourcefulness are problematic in their own right because of their position in a discourse of post-crisis capitalism that has emerged since the 2008 global financial crisis. In the wake of the financial crisis, gendered accounts of the crisis gained attention: macho cultures of excessive risk had led to the crisis, they argued, and post-crisis finance should prioritize gender diversity because women are more prudent and risk-averse (Prügl 2012). These are powerful tropes that have resonated outside of finance, and been influential in global development as well. In line with the search for a post-Washington Consensus mode of development that centers on the human, women have been elevated as economic agents of a more sustainable and equitable future. This narrative is not unique to the World Bank: across national and international financial institutions, women feature as "archetypal neoliberal subjects" because they are attributed the ability to usher in an era of sustainable capitalism which might avert another global crisis (Elias 2013: 153). The current Gender Action Plan for the Bank, covering 2016–2021, focuses primarily on gender equality resilience in the context of climate change and natural disaster. Coupled with the World Bank Group's 2015–2023

Gender Strategy, it calls for the Bank to focus on developing "gender-smart solutions to climate change" (World Bank 2015). Building on the model established in the 2012, where gender equality is represented as a function of freer markets and fewer market obstacles, the 2016–2021 Gender Action Plan argues that gender equality will drive both growth and resilience. The equation of women with resilient post-crisis capitalism rests on the belief that women and girls – given sufficient investment – will embody a different form of economic agency that is more risk-averse and produces better outcomes for states and firms.

The narratives of post-crisis renewal sit at the heart of the "Business Case for Gender Equality" that institutions like the World Bank, World Economic Forum, International Monetary Funds, and others advocate. They hinge on the idea that women's resources are currently "untapped" and can be accessed through investment or development interventions. The activation narrative purports to empower women in two specific ways: firstly, it promotes the idea that women represent an as-yet-undiscovered pool of labor power that can be harnessed for growth. Secondly, it presents women as a large and powerful consumer group whose customer loyalty should be secured by women-friendly policies.

> "Women – especially educated women – present an untapped pool of resources in the search for talent and skills."
>
> [238]

> "… [G]ender equality has become a desirable trait that customers and investors look for. Corporate social responsibility is an avenue for firms to enhance competitiveness by differentiating products and capturing the loyalty of women's growing market share."
>
> [331]

This same relationship of activation underpins the 2012 WDR.[1] If human capital theory strives to identify ideal subjects of investment, for future growth, this means looking for the subjects who have been overlooked by development. Who represents the "greatest untapped resource"? Human capital theory then proposes to identify the kinds of interventions are proposed in the in order to catalyse and activate the qualities of this subject. In the 2012 WDR, this means looking for the development interventions that are proposed to harness the potential of girls and women, to bring them into economic life as the Bank sees it.

Inculcating market mentalities

Smart Economics development strategies, dependent as they are upon the promise of profitability and mutually beneficial relations between corporations and poor populations, are discursively structured around the notion of discovering new markets and facilitating greater inclusion into the market. On these terms, women represent one of the primary spaces that have yet to be "colonized by the formal market" and therefore the claim that women exist outside of markets features prominently in the wider Smart Economics discourse (Roberts and Soederberg 2012: 958). Development interventions like microfinance or Conditional Cash Transfers have similarly been popularized in order to economize social relations and bring women "closer" to markets (Rankin 2001; Molyneux 2006). This marginality is alternately attributed in the 2012 WDR to cultural prejudice, gender disparities in human capital, and women's lack of knowledge about business culture. The 2012 reproduces some core assumptions of early gender frameworks in development because it imagines women as a group who have benefitted to some extent from development gains, but in some areas have failed to benefit because of "muted" market signals, their marginality from the market, and the changes wrought by markets [76, 270, 272, 254]. The relationship between women's marginality from markets, the process of their discovery, and the profitability of their integration rests on an unproblematized and depoliticized notion of development as a teleological process in which various groups are enveloped and thereby developed.

The 2012 WDR promotes instilling market mentalities into women who supposedly lack the skills and aptitudes to participate in market life. This includes a variety of skills related to commerce, but includes a wider range of behaviors and attitudes that are understood to inhibit women's market participation. This expansion of empowerment interventions into the realm of emotion and aspiration is a familiar feature of human capital-building interventions, because these qualities can be re-interpreted as components of human capital that will produce future growth or future losses. When there is no "outside" of capital, and when everything can be calculated in terms of its contribution to economic growth, it follows that affect and emotion may become intelligible through their role in production (see Anderson 2016). The subject constructed through human capital theory is a subject of unrealized potential, but whose potential can be activated through interventions to shape their disposition, habits, and behaviors. In the 2012 WDR, interventions proposed to teach women appropriate market behaviors and skills demonstrate the gendered dimensions of this control, in particular because they seize on the essentialist assumptions about female bodies and subjectivities established in the above two sections. Girls and women, in human capital-centric development discourses, are uniquely adaptable figures whose potential can be unlocked when their behaviors and dispositions are appropriately shaped for economic empowerment.

Among the mechanisms proposed for the activation of female labor power, the report accords a prominent position to discussing the benefits of globalization and restructuring on women's economic empowerment. Globalization, it argues, has worked to "lift some of the constraints" to gender equality but women are still affected by existing constraints and "risk being left behind in the absence of public action" [102]. Women are therefore positioned as potential beneficiaries of the forces of globalization, if only its forces can reach them:

> "In today's globalized world, forces such as trade openness and the spread of cheaper information and communication technologies have the potential to reduce gender disparities by connecting women to markets and economic opportunities, reshaping attitudes and norms among women and men about gender relations, and encouraging countries to promote gender equality. But their impact will be muted without effective domestic public action."
>
> [xxi]

To this end, the report proposes a range of public actions that can connect women with markets, expose them to market signals, and harness their talents and skills for shared benefits. These interventions include regulatory reforms around finance, property, and labor in order to allow female entrepreneurs to start businesses more easily. It also involves a range of interventions to shape and train women whose entrepreneurial success is constrained by their social position. The model of economic agency within the Bank is normatively masculine insofar as it employs a classical model of rational economic man that associates economic productivity, rationality, and interest-maximizing behaviors with masculinity and men; non-men and non-masculine people are attributed an unproductive, pre-market subjectivity. Although the Bank's logic of growth implicitly valorizes masculine economic behaviors, it does advocate that (some) women can be "inculcated with a limited rationality such that they operate as better workers" (Bedford 2005: 295).

Women's marginality from the market is a problem in the report because it means their talents and skills are still "untapped": they must be harnessed for growth. The 2012 WDR, while not a policy report in itself, is written in a policy-focused language that employs an activation narrative that works to acknowledge women's marginality and present a solution to it. In the report, women's labor is generally understood as "under used or misallocated" [3, 47] in low wage or low productivity jobs. Throughout, the report conflates low wage and low productivity jobs, so the claim that women's work is misallocated refers to their confinement to low-wage formal employment, informal or entrepreneurial employment, and unpaid care work [26, 80, 201]. It places heavy and repeated emphasis on the potential contribution that women's "talents and skills" can make when properly applied: when markets work well women's talents and skills can be allocated to "activities which make the best use of those abilities" [3, 47, 100]. Countries and companies that fail to recognize the potential value of women's talents and skills and therefore fail to "capitalize" on this potential will face high and rising costs [254, 271, 272, 47, 3, 331, 334]. This is the most basic and structural principle of the Smart Economics policy agenda and constitutes its central claim: women's empowerment is a "smart economic" strategy precisely because of its potential to increase profits, generate productivity gains, and secure competitive advantage for countries and companies operating "in a more competitive and globalized world" [3].

Despite the presumed naturalness of market relations and mentalities, Bank development interventions begin from the premise that women are insufficiently rational and require specific interventions to instil market mentalities. As the feminist critique of human capital demonstrates, gendered human capital narratives which dominate the Smart Economics agenda identify women with a range of dormant qualities that can be harnessed through intervention. This section therefore undertakes an analysis of the "acquired skills" and "learned behaviors" (in Foucault's terms) that the report proposes for women in order to catalyze the empowerment process. Inculcating market mentalities extends beyond the provision of training, coaching, mentoring, or socialization into masculine networks; it involves the development and promotion of new subjectivities, or ways of interacting with the market. It promotes a skill set compatible with the ethos of responsibilization and self-care. Training in employment, financial, and life skills works to instill this rational economic subjectivity in women and to responsibilize them. By targeting certain groups (assumed to be) marginal to markets for training in appropriate market mentalities, these interventions serve to "culturalize" rationality and attribute capitalist failures to "attitudinal inadequacies" (Bedford 2009: 139). This is evident firstly in the report's frequent references to "job and life skills training" for women and secondly in its tendency to represent women's subjectivities as insufficiently market-oriented and to prescribe interventions for creating more aspirational, ambitious women.

Because it begins from the premise that women are predisposed to activity in the domestic sphere and largely confined to reproductive work, the WDR 2012 assumes that women require "job training" and "life skills training" in order to transition into productive work in the labor force. It follows, then, that the report imagines job training as an important piece of the agenda to promote gender equality. It suggests that successful interventions that enable women to enter or reenter the workforce will require job training, broadly conceived [28, 30, 35, 203, 300, 303], marketing training [27], financial literacy training [302, 303], among other forms of training. Job and skills training is advocated in order to improve employment opportunities [314], increase earnings in the formal sector [28–29], correct the gender skills gap [270], increase overall firm revenue [302] and promote economic empowerment [33]. Training interventions are associated with increased economic and social agency: "… interventions in [rural areas] need to focus on building life skills, including social capital for adolescent girls, improving their aspirations and agency, and reducing risky behavior" [317].

This panoply of interventions constitute "micro-level attempts to create economic rationality" and are characteristic of Bank policy, insofar as they aim to change individual and community behavior into more rational modes of being (Williams 1999: 93–94). Business, finance, and the "professional" realm are constructed as masculine domains and women are assumed to require training in order to overcome their innate unfamiliarity with the skills needed to enter these domains. In the report's reading of gender inequalities, wage and job disparities are the product of women's lack of familiarity with markets and their lack of market skills. Beyond job training, the report advises that women should be socialized into gendered business networks. Most prominently, on-the-job training or apprenticeship placements are understood to function as mechanisms for moulding women into effective entrepreneurs and business people, while correcting for "information deficits" among employers:

> "For example, a recent female graduate in industrial engineering may fail to get a job in a private company because the potential employer is not sure how well a female worker will fit into an otherwise all-male company. In other words she may not get the job because the employer has too little information about her potential performance."
>
> [231]

Programs like this therefore address barriers to employment by "allowing participants to overcome information problems by communicating their abilities to employers" [300]. The report repeatedly contends that discrimination results from information deficits, where women are less able to communicate or convey their skills to employers or are insufficiently represented in the firm to provide this information [18, 231, 239, 300]; training is suggested to remedy this problem [342, 300, 29, 301]. The report's discussion of employment and training further suggests that women be coached and introduced to male business networks in order to "help them master the dominant social codes and nurture their ambition" [342]. The entrepreneurial woman is represented here as existing on the fringes of masculine business networks, but possessing the requisite pre-market mentality and ambition which can be cultivated; furthermore, the gendered language of "nurturing" ambition signals an association between maternal and market subjectivities.

The report places great emphasis on the need to socialize women into market cultures to unlock their potential productivity; to this end, it presents an example from a successful programme in Peru where women received training on "business strategy", "managing the firm", and "finance and enterprise training" which led to increased revenues and helped to overcome "gendered networks" from which they had been excluded as women [302]. In a Liberian programme, girls attended a job fair where "private sector human resource and career development specialists" met individually with girls to coach them on "professionalism" [34]:

> "Private sector human resource and career development specialists met with trainees individually to impart their knowledge about the industry,

coach them on professionalism in the workplace, and give constructive feedback on the skills demonstrated."

[34]

It identifies a gap in aspirations between men and women, both in adolescence [317, 32–32] and later in their careers [235–236]. Training and other interventions are advocated to instil "professionalism" [34], "positive thinking" [29, 301], "nurture their ambition" [342], and enable women to "better communicate their abilities to employers" [28–29, 300]. Ambition, aspiration, and overall mentality are represented as integral pieces of a rational economic subjectivity:

> "Employability skills training augments the technical skills graduates learn in community college with the practical skills for finding and succeeding in employment. Employers often say recent graduates lack interpersonal and other basic job skills. So, students in the pilot program received 45 hours of instruction in team building, communications, presentations, business writing, customer service, resume writing, interviewing, and positive thinking."
>
> [29, 301]

Shifts in aspiration and attitude are paired with, and complementary to, a further range of "life skills" training interventions promoted in the report that constitute a range of expanding techniques to manage and discipline the self. The report moves between promoting job training, employability skills, and "life skills", sometimes conflating these [xxiii, 33, 34, 35, 315, 316, 317]. Interventions to teach life skills to girls are frequently associated with a reduction in pregnancies [33, 317] and risky sexual behavior [317]; this life skills training is linked to the goal of increasing women's economic independence [34]. Life-skills training for girls, promoted alongside "hard" skills training, aims to shape girls' subjectivity and activate their dormant potential in order to promote economic participation. This skills training programme is advocated in order to make girls and women more employable, by training them in "soft" skills – "team building, communications, presentations, business writing, customer service, resume writing, interviewing, and positive thinking" [29, 301] – that complement "hard", technical skills. Employability here refers to a broad spectrum of attributes that extend beyond financial skills or literacy training and comes to encompass general attitude and personality; it reflects the notion that capitalist success requires a particular attitude characterized by ambition, aspiration, and willingness to take on risk in order to pursue profit.

Conclusion

Familiar metaphorical representations of women and girls as untapped resources opened this chapter. Female bodies as dormant, hidden treasures, waiting to be unlocked and harnessed for growth: this is a frequently used narrative trope in gender equality policy discourses today. This approach to gender equality, feminist scholarship has noted, is not only reductive and instrumental but also rhetorically violent (see Sjoberg 2014). The call to "tap" women's resources evokes sexual imagery and associations with extractive industries, neither of which provides a useful metaphor to stress the moral urgency of gender equality issues. Girls and women might gain increased visibility in policy discourses when their agency is re-imagined as a valuable resource that must be accessed to spur growth, but ultimately this metaphor falls short. It both mischaracterizes women's economic contributions by hiding the forms of undervalued feminized work that women do, and it presents a misguided equation of economic exploitation with gender equality. Women's liberation, as Marxist feminists have long reminded us, will not be achieved when their labor is as thoroughly exploited in the market as men's labor.

The call to "tap" women's resources is undoubtedly a reductive rhetorical strategy to frame gender equality goals as converging with economic goals. The mode of visibility that human capital framings afford to women is one that aligns with the need to quantify their economic capacities and does, to some extent, make girls and women visible as development agents, roles that were previously unavailable to them. Yet, when we examine the role of human capital theory in formulating this trope, and bring a feminist critique of human capital to bear on the discourse, we can see the power relations at work. In other words, rather than simply standing in as a convenient framing of the issue that will appeal to gender-skeptic organizations in development or business, the discourse of women's untapped human capital does a significant amount of work to construct and reproduce power relationships, as well as to legitimize a set of interventions.

A feminist critique of human capital alerts us to the essentialist tropes that underpin women's visibility: they are either mothers or pre-mothers, and either way attributed an intrinsic maternal subjectivity that can be relied upon to promote equitable and sustainable modes of income generation and distribution. The values of motherhood are associated with positive outcomes and family wellbeing, in contrast to earlier development policymaking assumptions about mothers as passive victims of poverty or reproductive vessels for population growth. Motherhood is instead valorized as an ideal mode of economic agency, because it is attributed a variety of benevolent and community-minded traits that are contrasted with rigid and self-interested masculinities. Yet, motherhood also presents problems for the Smart Economics account of full female empowerment, because reproductive and productive forms of work are often understood to be in tension with each other. Women must therefore balance reproductive responsibilities with productive work and make choices that maximize their ability to do both. Heightened visibility for girls and women is one product of the human capital framing and its valorization of a supposedly intrinsically maternal disposition; the other side of this coin is the invisibility of women who fall outside of this category, whether that is because they are childless, heterosexual, or outside of the childbearing age range that the Bank's framework deems significant. The intrinsic qualities attributed to women that underpin their position in a human capital framework are limited to some women, and exclusive of others.

Of course, the purpose of identifying women's talents and skills as untapped and yet-to-be-harnessed is to prescribe ways that their resources can be accessed. If women are understood in this discourse as pre-empowerment subjects who possess the potential for productivity, but lack the appropriate tools or behaviors, then empowerment interventions are required to equip them with the tools for economic agency. In Foucault's terms, this is the relationship between analytical and programmatic axes of human capital: identifying the intrinsic qualities that make subjects of potential, and authorizing a set of interventions to activate the potential of those subjects. In the 2012 WDR, the proposed interventions are those that shape women's attitudes and aspirations to be compatible with market cultures, and to allow them to demonstrate their capacities in the marketplace. This involves the prescription of interventions that will equip women with the required attributes for market success. Not only is women's human capital an untapped resource for growth, in this discourse, but part of the reason for the lack of recognition of their capacities is because they are unable to communicate that potential in appropriate ways. Human capital theory affords girls and women new modes of development visibility, but it does so in ways that produce clear boundaries around female subjects who are ideally positioned for empowerment, and those who are not. Moreover, it does so through the legitimation of a variety of interventions to activate and harness those capacities. In this regard, it is part of a broader trend of private-sector authority in Gender and Development governance that will be addressed in the following two chapters.

Note

1 Furthermore, as Roberts and Soederberg point out, this same relationship of activation for women as investors and entrepreneurs underpins the Goldman Sachs "Womenomics" investment theme, which proposes the economic empowerment of women for corporate profitability (2012: 958).

References

Anderson, Ben. 2016. "Neoliberal Affects." *Progress in Human Geography* 40(6): 734–753.

Bedford, Kate. 2005. "Loving to Straighten Out Development: Sexuality and Ethnodevelopment in the World Bank's Ecuadorian Lending." *Feminist Legal Studies* 13(3): 295–322.

Bedford, Kate. 2009. *Developing Partnerships: Gender, Sexuality, and the Reformed World Bank*. Minneapolis, MN: University of Minnesota Press.

Benería, Lourdes. 2012. "The World Bank and Gender Inequality." *Global Social Policy* 12(2): 175–178.

Bergeron, Suzanne. 2006. "Colonizing Knowledge: Economics and Interdisciplinarity in Engendering Development." In *Feminist Economics and the World Bank: History, Theory, and Policy*, edited by Edith Kuiper and Drucilla Barker, 127–141. Abingdon: Routledge.

Bergeron, Suzanne. 2016. "Transgressing Gender and Development: Rethinking Economy Beyond 'Smart Economics.'" In *Social Sciences for an Other Politics*, edited by Ana Cecilia Dinerstein, 65–77. New York: Springer.

Brickell, Katherine, and Sylvia Chant. 2010. "'The Unbearable Heaviness of Being': Reflections on Female Altruism in Cambodia, Philippines, The Gambia and Costa Rica." *Progress in Development Studies* 10(2): 145–159.

Calkin, Sydney. 2015. "'Tapping' Women for Post-Crisis Development: Evidence from the 2012 World Development Report." *International Feminist Journal of Politics* 17(4): 611–629.

Chant, Sylvia. 2012. "The Disappearing of 'smart Economics'? The World Development Report 2012 on Gender Equality: Some Concerns about the Preparatory Process and the Prospects for Paradigm Change." *Global Social Policy* 12(2): 198–218.

Chant, Sylvia. 2013. "The Long Shadow of 'smart Economics': The Making, Methodologies and Messages of the World Development Report 2012." In *The International Handbook on Gender, Migration and Transnationalism*, edited by Laura Oso and Natalia Ribas-Mateos, 97–126. Cheltenham: Edward Elgar.

Clegg, Liam. 2010. "Our Dream Is a World Full of Poverty Indicators: The US, the World Bank, and the Power of Numbers." *New Political Economy* 15(4): 473–492.

Elias, Juanita. 2013. "Davos Woman to the Rescue of Global Capitalism: Postfeminist Politics and Competitiveness Promotion at the World Economic Forum." *International Political Sociology* 7(2): 152–169.

Elson, Diane. 2009. "Gender Equality and Economic Growth in the World Bank World Development Report 2006." *Feminist Economics* 15(3): 35–59.

Elson, Diane. 2012. "Review of World Development Report 2012: Gender Equality and Development." *Global Social Policy* 12(2): 178–183.

Evans, Alice. 2012. "World Development Report 2012: Radical Redistribution or Just Tinkering within the Template?" *Development* 55(1): 134–137.

Griffin, Penny. 2009. *Gendering the World Bank: Neoliberalism and the Gendered Foundations of Global Governance*. Basingstoke: Palgrave Macmillan.

Harcourt, Wendy. 2009. *Body Politics in Development: Critical Debates in Gender and Development*. London: Zed Books.

Harcourt, Wendy. 2012. "Review Essay: Beyond 'Smart Economics': The World Bank 2012 Report on Gender and Equality." *International Feminist Journal of Politics* 14(2): 307–312.

Mawdsley, Emma, and Jonathan Rigg. 2002. "A Survey of the World Development Reports I: Discursive Strategies." *Progress in Development Studies* 2(2): 93–111.

Molyneux, Maxine. 2006. "Mothers at the Service of the New Poverty Agenda: Progresa/ Oportunidades, Mexico's Conditional Transfer Programme." *Social Policy & Administration* 40(4): 425–449.

Naraya, Deepa, Raj Patel, Kai Schafft, Anne Rademacher, and Sarah Koch-Schulte. 2000. *Voices of the Poor: Can Anyone Hear Us?* Washington, DC: World Bank. http://documents.worldbank.org/curated/en/131441468779067441/Voices-of-the-poor-can-anyone-hear-us.

Prügl, Elisabeth. 2012. "'If Lehman Brothers Had Been Lehman Sisters…': Gender and Myth in the Aftermath of the Financial Crisis." *International Political Sociology* 6(1): 21–35.

Prügl, Elisabeth. 2017. "Neoliberalism with a Feminist Face: Crafting a New Hegemony at the World Bank." *Feminist Economics* 23(1): 30–53.

Pupavac, Vanessa. 2005. "Human Security and the Rise of Global Therapeutic Governance." *Conflict, Security & Development* 5(2): 161–181.

Rankin, Katharine. 2001. "Governing Development: Neoliberalism, Microcredit, and Rational Economic Woman." *Economy and Society* 30(1): 18–37.

Razavi, Shahra. 2012. "World Development Report 2012: Gender Equality and Development – A Commentary." *Development and Change* 43(1): 423–437.

Repo, Jemima. 2015. *The Biopolitics of Gender.* Oxford: Oxford University Press.

Roberts, Adrienne, and Susanne Soederberg. 2012. "Gender Equality as Smart Economics? A Critique of the 2012 World Development Report." *Third World Quarterly* 33(5): 949–968.

Sjoberg, Laura. 2014. "Commodify Women Much? Care.org and Tapping Women." *Relations International* Blog. Published 29 May 2014. http://relationsinternational.com/tapping-women/.

United Nations. 2012. "Female Energy, Talent, Strength Represent Humankind's Most Valuable Untapped Resource, Secretary-General Says in Message for International Women's Day." Press Release *SG/SM/14140*. www.un.org/News/Press/docs/2012/sgsm14140.doc.htm.

Williams, David. 1999. "Constructing the Economic Space: The World Bank and the Making of Homo Oeconomicus." *Millennium-Journal of International Studies* 28(1): 79–99.

World Bank. 2012. *World Development Report 2012: Gender Equality and Development.* Washington, DC: World Bank. https://openknowledge.worldbank.org/handle/10986/4391.

World Bank. 2015. "World Bank Group Gender Strategy (FY16–23): Gender Equality, Poverty Reduction and Inclusive Growth." Washington, DC: World Bank. https://openknowledge.worldbank.org/handle/10986/23425.

World Bank. 2016. "Gender action plan: 2016–2021." Washington, DC: World Bank. http://documents.worldbank.org/curated/en/243921492664887890/Gender-action-plan-2016-2021.

5 Girl Effects

Introduction

In November 2013, the British right-wing tabloid *The Daily Mail* published a series of stories that railed against the UK Department for International Development (DfID). The subject of its ire was a project in Ethiopia called Yegna, funded through the Girl Hub collaboration between the DfID and the Nike Foundation. Yegna is a multi-platform campaign of TV, radio, and musical programs aimed at Ethiopian girls and young women. Yegna aims to use pop culture to challenge social norms and provoke conversations about the "positive role girls can play in Ethiopian society" (Girl Effect, Yegna n.d.). *The Daily Mail* ran a series of outraged articles about Yegna, lamenting the fact that "UK taxpayers have picked up a £4million bill to fund Ethiopia's own Spice Girls" (Brown 2013). *The Sun* charged DfID with wasting its funding "so pop stars can have their own chat show" rather than spending the funding to support elderly British citizens or "halt the migrant tide to Europe" (Harper 2016). Conservative Members of Parliament dubbed Yegna a "blood boiling" waste of money and a "vanity project" (Ibid.). The scandal was renewed in late 2016, when it emerged that DfID had awarded another grant to Yegna. After further tabloid coverage, the UK government publicly ended the Girl Hub program and cut its funding to Yegna. In explaining its decision, DfID promised to find "more effective ways to invest UK aid and to deliver even better results for the world's poorest and value for taxpayers' money" (Department for International Development (UK) 2017a). The UK's international development agenda under the current Conservative government has committed itself to "drive taxpayer value" and identify opportunities for foreign aid to cultivate Britain's soft power in the run up to Brexit (Priti Patel quoted in BBC 2016).

The Yegna scandal is instructive of a growing trend in Gender and Development, which has been termed the "girl-powering of development and humanitarianism"; this indicates the status of adolescent girls as a separate category of development interest and the central position of girls in current discourses of post-crisis growth (Koffman and Gill 2013: 86). Girl-power discourses, with a particular focus on the empowerment of girls in the global

South, now animate a wide range of humanitarian and development campaigns, advertising campaigns, corporate social responsibility initiatives, and gender equality policies. The Yegna scandal illustrates the politics of respectability at work in "girl-powered" development discourses which stress girls' diligence, productivity, and community spirit as a means to advocate for their empowerment through interventions to improve productivity and control fertility. Girls are highly visible subjects of development interventions, and widely recognized by development and financial institutions as worthy targets for anti-poverty investments. Yet, the mode of visibility for girls and the agency permitted to them is severely limited by the dominance of an instrumental, investment-based rationale that centres on girls' potential productivity through controlling their reproductivity. Girls can be situated in a development rationale that stresses efficiency, productivity, and the "Business Case" for empowerment, but their position in this narrative is fraught with tension and ultimately reproduces highly conservative boundaries for appropriate girlhoods.

Girls' visibility as development agents today is unprecedented, but it is constrained by its relationship to human capital calculations. As such, certain girls and women are written out of economic life, while others appear as idealized agents of growth. The previous chapter demonstrated this process in the 2012 World Development Report, where economic agency is interpreted through a narrow human capital account of interventions to activate their unique productive capacities. Age is an important axis of difference in this process, because gender equality is frequently framed as a strategy for intergenerational change and thus for the achievement of long-term development outcomes. Human capital theory has historically provided a core narrative to link youth, gender, and development futures together: girls' education was a key issue through which human capital theory moved into Gender and Development policymaking in mainstream development institutions (see Chapters 2–3). Young girls and adolescents have been accorded a special visibility in development policy as human capital *in formation* whose productive capacity tomorrow can be improved today (Mahon 2010). Such future-oriented analyses of productivity over the lifespan facilitate a focus on girls as a key site of investment and development intervention.

This chapter employs a feminist critique of human capital theory to examine the girl-powering of the development landscape and the modes of governance therein. Human capital theory has been essential in creating the current mode of girls' policy visibility, because it has provided a language and set of metrics through which girls' productive potential (and reproductive risks) can be translated into a familiar policy language of gender equality as efficiency. It has also provided a framework through which girls' economic agency is made intelligible as a source of profit. In essence, girl-powered development discourses present a future-oriented rubric for understanding girls' lives and value: girls appear as the workers AND mothers of the future, and thus carry a double incentive to invest. The feminist critique of human capital asks us to look for the relationship between the kinds of intrinsic qualities ascribe to women and the interventions designed to elicit particular behaviors and skills from them. This chapter argues that girls are discursively positioned as risky subjects who encapsulate the potential for development successes or failures, and whose possible outcomes are mapped onto their bodies. Girls' intrinsic qualities (to return to the terms of Foucault's critique) resonate with the tropes of female altruism and responsibility: girls are attributed the essentialist qualities of their mothers, in terms of the assumption that they are naturally more community-spirited and productive. And yet, they are identified as uniquely risky subjects who are on the cusp of either an empowered, productive adulthood or disempowered, reproductive adulthood. As such, they are subject to surveillance and forms of intervention that aim to catalyze their economic potential while reducing the risk of pregnancy. The call to intervene in girls' lives to secure their future productivity often appears in the form of a call to invest in their human capital in order to reap the rewards later. However, as I demonstrate, the kinds of interventions prescribed to empower girls and unlock their transformative development potential reproduces a familiar set of projects to train girls as entrepreneurs and consumers, as part of a broader de-politicized vision of empowerment.

The landscape of global girl power

New trends in development came about in response to perceived failures or oversights. Reform agendas in the post-Washington Consensus era responded to the criticism that development had pursued economic growth without concern for human wellbeing. The embrace of participatory development rhetoric responded to the critiques of marginalized groups at the grassroots who rejected policy imposed from above. The current "Gender Equality as Smart Economics" agenda responds, in part, to the criticism that women have been overlooked as an engine of development growth – hence the rhetoric of women as buried resources who must be mined and extracted. A similar process can be seen in operation around girls and girlhood. During the 1990s, girls were "discovered" by the international development community and have since acquired increased visibility as privileged subjects of development. At once, several high-profile development actors emerged as the champions for young girls and with the professed mission to put girls on the agenda and show their potential as development agents. It is a movement that has since grown to include a wide array of global, national, private sector, charitable, and cross-sector initiatives. It is not just the number of girl-focused programs and campaigns that is notable, but the new coalitions of actors coming together on the issue and the growing orientation towards a private-sector emphasis on girls as consumers. In the development policy literature, this inclusion of girls in this agenda is pitched as the extension of the Smart Economics agenda to "*Smarter* Economics" in which more efficient development is driven by investment in younger generations (Chant 2016). As a development discourse, its influence crosses sectors and brings together traditional development institutions with a range of non-state actors: this includes development and economic governance institutions, national governments, charities, private firms, social media platforms, and more.

A 1990 policy decision by UNICEF to develop a specific strategy for girls marks something akin to the starting point for this trend in policy terms, which has expanded enormously in the intervening years (Croll 2006). From the early 1990s, international development agencies and NGOs coalesced around a message of girls' education and focus on the "girl child" at the centre of development discourses. UNICEF's 1990 girl-focused strategy marks a starting point for the growth of girls as development agents on the global stage and also signals the central place of education on this agenda. Recognition of girls as potential agents in economic and political life, and as necessary targets of development aid, has been inseparable from a focus on girls' schooling; this slippage is a much-noted and much-critiqued element of the discourse (Croll 2006; Cobbett 2014). As previously noted, human capital theory has played an important role in this trend in mainstream institutions, because it allowed for the quantification of educational benefits and legitimized development focus on girls through education. Its influence is widespread: the human capital framing is employed on education issues by dominant international institutions working in the global South, although their policy positions on the need for public financing of such human capital investments vary (White 2011: 292). The focus on girls that began with UNICEF has spread across the many institutions of the United Nations and beyond. In 2007, UNICEF, UNIFEM (now UN Women), ILO, UNFPA and the World Health Organization established a UN Interagency Taskforce on Adolescent Girls that aimed to raise awareness of "invisible girls" who are not included in development statistics or policies. The taskforce aims to "unleash the power of girls" who are "the unexpected solution to many of the world's most pressing problems" by strengthening interagency collaboration across the UN and facilitating effective development programs on these issues (UNFPA 2011). The United Nations Girls' Education Initiative, led by UNICEF, monitors and evaluates national education systems with the goal of expanding girls' access to schools, in partnership with other UN agencies, the World Bank, national governments, and NGOs (UNGEI n.d.). In addition, October 2012 saw the United Nations establish the first UN-designated International Day of the Girl Child, with the broader theme of 2012 declared as the UN Year of Ending Child Marriage.

At the national level, governments contribute funding to a wide range of multi-lateral projects like the above-named UN programs. National development agencies also lead their own girl-centred projects, as part of broader gender and development agendas. Development donors like the Nordic states have long had a gender focus in their policymaking, although it is notable that other donors have more recently adopted a focus on empowerment. For instance, the American government's Gender and Development programming places an increasing focus on girl children and adolescent women. USAID opened its Women's Empowerment Office in 2012, from which it runs development programs and partnerships on girls' education and health. In 2015, the US government introduced its Global Strategy to Empower Adolescent Girls that included components implemented by the State Department (on diplomatic issues), USAID (on development spending), US Peace Corps, and Millennium Challenge Corporation (on bilateral aid spending). Michelle Obama launched the "Let Girls Learn" program to expand access to education for girls, from which the Trump administration threatened to withdraw funding in early 2017 (USAID n.d.; McCarthy 2017). In the United Kingdom, the Department for International Development in 2010 launched the "Girl Hub" collaboration with the Nike Foundation, the closure of which was discussed in the introduction to this chapter. Girl Hub had previously been subject to criticism in 2012 from the Independent Commission for Aid Impact, who raised concerns about its lack of clarity around the program's aims, strategy, and weak accountability mechanisms (Independent Commission for Aid Impact 2012). Since 2011, DfID has run a program called Leave No Girl Behind as part of its Girls Education Challenge, which funds NGO projects in the global South and includes "strategic partnerships" with corporations like Coca Cola, Microsoft, and Ericsson (Department for International Development (UK) 2017b). With Coca Cola, for example, DfID will fund an entrepreneurship scheme in Nigeria to build girls "financial, entrepreneurial and leadership skills" and help them start businesses, including as retailers of Coca Cola products (Department for International Development (UK) 2014; Coca Cola 2014).

Private sector partnerships in the field of girl-powered development abound, joining together public, private and third sector actors in collaborative initiatives. This is partly driven by financial issues: private sector partnerships have been welcomed by multilateral institutions who are eager to fill funding gaps in the field of girls' education and development (Draxler 2016; Unterhalter 2017). The World Bank in particular has been a leader of girl-centred partnerships with private sector organizations and charitable foundations. In 2008, the World Bank and private sector partners launched the Adolescent Girls Initiative to "promote the transition of adolescent girls from school to productive employment" which ran from 2008–2015; it was supported by the Nike Foundation and eight national governments (World Bank 2009b). Gender-equality programing has been an important part of the Bank's private-sector collaborations, particularly in the wake of the 2008 global financial crisis (see Roberts and Soederberg 2012). The Bank's private sector partnerships are an area marked out for growth: the recommendation to expand private sector partnerships was a key aspect of the 2007–2010 Gender Action Plan and 2012 World Development Report (see Chapters 3–4). Similarly, the World Economic Forum is an important site of girl-powered development where the discourse of investment in girls is shaped and promoted to the private sector. In 2006, the World Economic Forum, in partnership with its Competitiveness and Women Leaders Programs began releasing an annual report called "Women's Empowerment: Measuring the Global Gender Gap" of which girls' education is a major component (Elias 2013). In 2011, UN Women released its own *Gender Dividend* report that encouraged states to understand gender equality as a national competitiveness issue (Roberts 2015). In 2009, the WEF hosted a plenary session in which corporate, foundation, government and NGO leaders discussed gendered poverty and investment in girls, citing the "an irrational investment gap" in this area (World Bank 2009a).

Multi-national corporations and their charitable foundations have been significant leaders in broadening the appeal of girl-powered development beyond United Nations institutions and national governments, although they often do so through partnerships with public institutions. Since its establishment in 2004 by Nike, the Nike Foundation has been a major source of influence in this field, in part because its work is focused exclusively on adolescent girls. In 2005, it joined with the United Nations Foundation to launch the Coalition for Adolescent Girls to "address adolescent girls' need for support and their potential to change the world" (Coalition for Adolescent Girls n.d.). The Nike Foundation is best known for its Girl Effect campaign, dedicated to raising awareness and promoting "social norm change" that empowers girls. Numerous corporations run girl-centred projects through their CSR wings or private foundations; these projects take diverse forms including social media campaigns, branding campaigns, NGO partnerships, research reports, investment guidelines, and social enterprises (see Koffman and Gill 2013; Koffman et al 2015). It should also be noted that as interest – across public and private sectors – in the "Business Case" for girls' empowerment grows, so too does the consultancy industry around this issue, comprised of high-profile global financial and accountancy firms whose publications influenced private-sector interest in the issue. These include: Goldman Sachs' *Womenomics* report (1999); McKinsey and Co.'s *The Business of Empowering Women* (2010); Ernst and Young's series *Groundbreakers: Using the Strength of Women to Rebuild the World Economy* (2009); and Deloitte's *The Gender Dividend: Making the Business Case for Investing in Women* (2011). More recently, the Nike Foundation and UN Foundation have commissioned MapleCroft data consultancy to build a proprietary "Girls Stats" database that maps data on girls' vulnerability and risks across the world, so that "unique, targeted programs" can be designed (quoted in Murphy 2017: 127). The growing field of private sector gender expertise on the "Business Case" for gender equality provides firms with guidance on accessing female consumer markets, capturing female expertise within the corporate structure, and investing strategically in gender-related areas.

The girl-powering of development captures more than a rhetorical trend or a heightened visibility for particular girls in development branding. It tracks on to transformations in development funding and authority that accord greater authority to private-sector entities through partnerships on social responsibility and development projects; the material effects of these partnerships the subject of Chapter 6. As the review above has shown, girl-powered development and humanitarian initiatives are on the rise. Space limits preclude attention to every relevant initiative in this area, so the analysis that follows focuses on four initiatives that provide a representative example of the most distinctive features of the trend: they comprise hybrid and cross-sector partnerships, heavy emphasis on branding through social media and corporate links, and center their campaigns around promoting awareness of girls' economic agency. The four initiatives, detailed below, are: the Girl Effect; Girl Rising; Girl Up; and Because I Am a Girl.

1) The Girl Effect is undoubtedly the best known of the many girl-power development initiatives, because it has been an extremely high-profile and influential project that has gained attention in media, policy, and academic spheres. It launched in 2009 as a project of the Nike Foundation, the charitable wing of Nike Inc., although it became an independent NGO in 2015 (with continued financial support from Nike). The Girl Effect began as a campaign to raise awareness of the "potential of girls to end poverty," although it has since changed from publicity and awareness-raising to funding development projects through partner NGOs. Currently, the Girl Effect works in two areas: first, building "culture brands" (TV, radio, and magazine content) that promote positive messages about girlhood. Its second focus is mobile technologies that connect girls with educational content, mentoring, and communication; this includes mobile platforms that encourage girls to research and collect data on their lives for development projects. In its early years, the Girl Effect described itself as a "movement" whereas today it calls itself a "creative social business." (Girl Effect n.d.)

2) Girl Rising is a "global social action campaign for girls' education and empowerment" that uses "storytelling" through film and media. It was founded by the Intel Corporation, the Documentary Group, Vulcan Productions, and 10x10, a campaign for girls' education, among other private, public, and third sector partners who subsequently joined. Girl Rising is best known for its 2013 film *Girl Rising* that combined documentary footage with celebrity voiceovers to tell the stories of nine fictional girls across the global South. The Girl Rising initiative, and its film, aim to "raise awareness about the issue, inspire action, and drive resources" (Girl Rising n.d., "Girl Rising" and "Fuel the Movement"; see also Bent and Switzer 2016). Girl Rising measures its impact through "social media impressions" and viewing figures for its media (Ibid.); it does not fund specific development projects, but re-invests revenue back into the campaign. Its programs today involve collaborations to produce and distribute new films, fundraise through film screenings, and campaigning for educational issues.

3) Girl Up is a campaign launched in 2010 by the United Nations Foundation with the mission of "engag[ing] girls to stand up for girls, empowering each other and changing our world" (Girl Up 2016). Girl Up uses social media and campaigning events to "raise awareness and funds" for United Nations programs that target girls. Girl Up therefore shares a public-orientation with the above campaigns, but its distinctive dimension is its target audience: Girl Up is driven by the mantra of "for girls, by girls" that "encourages

American girls to become forces of global change" (Girl Up n.d.). Its agents are "philanthro-teens" who are called upon to hold events, form clubs, and begin campaigns to raise funds for Girl Up, as well as to host events that will benefit girls in their local area (Girl Up 2012; Girl Up n.d.). To this end, it includes events that train young women in fundraising, public speaking, and leadership mentoring to help them begin local Girl Up clubs. It also has a strong element of celebrity advocacy, hosting events with actors, musicians, and socialite-philanthropists like Queen Rania of Jordan, Ivanka Trump and a range of celebrity-branded products that girls can buy to contribute to the campaign.

4) "Because I Am a Girl," is a campaign run by Plan International, a global development charity based in Britain whose work focuses primarily on children's rights. Plan directly funds development projects through fundraising and publicity campaigns. In 2007, it launched a report on girls around the world, and with it a campaign called "Because I Am a Girl." The campaign is notable for its highly visible public face, which included a poster campaign across Canada (from PlanCanada), a film called #LearnWithoutFear (from PlanUK), a charitable shoe line (from PlanUSA), numerous video spots, celebrity advocacy, and a campaign for the establishment of the International Day of the Girl Child. Plan too sees its work as a "movement" which has developed out of the original "Because I Am a Girl" campaign: this movement aims to promote girls, "voices and visibility" by influencing policy outcomes, building partnerships, and driving "investments in their futures" (Plan n.d.; Plan 2015). Its projects include drives to collect data on girls, publication of a girls' rights manifesto, and the publication of annual reports that address different dimensions of girls in development (Plan 2009).

Divergent girlhoods

The bodies of girls are "always understood as potentialities, in need of regulation and evaluation" (Banet Weiser 2015: 56). In this policy discourse, girls are understood as vulnerable subjects in crisis, but also as subject who embody a unique productive potential. Scholarship in the field of girlhood studies has identified this language of risky girlhood as part of a governing logic for girls in the global North. Discussions of girls are structured around two types: girls may occupy the role the successful girl (entrepreneurial, empowered, consumerist) or the girl at risk (characterized by poverty, vulnerability, and generally racialized). These "Can Do" and "At Risk" girls are conceptual constructs that can be applied to the same girl: the two types are oriented around girls' choices, where disempowering choices can turn the girl into a risky figured (Harris 2004). The Can Do and At Risk girls not only provide a conceptual framework for understanding the representational binaries that structure this discourse, but they also serve to justify new modes of surveillance around girls. Surveillance of girls aims to identify which of these paths – success or failure – girls follow, and to intervene in their bodies and social behavior to shape these paths (McRobbie 2009). The dualities that structure girls' representations contain clear echoes of the human capital logic that has been essential in their heightened visibility as promising subjects of future productivity: dormant resources in need of cultivation. Tropes of the successful and risky girl resonate in development discourses as well, although these politics take a slightly different cast, however, because they are played out against the backdrop of poverty: girls in the global South are imagined as being anti-poverty solutions and thus responsible for poverty eradication. The stakes are raised, in a sense, because the success or failure of girls in the global South is writ large as a development success or failure. Today, girlhood is understood through the pairing of "possibility and challenge" (Banet Weiser 2015: 57).

The discourse of girl-powered development hinges on the idea that girls' human capital is ideally placed for investment, which will generate returns as she grows, as long as appropriate interventions guide her towards a path of productivity. It holds that well-timed interventions can catch girls at the tipping point in their lives and capitalize on the uniqueness of girls to generate widespread prosperity. The duality of potential and challenge that structures this discourse is productively illuminated by a feminist critique of human capital that points to the analytical and programmatic axes of human capital, or the kinds of innate predispositions that are ascribed to girls and the modes of appropriate behaviors and acquired skills that are proscribed through development intervention. The particular visibility of girls as ideal development subjects is generally underpinned by the contention that girls are uniquely suited for development leadership: that they are different from boys and therefore more caring and worthy. Girl-powered development material is replete with claims about the uniqueness of girls that makes them especially worthy and community-minded recipients of development attention (see MacDonald 2016; Chant 2016). The tropes of altruism, productivity, and responsibility attributed to women are similarly applied to girls through a future-oriented logic that stresses the need to cultivate these traits for future returns. By extension, a series of programmatic interventions are prescribed to capitalize on these traits and cultivate girls' skills for economic participation. The same forms of visibility that accord girls a newfound status as subjects of political concern subject them to an "unprecedented level" of interventions to shape their bodies, sexualities, behaviors, and modes of economic agency (McRobbie quoted in Harris 2004: 14). Positioned within a broader anti-poverty discourse, girls are tasked with the job of eradicating poverty through the choices they make between success and failure.

The kinds of conceptual dualities illustrated in the Can Do/At Risk frame run throughout girl-powered development discourse: girls in the global South are often represented as positioned at a fork in the road from which divergent girlhoods emanate. They convey the idea that girlhood is a ripe moment for intervention into the lives of girls, from which point they can be transformed for a life of productivity. Absent these interventions, it follows, they will be consigned to a life of poverty and disempowerment from which there can be no respite. The Girl Effect campaign, for example, relies on this duality as one of its main rhetorical tools. Its vision of girls employs the binary of entrepreneurial/risky girls, who are either saved by development interventions or lost to development forever. Maria Eitel, the former CEO of the Girl Effect, uses this logic to explain why girls are the particular focus of the Nike Foundation's efforts:

> "[The adolescent girl] has the opportunity to break that intergenerational cycle and that's very unique to an adolescent girl. What happens to her at that transitional moment will determine whether her family is on an upward spiral or a downward spiral."
>
> (Eitel quoted in Kanani 2011)

The Girl Effect positions adolescent girls at a fork in the road of the life course, where the girl either heads towards empowerment or disempowerment. The choices she makes are linked together in a succession of events, where education, employment, entrepreneurship and empowerment directly flow from each other. By extension, the welfare of her family, community, and country is linked to her choices at this pivotal moment. The right choice means empowerment for her and the whole community, while the wrong choice (or a failure to intervene in her life at the right moment) will leave them all mired in a cycle of poverty. Girls across the global South are widely attributed this unique "Third World potential", which assigns them the sole responsibility for poverty eradication (Moeller 2013). The idea that girlhood is understood as a crucial moment of development success or failure may sound hyperbolic, but in fact the discourse of girl-powered development turns on this overheated rhetoric that makes claims about the astonishing new discovery of girls and the absolute urgency of immediate intervention to stave off poverty. Girls are invested with special potential and enormous risk here: they either represent development's saviours or its destructors, depending on the educational and reproductive decisions they make in adolescence. This duality is explicitly mapped out in the Girl Effect's promotional material that presents girlhood as a series of decision points where empowerment is begun or disempowerment cemented. An early mission statement from the Girl Effect set this up as a "crossroads" where the adolescent girl can follow one of two paths: either "she gets the opportunity to raise the standard of living of her family" or "she and her family are struck in a cycle of poverty" (cited in Shain 2013). The diverging trajectories metaphor continues in the Girl Effect's more recent promotional material, which articulates the binary as Old versus New Normal.

With its recent change in status and re-brand, the Girl Effect issued a new series of graphics to showcase its mission. These graphics use the headings of "Old Normal" and "New Normal" to showcase the changes in girls' lives. The "Old Normal" shows a girl's figure inside a spiral, surrounded by the words: Pre-determined outcomes, protection, control, dependency, and violence. By contrast, the girl's figure in "New Normal" is raising her arms in a triumphant pose, surrounded by words including: agency, autonomy, empowerment and new opportunities (Girl Effect 2016). Creating a "New Normal" is the mission of the Girl Effect, though the catalyst for these changes is vague. The clearest implication is the assumption that without intervention, girls will follow a life of "pre-determined outcomes" (Eitel quoted in Kanani 2011). This is a message that CEO Maria Eitel also often returns to, where she emphasizes the abstraction of the girl as a singular moment for intervention. If this fails, she suggests, poverty continues:

> "The other more common path is where she turns 12 and all of her opportunities are shut down. She gets pulled out of school to face early marriage, pregnancy, risk of HIV infection. When that happens, things are pretty much set for her and for the next generation."

In these representations, the singular girl of the global South comes to embody all the promise and peril of development. She is invested with anticipation and anxiety for the future of the global economy, because her choices could trigger the chain reaction that ends poverty. She is development in a corporeal form, where the kinds of violence written on her body stand in for larger development failures. The prevalent narrative of divergent girlhoods argues that an adolescent girl's life is characterized by two outcomes: either productivity (delayed childbirth and marriage) or reproductivity (early childbirth and marriage). By equating girls' lives with broader development outcomes, it performs the rhetorical trick of attributing development failures to cultural practices or kinship structures (Hickel 2014). Such tropes are at work in the Girl Effect's high-profile video campaign: in the eponymously titled "Girl Effect" video, the girl is represented as a figure who is literally crushed by a husband, hunger, and HIV. The girl figure holds a baby, as flies swarm around them; her figure shrinks as these things pile up on top of her (see Girl Effect 2008b). In another Girl Effect video, titled "Clock is Ticking", a girl is chased by grasping hands that represent men trying to pull her into prostitution and infect her with sexually transmitted diseases. The text across the screen reads: "If she survives childbirth, she might have to sell her body to support her family, which puts her at risk for contracting and spreading HIV" (Girl Effect 2010).

This video imagines the same girl on two timelines: in one, she becomes pregnant, gives birth, falls into prostitution, and contracts HIV. In the alternate timeline, she avoids pregnancy until later in life, gets an education, and starts a business. Broader anxieties about development, security, and disease are at work in these representations of girlhood because they invest the figure of the girl child with such responsibility for development, and subsequently with a cataclysmic series of failures that will follow from her disempowerment. As in the 2012 WDR, economic productivity is set in opposition to biological reproductivity, where girls and women are asked to manage their choices carefully to become both productive workers and responsible mothers. The trajectories laid out here establish long chains of effects that result from girls' decisions: either "autonomy, productivity and promise" or "tradition, confinement, reproductivity, and peril" (Switzer 2013: 347). The duality of the Can Do and At Risk girls structures this moment, infused with suspense and contingent on appropriate interventions. Which way will she go?

The representations of divergent girlhoods here work on a set of dualities. These are mapped onto visions of temporal and spatial difference. Temporally, the figure of the disempowered girl is represented as poised at a crucial turning point in her life, from which she can be empowered or disempowered. This kind of temporal frame is evident in the messages of investment and future profit, as well as through the oft-repeated claim that girls are at a "transitional moment" (Eitel in Kanani 2011). Sometimes, the temporality of empowerment/disempowerment is bluntly visually represented with a clock, as in the Girl Effect "Clock is Ticking" video (Girl Effect 2010). But this duality is also mapped spatially, in terms of the lines of different between the girl in the global South and her American or European counterpart. In essence, it uses a modernization framework to imagine girls as growing up into empowered and productive forms of womanhood, and thus spatially eliminating the distances between Western womanhood and the "rest." These forms of temporal and spatial difference are collapsed into the figure of the "Third World Woman" trope, who is represented as the future incarnation of the promising girl. The kinds of images and narratives of girlhood in the global South, contrasted with the representations of empowered girlhood, convey a call to "save" girls in the global South from the future that awaits them as stereotypical girls in the global South.

"Girls Mean Business"

This girl-powered account of anti-poverty imagines girls as a transformative force who can be "unleashed" to eradicate poverty. In doing so, it equates gender inequality with economic stagnation and crisis, thereby asserting a clear link between gender equality and economic growth. This link is not simple or straightforward, nor is it the case that economic growth directly drives improvements in gender equality (see Kabeer and Natali 2013). Yet, girls are attributed a unique ability to end poverty through their newfound agency, as the Girl Rising project explains: "Around the world, girls face barriers to education that boys do not. But educating girls can break cycles of poverty in just one generation" (Girl Rising n.d.). The power of girls and women is framed as "one of the most powerful development multipliers" (World Bank 2012), "the world's greatest untapped resource" (Girl Effect 2012: 3). The policy visibility of the girl stems from a new reading of her lifespan: she is inserted into a longer chain of correlation that links her personal decisions with broader community development outcomes. The proposed solution is to "tap" the resources of girls and women whose economic contribution has not been adequately harnessed. A graphic produced by the Nike Foundation for the Girl Effect, for instance, uses the recognizable green EXIT sign with the image of a girl as the figure running out (see Provost 2012). The caption reads "In case of global poverty, set me free!" The policy visibility of girls has been facilitated by the insertion into a logic of calculation and intervention. As such, their relevance to development outcomes is represented primarily in terms of their ability to contribute economically as empowered workers, and to raise productive children as empowered future mothers.

A 1992 speech by then-Vice President of the World Bank Lawrence Summers provides an early example of this logic. During his time at the Bank, Summers was a prominent advocate of the economist's case for gender equality; he was generally careful to bracket off moral questions about women's status as citizens in favour of an argument about the benefits of their economic enfranchisement (Summers 1994; see also Chapter 3). In a speech at the Eighth Annual General Meeting of the Pakistan Society of Development Economists, Summers argued that investment in girls' education "may well be the highest return on investment available in the developing world" (Summers 1992: 1). To advance this argument, Summers calculated the costs and benefits of different interventions in girls' life. He calculated that a $30,000 investment in girls' schooling could reduce fertility by the amount of 500 births. By contrast, he estimated that it would take $33,000 investment in family planning programs distributing contraception to achieve the same reduction of 500 fewer births (Ibid.: 6–7). Investing in girls' education, Summers concluded, delivered social benefits that were "more than sufficient to cover its costs" (Ibid.: ii). These kinds of calculations, which today sound commonplace and proliferate in the publications of governments and NGOs, crystallized in the 1990s. They introduced a new "tabulation of economic life" and prescription for economic agency, whose visual and rhetorical touchstone was the poor girl of the global South (Murphy 2017: 114). Notably, Summers' economistic framework introduces a logic of girlhood that is powerful today: it identifies dormant potential, risky behaviors that would lower productivity, and calculates the cost/ benefit of intervening to incentivize other behaviors. Moreover, it does so in a dispassionate language that leaves aside moral questions about freedom, equality and agency.

Human capital theory proposes a shift in the way we understand the laborer and her labor: rather than selling her labor for a wage, the laborer becomes an asset in which she can invest and reap rewards. The wage she earns is re-imagined as the income stream off that capital, which could be improved in the long term with strategic investments to raise the value of capital. In short, human capital theory proposes a re-imagining of human life. Human capital theory has performed a similar function for girls, by allowing girls to become legible as subjects of *future* economic productivity. This is especially evident in the frequent equation of girls and their growth with the growth of investment portfolios. In a Plan International ad, a girl asks the viewer to "Invest in me: it makes sense. Start when I'm very young and watch your investment grow as I do. Because you see my potential" (Plan International 2016). The maturation of an adolescent girl into an adult woman (and a mother to the next generation) is mapped onto the maturation of a stock or bond. Girls here are caught up "in a cloud of anticipatory calculations" in which dimensions of a girl's life and her relationships are positioned in a chain of correlation that equate education, delayed marriage, lower morality, and raised wages (Murphy 2017: 114). Education, employment, and pregnancy are directly linked together in this policy discourse, through the contention that appropriate interventions can trigger the chain of events that results in greater productivity. The association of girls and women with savvy investments potentially opens up space for a consideration of women's economic agency, but at a steep cost because such discourses are often profoundly de-humanizing. It sells a truncated version of women's agency because they equate her body with greater or lesser financial returns, sometimes in the bluntest terms. This is apparent in an image from a 2012 Girl Effect brochure that shows a woman holding a baby. She is standing next to a baby carriage stuffed with money; the caption explains that "with nearly four million adolescent mothers annually, India loses US$383 billion in potential lifetime income" (Girl Effect 2012). Similarly, a 2013 Girl Effect report contains an image of a piggy bank being stuffed with coins that resemble globes, with this message on the side of the piggy bank: "She'll get pregnant later which is great for her country's economy" (Girl Effect 2013).

The reliance on cost/benefit calculations to understand social inequalities is not unique to the area of gender policymaking, but is indicative of a broader neoliberal ideological climate in which it is expected that all dimensions of life should be governed according to business principles. It follows that the most widespread and influential discursive formulations of gender equality will be those that originate in market logic and work for the achievement of market goals. As such, much of the girl-power development discourse dispenses with appeals to justice or equality and instead advances its case through a calculation about the most efficient ways to achieve development outcomes. For example, this reasoning is used when girl-powered development initiatives provide explanations of why they focus on girls, rather than boys, or children generally. The answers tend to adopt an instrumental logic of strategic investment and efficiency of outcomes. Girl Rising, for example, explains that "Educating girls can break cycles of poverty in just one generation, making girls' education one of the smartest investment opportunity in the world today" (Girl Rising n.d.). Plan International's video campaign deploys a similar justification for girls, placing them at the center of development solutions. The female voiceover in Plan International's promotional videos explains: "Invest in me and the whole community will benefit. I'll be smarter, healthier and stronger. My work will add to the economy of the village, the country, our planet" (Plan International 2016). The girl's economic agency is continually understood here in terms of her future as a mother and carer in the community:

> "The "girl effect" theory of change hypothesizes that by investing in an adolescent girl, we not only transform her life chances, but also the life chances of her future children and her community. If we invest in enough girls, we can unleash the potential of whole nations."
>
> (Girl Hub n.d.)

The ability to re-imagine girls' future potential through human capital theory has given them a newfound importance in development discourses and made them legible to investors in the private sector. This performs a move that is familiar from early days to development: first women were understood as irrelevant to development, because they were imagined as passive victims of tradition and backwardness, who would suffer from poverty and inequality but had little role in contributing to economic change in their communities. A few things changed this: the "discovery" of a linkage between development, fertility, and economic agency meant that the wellbeing of women came to be seen as fundamentally important to the achievement of development goals. Women as mothers gained visibility in development because their performance of care duties impacted the health, education, and productivity of the next generations. Motherhood granted women a visibility in development, albeit a limited one that was largely instrumental and often essentialist. Girls have become visible as potential vessels of development (and risky figures who require intervention) through their inclusion in broader modes of Smart Economics reasoning: their lives have become legible through calculations that assess their potential productivity versus the risk of their reproductivity. At its core, this agenda is fueled by the idea that investment in girls can produce higher returns than other investments, but that the failure to adequately invest will have serious consequences for girls, their families, and the entire project that is global development. Through the logic of human capital theory, girls are subject to new forms of quantification through which their bodies and life trajectories are measured in terms of investment potential. This has given rise to a discourse of global girl power that hinges on saving girls from disempowerment, through which larger development failures are attributed to failed interventions in girlhood.

Familiar solutions

The narrative of girl-powered development can be paraphrased as follows: "Girls in the global South are at a crossroads, from which point they will become empowered entrepreneurs or join the disempowered mass of the global poor. Urgent interventions are required to empower girls and harness their potential economic power." However, the kinds of solutions that are proposed for girls' empowerment reflect a rhetorical shift, but fall short of substantive policy change. They often deploy the language of autonomy and empowerment, but still endorse a logic of intervention to instil girls and women with market-compatible behaviors. In fact, the solutions promised in girl-powered development tend to revolve around a familiar set of educational and financial development projects, limited to a narrow range of income-generating activities and job skills-training interventions linked to employability. Evidence from ethnographic studies of these development interventions demonstrates the tendency for such projects to translate poorly into practice because of over-reliance on pre-scripted empowerment narratives that do not conform to girls' lives. Moreover, they frequently reproduce a vision of feminist action as neo-colonial saving of distant others.

Despite public campaigns' insistence that girls are unique sources of development agency, or specially placed vessels for economic transformation, the kinds of intervention prescribed for them reflect entrenched development wisdom about unleashing entrepreneurship in order to catalyse broader economic growth. As part of its "Economic Powerhouse" funding stream, the Girl Effect sponsored a project in Brazil to provide entrepreneurship training for girls between the ages of sixteen and 24 in computer skills, math skills, literacy, and civic knowledge. Evaluation of its outcomes found that the project was largely unsuccessful at finding employment for the participants after, and those who did find employment were confined to low-wage work in supermarkets, bus companies, and call centres (Moeller 2013: 616). The project sought to catalyse the "Girl Effect" by equipping girls with employment skills, but this had little effect in the broader politico-economic context. Girl Effect projects focused on sport as an empowerment tool similarly emphasize the potential for development interventions to build entrepreneurial mentalities and self-reliance to equip girls with income-generating skills in unstable markets. They emphasize confidence-building exercises that will translate into economic agency and independent incomes, with knock-on effects on family income (Hayhurst 2014; Forde and Frisby 2015; Caron and Margolin 2015). Interventions designed to make girls and women more employable advocate forms of training that will allow girls to better communicate their skills to employers and navigate business environments where employers might be skeptical of their abilities (World Bank 2012). The kinds of gendered inequalities that girls and young women face are continually reduced to human capital-building interventions that will equip them with marketable skills. As such, these interventions tend to be focused on girls in isolation, and focused on income-generation skills to trigger broader economic growth, in much the same way that older development frameworks did; this provides evidence of the staying power of 1970s WID frameworks (Chant 2016). They embrace a new language of empowerment, confidence, and self-esteem, but the kinds of interventions that fall under the girl-power development program in fact reproduce an older set of education and training programs that focus on entrepreneurship, education and training as a means to income-generation and self-reliance.

Girls' visibility as key development agents depends on the understanding that the adolescent girl is positioned at a crossroads in her life, at which point essential interventions can be made to set her on the path of empowerment. Absent interventions, disempowerment will follow. As Girl Effect CEO Maria Eitel describes it, the 12 year old girl living in poverty occupies a moment of transition after which follows an "upward spiral or a downward spiral" (quoted in Kanani 2011). The Girl Effect therefore aims to intervene in this crucial moment to change the trajectory of the twelve-year-old girl's life – "before it is too late." Yet, in practice, this proves an unworkable model. A Brazilian recruitment drive for a Girl Effect project provides a concrete manifestation of these narratives, and the dissonance with which they map onto girls' lived experiences (Moeller 2014). The project tried to locate the population of girls theorized by the Girl Effect's model of change, but in practice, this model appeared to be poorly suited to the lived reality of its supposed beneficiaries. Officially, the project sought to recruit 100 girls with the following characteristics: "Female sex, 16–24 years old, likes sports, and interested in entering the labor market or becoming an entrepreneur." Yet the recruitment process was shaped by a variety of unofficial characteristics including "race, class position, education level, employment status, and fertility" (Ibid.: 590). The project sought girls who were below the poverty line, but not destitute; Afro-Brazilian girls racialized as black; girls in state school but who had not graduated or pursued further study; unemployed or in low-wage employment; and girls who were not pregnant or mothers. These restrictions, among other factors, meant that only 70 girls were recruited by the deadline and numbers declined as the program ran (Ibid.: 587). When girls were identified and recruited into the program, they were required to complete questionnaires that mapped them on to these "universal indicators" of empowerment (Moeller 2013). The model of adolescent girlhood that drives the Girl Effect's campaign and underpins its policy documentation envisions adolescent girl as *tabula rasa*: she is yet unblemished by disempowering attributes that will harm her future productivity, and can therefore be brought into development projects that will capitalize on her potential. This vision appears to be a convenient fiction for marketing purposes, with less ability to translate into girls' lives. This dissonance, however, was not a problem from the Girl Effect's perspective: Moeller's (2013) findings show that when Girl Effect projects failed to improve the lives of enrolled participants, project managers still saw the effort as successfully raising awareness of the NGO's message among big donors.

Girl-power development is a public-oriented and high-profile set of campaigns and messages, whose dominant narrative about girls' and women's empowerment valorizes particular forms of female economic agency, but it excludes those women whose bodies or lives cannot be "read" as sufficiently productive. Such policy discourses perform the function of setting boundaries around who can be the subject of Gender and Development knowledge. Narratives like these shape the development practitioner too, and impact the kinds of voices that can be "heard" in the development process. For all the messaging about raising awareness of girls and making their voices heard, these narratives actually serve a limiting effect so that only particular narratives of empowerment can be heard as authentic. In the Girl Effect's *Girls' Voices* project from Pakistan, project leaders found that the girls' voices highlighted in the project tended to conform to ideas about repression and intervention. The girls' testimonies included in the project's public-facing showcase reinforced the "history and authority" of the Girl Effect's campaign by featuring girls who reaffirmed the need for interventions of transnational institutions, and whose accounts of future aspirations conformed to narratives about the liberation of Muslim girls from oppressive societies through entrepreneurship. Girls who articulated alternative narratives that did not center economic independence or income-generation were excluded from the project's publicity material (Khoja-Moolji 2016: 747–748). The approved narratives in the project called forth a trajectory of disempowerment by oppressive cultures, interventions for education and empowerment, followed by economic independence and community transformation.

These prescribed narratives of girl-power and empowerment do not map onto the lives of the girls to whom they refer: they present "distorted, stylized versions" of girlhood that enforce conceptual binaries between different kinds of girls and the futures which naturally follow from their adolescent years (Switzer 2013: 346). The model of empowerment produced and reproduced in girl-power projects is premised on a rigid understanding of girlhood and transition to economically productive womanhood. This model struggles, in practice, to translate into meaningful metrics for understanding the lives of girls in the global South. This is partly because they are based on ideas about universal indicators for empowerment, but also because they are deeply rooted in a modernization narrative that imagines girls in the global South as passengers on a journey to become more like "us." Girl-power discourses depend on the idealized adolescence of the Western teenager to anchor their reference points about empowerment and economic fulfilment. The kinds of divergent girlhoods are imagined less in temporal terms (Future life A vs. Future life B) than geographical ("our" girls vs. "their" girls). Girl-powered development is replete with conceptual binaries that separate the empowered girl from the disempowered girl, the Western woman from the oppressed non-Western woman, the Can Do entrepreneur from the At Risk teen. This is a hallmark of what Angela McRobbie (2009) describes as post-feminist politics. Post-feminist culture offers young women in the West a highly conservative mode of empowerment characterized by sexual and economic freedoms, in which they are positioned *against* gender arrangements in other cultures and called upon to participate in empowering (saving) victimized, non-Western women in the rest of the world. "Our" young women are encouraged to understand themselves as "grateful subjects of modern states and cultures", in opposition to distant others who lack access to Western freedoms (McRobbie 2009: 27–8). The narratives of divergent girlhoods are frequently located in the body of the adolescent girl at the center of development campaigns – whose life stands in for broader development outcomes – but they are also apparent in girl-power discourses that spatialize girlhoods along geographical lines. In post-colonial terms, this relationship hinges on a "missionary Girl Power" evoked by empowerment campaigns (Sensoy and Marshall 2010; see also Caron and Margolis 2015; MacDonald 2016). Development hierarchies are not transformed, but filtered through the language of girl-power and the urgency of saving at risk girls abroad.

The UN Foundation's Girl Up project relies on this kind of logic, where American girls are told that they are truly empowered and can therefore lead the charge to empower oppressed girls around the world. Girl Up highlights the importance of connections between different girls (and conceptions of girlhood) in these initiatives, which often contain a strong element of awareness raising on the part of girls in the global North about gender inequality in the global South. The Girl Up project encourages "American girls to become forces of global change" because they are "more educated, socially connected and empowered today than ever before in history" (UN Foundation 2010). Girl Up asks American girls to act as leaders and "philanthro-teens" who have the power to empower girls around the world through social media awareness, local meet ups, and fundraising. It invites girls to see themselves as having achieved equality, which can now be shared:

> "With Girl Up, you can join the fight for every girl's right to be respected, educated, healthy, safe and ready to rule the future. Just like you."
>
> (United Nations Foundation 2009)

Beneath the surface of the girl-power rhetoric lies a familiar development paradigm. We can trace is evolution through modernization frameworks, welfarist frameworks, Women in Development, to today's Gender Equality as Smart Economics. The representations at play here evoke the most stereotypical representation of the disempowered "Third World Woman" evoked by Chandra Mohanty: this woman is sexually constrained, "ignorant, poor, uneducated, tradition bound, religious, domesticated, victimized, etc." (Mohanty 1988: 65). Mohanty's critique of the Third World Woman does not just condemn essentialist or imperialist images of female subjugation: it asks Western women to examine their complicity in the construction of this figure, and asks us to understand the way that the Third World Woman is constituted in relationship to her. In the case of girl-powered development material, the evocation of divergent girlhoods is not only about representing girls in the global South as vessels for development (or continued poverty), but about positioning girls in the global South as lacking access to the right kind of childhood. The narrative of diverging girlhoods maps on to broader modernization tropes in development, where girlhoods around the world are assessed in relation to "our girls" and their lives. The representational modes used here have the potential to evoke solidarity, in asking viewers to reflect on their position of privilege or their relationship to distant others. However, the utterly de-politicized discourse of girl-power avoids any political or structural critique of the vast gulf of inequality that separates "us" from "them" and instead positions viewers as the empowered agents who can save others (Calkin 2015). The relationship is instead suffused with a post-feminist sensibility that resists solidarity by relying on civilizational hierarchies.

Conclusion

Girls around the world face compounded forms of disadvantage, where their age and sex situate them at the bottom of a social hierarchy that subjects them to numerous forms of violence. No account of Gender and Development can robustly address gendered inequalities without giving special attention to the numerous forms of violence and inequality faced by girls and young women. Feminists have advocated for the inclusion of girls on the global policy stage for decades, with increased prominence since the 1990s. More recently, girls and young women have acquired dramatically increased visibility as subjects of a girl-power discourse that spans public and private institutions. This chapter has demonstrated that the current visibility of girls – their discovery as "worthy" subjects – is oriented around the idea that girls constitute a unique site of future potential as well as risk. Their transformation from promising, but uncultivated, subjects into productive, empowered actors hinges on a set of interventions to catalyse their potential and guide them past the obstacles that hinder their progress. At each stage, the conception of girlhood here is positioned as a transition point between two futures: empowerment or disempowerment. The idea of divergent girlhoods that frames so much of the girl-power discourse in development owes its conceptual premise to human capital theory, because of its emphasis on investments and interventions to capitalize on girls' resources. Girls represent future women, and are thus attributed female essentialisms that correspond to productivity, but they are constrained by social institutions and market failures that can be overcome with adequate behavioral changes.

The search for a "silver bullet" to eradicate poverty is a perennial feature of development policymaking. Today, the object of the silver bullet rhetoric, enthusiastically framed as the solution to poverty, is the adolescent girl. Girls are held up as uniquely powerful solutions to end inter-generational poverty, and as particularly profitable sites for investment. World Bank Managing Director Ngozi Okonjo Iweala crystallized the message of girl-powered development on a World Economic Forum panel in 2009, where she explained: "Investing in women is smart economics, and investing in girls, catching them upstream, is even smarter economics. If you invest in girls, if you educate girls, if you get girls into jobs, you solve so many problems" (World Bank 2009a). Girls are represented as powerful agents for economic growth, catalysts for accelerated development, and unique problem solvers who can achieve change without the assistance of bigger institutions. Yet this discourse is also animated by a particular form of respectability that stresses girls' diligence, productivity, and community spirit: emphasis on education, job training, and entrepreneurship sets the boundaries of girls' empowerment.

Girls are being touted as the solution to global problems, through the call to recognize, invest in and unlock their capacities. As the Girl Effect's most popular video proclaims: "The world is a mess. Poverty. AIDS. Hunger. War. So, what else is new? So what if there was unexpected solution? … It's not the internet. It's not science. It's not the government. It's not money. It's (dramatic pause) a girl." (Girl Effect 2008b). This not only serves to displace responsibility on to girls' shoulders, but it creates a radically de-politicized environment for girls to solve the world's problems. This formulation of girls as the superheroes who will solve intractable global problems is, of course, the hyperbole of a publicity campaign. But its message is important, not because of the role it envisions for girls, but because of its insistence that neither the government nor money will solve existing problems. Girls' potential must be unlocked, but how?

The ascendance of girl-powered development and humanitarianism takes place in the context of broader shifts in development governance. The growth of private sector authority in development, and the implications of this trend in Gender and Development, is the subject of the next chapter. The recognition of girls as a valuable site of human capital investment has accorded significant attention and funding to programs for girls' schooling and economic empowerment. Private sector partners are a prominent force in the girl-power development field, with numerous cross-sector partnerships launching in the past fifteen years for the empowerment of adolescent girls. However, these partnerships are seriously limited by their focus on girls as sites of investment and productivity: they promote girls' agency through instrumentalized and truncated accounts of girls as anti-poverty solutions, while advancing a familiar set of market-driven policies. Moreover, these partnerships raise questions about the kinds of development authority that dominate in Gender and Development today. The private sector has taken a larger role in Gender and Development in recent years, aided in part by a widespread embrace of "Business Case" accounts of gender inequality that stress the coupling of gender equality with financial benefit for investors. This change has major implications for democracy, transparency, and equality in development.

References

Banet-Weiser, Sarah. 2015. "Media, Markets, Gender: Economies of Visibility in a Neoliberal Moment." *The Communication Review* 18(1): 53–70.

BBC. 2016. "Aid to be cut unless it is value for money, says Patel." *BBC News Online.* Published 25 October 2016. www.bbc.co.uk/news/uk-politics-37758164.

Bent, Emily, and Heather Switzer. 2016. "Oppositional Girlhoods and the Challenge of Relational Politics." *Gender Issues* 33(2): 122–147.

Brown, Larisa. 2013. "How you pay £4m to fund the Ethiopian Spice Girls: New aid storm over project that's even ridiculed in African country." *The Daily Mail Online.*

Published 15 November 2013. www.dailymail.co.uk/news/article-2508063/UK-pay-4m-fund-Ethiopian-Spice-Girls-New-aid-project-Yegna-ridiculed.html.

Calkin, Sydney. 2015. "Post-Feminist Spectatorship and the Girl Effect: 'Go Ahead, Really Imagine Her.'" *Third World Quarterly* 36(4): 654–669.

Caron, Cynthia, and Shelby Margolin. 2015. "Rescuing Girls, Investing in Girls: A Critique of Development Fantasies." *Journal of International Development* 27(7): 881–897.

Chant, Sylvia. 2016. "Galvanising Girl for Development? Critiquing the Shift from 'smart' to 'Smarter Economics.'" *Progress in Development Studies.* 16(4): 314–328.

Coalition for Adolescent Girls. n.d. "About Us | The Coalition for Adolescent Girls." Accessed 18 October 2016. http://coalitionforadolescentgirls.org/about-us/.

Cobbett, Mary. 2014. "Beyond 'victims' and 'heroines': Constructing 'girlhood' in International Development." *Progress in Development Studies* 14(4): 309–320.

Coca Cola. 2014. "The Coca-Cola Company and the U.K. Government of International Development Partner to Empower Young Women in Africa." *Coca Cola Company 5by20*. Published on March 7 2014. www.coca-colacompany.com/stories/the-coca-cola-company-and-the-uk-government-of-international-development-partner-to-empower-young-women-in-africa.

Croll, Elisabeth J. 2006. "From the Girl Child to Girls' Rights." *Third World Quarterly* 27(7): 1285–1297.

Department for International Development (UK). 2014. "The Coca-Cola company and the UK government strengthen girls' education and economic opportunities in Nigeria." Press Release. Published on 7 March 2014. www.gov.uk/government/news/the-coca-cola-company-and-the-uk-government-strengthen-girls-education-and-economic-opportunities-in-nigeria.

Department for International Development (UK). 2017b. "Girls' Education Challenge" *UK Department for International Development.* Website last updated 2 August 2017. www.gov.uk/guidance/girls-education-challenge.

Department for International Development (UK). 2017a. "Update on DFID's partnership with Girl Effect." *UK Department for International Development.* Posted on 6 January 2017. www.gov.uk/government/news/update-on-dfids-partnership-with-girl-effect.

Draxler, A. 2016. "Public-Private Partnerships and International Education Policies." In *Routledge Handbook of International Education and Development*, edited by Simon McGrath and Qing Gu, 443–451. Abingdon: Routledge.

Elias, Juanita. 2013. "Davos Woman to the Rescue of Global Capitalism: Postfeminist Politics and Competitiveness Promotion at the World Economic Forum." *International Political Sociology* 7(2): 152–169.

Forde, Shawn D., and Wendy Frisby. 2015. "Just Be Empowered: How Girls Are Represented in a Sport for Development and Peace HIV/AIDS Prevention Manual." *Sport in Society* 18(8): 882–894.

Girl Effect. n.d. "About the Girl Effect." *The Girl Effect.* Last accessed 20 July 2017. [The content of this site changes frequently] www.girleffect.org/about/.

Girl Effect n.d. "Yegna." *The Girl Effect.* Last accessed June 14 2017. www.girleffect.org/what-we-do/yegna/.

Girl Effect. 2008a. "The Girl Effect: I Dare You to See I Am the Answer." YouTube video. Uploaded 22 May 2008. https://youtu.be/-Vq2mfF8puE.

Girl Effect. 2008b. "The Girl Effect." YouTube video. Uploaded 24 May 2008. https://youtu.be/WIvmE4_KMNw/.

Girl Effect . 2010. "The Girl Effect: The Clock Is Ticking." YouTube video. Uploaded 13 September 2010. https://youtu.be/1e8xgF0JtVg.

Girl Effect. 2012. "Smarter Economics: Investing in Girls." Brochure. Originally posted at www.girleffect.org/download?downloadType=a&id=2231. [No longer available online].

Girl Effect. 2013. "Economically Empowered Girls Can Stop Poverty Before It Starts." Brochure. Originally posted 31 January 2013. www.girleffect.org/media/1163/girl_effect_infographic_economically_empowered.pdf [No longer available online].

Girl Hub. n.d. *Business Case and Intervention Summary.* London: Department for International Development. iati.dfid.gov.uk/iati_documents/3763610.odt.

Girl Rising. n.d. "Fact Sheet: India." http://girlrising.in/assets/9.%20GR_India_NGOFactSheet.pdf.

Girl Rising. n.d. "Girl Rising." Online. Last accessed 19 September 2017. http://girlrising.com/our-mission/.

Girl Rising. n.d. "Fuel the Movement." Online. Last accessed 19 September 2017. http://girlrising.com/grow-the-movement/.

Girl Up. n.d. "Fact Sheet." www.unfoundation.org/assets/pdf/girl-up-fact-sheet.pdf.

Girl Up. n.d. "Girl Up: Uniting Girls to Change the World: United Nations Foundation." Online. Last accessed 10 September 2017. https://girlup.org/.

Girl Up. 2012. "Girl Up and CLEAN & CLEAR® Partner to Help Teens Get Ready for the New School Year." Press Release. Published 17 July 2012. https://girlup.org/about/press-releases/girl-clean-clear-partner-help-teens-get-ready-new-school-year/.

Girl Up. 2016. "Campaign Overview: Uniting Girls to Change the World." Online. https://girlup.org/wp-content/uploads/2016/03/Girl-Up-Campaign_Overview.pdf.

Harper, Paul. 2016. "BAND AID: Britain pays £5 MILLION to 'Ethiopian Spice Girls' Yegna – so pop stars can have their own chat show." *The Sun Online.* Published 19 December 2016. www.thesun.co.uk/news/2432344/uk-aid-ethiopia-spice-girls-africa-taxpayer-funding/.

Harris, Anita. 2004. *Future Girl: Young Women in the Twenty-First Century.* Abingdon: Psychology Press.

Hayhurst, Lyndsay. 2011. "Corporatising Sport, Gender and Development: Postcolonial IR Feminisms, Transnational Private Governance and Global Corporate Social Engagement." *Third World Quarterly* 32(3): 531–549.

Hickel, Jason. 2014. "The 'girl Effect': Liberalism, Empowerment and the Contradictions of Development." *Third World Quarterly* 35(8): 1355–1373.

Independent Commission for Aid Impact. 2012. "Girl Hub: A DFID and Nike Foundation Initiative." London: ICAI. http://icai.independent.gov.uk/report/girl-hub-a-dfid-and-nike-foundation-initiative/.

Kabeer, Naila and Luisa Natali. 2013. "Gender Equality and Economic Growth: Is there a Win-Win?" *IDS Working Papers* 417: 1–58.

Kanani, Rahim. 2011. "The Nike Foundation on Unleashing the 'Girl Effect.'" *Huffington Post.* Published 20 April 2011. www.huffingtonpost.com/rahim-kanani/nike-foundation-girl-effect_b_850551.html.

Khoja-Moolji, Shenila. 2016. "Doing the 'work of Hearing': Girls' Voices in Transnational Educational Development Campaigns." *Compare: A Journal of Comparative and International Education* 46(5): 745–763.

Koffman, Ofra, and Rosalind Gill. 2013. "'The Revolution Will Be Led by a 12-Year-Old Girl': 1 Girl Power and Global Biopolitics." *Feminist Review* 105(1): 83–102.

Koffman, Ofra, Shani Orgad, and Rosalind Gill. 2015. "Girl Power and 'selfie Humanitarianism.'" *Continuum* 29(2): 157–168.

MacDonald, Katie. 2016. "Calls for Educating Girls in the Third World: Futurity, Girls and the 'Third World Woman.'" *Gender, Place & Culture* 23(1): 1–17.

McCarthy, Tom. 2017. "Trump Administration May Scrap Michelle Obama's Health and Education Programs." *The Guardian*. Published 3 May 2017. www.theguardian.com/us-news/2017/may/01/michelle-obama-school-lunch-let-girls-learn-scrapped-trump.

Mahon, Rianne. 2010. "After Neo-Liberalism? The OECD, the World Bank and the Child." *Global Social Policy* 10(2): 172–192.

McRobbie, Angela. 2009. *The Aftermath of Feminism: Gender, Culture and Social Change*. London: Sage.

Moeller, Kathryn. 2013. "Proving 'The Girl Effect': Corporate Knowledge Production and Educational Intervention." *International Journal of Educational Development* 33(6): 612–621.

Moeller, Kathryn. 2014. "Searching for Adolescent Girls in Brazil: The Transnational Politics of Poverty in 'The Girl Effect.'" *Feminist Studies* 40(3): 575–601.

Mohanty, Chandra Talpade. 1988. "Under Western Eyes: Feminist Scholarship and Colonial Discourses." *Feminist Review* 30: 61–88.

Murphy, Michelle. 2017. *The Economization of Life*. Durham, NC: Duke University Press.

Plan International. n.d. "Because I Am a Girl." *Plan International*. Last accessed 10 September 2017. https://plan-international.org/because-i-am-a-girl.

Plan International. 2009. Girls in the Global Economy: Adding It All Up. London: Plan International. https://plan-international.org/publications/state-worlds-girls-2009-girls-global-economy.

Plan International. 2015. The State World's Girls 2015: Unfinished Business. London: Plan International. https://plan-international.org/publications/state-worlds-girls-2015-unfinished-business.

Plan International. 2016. "Invest In Me." YouTube video. Uploaded 24 June 2016. https://www.youtube.com/watch?v=zuTBaJ4xmAI.

Provost, Claire. 2012. "Watchdog raises questions over impact of Nike's Girl Hub." *The Guardian*. Published 23 March 2012. https://www.theguardian.com/global-development/poverty-matters/2012/mar/23/girl-hub-strength-weaknesses.

Roberts, Adrienne. 2015. "The Political Economy of 'Transnational Business Feminism.'" *International Feminist Journal of Politics* 17(2): 209–231.

Roberts, Adrienne, and Susanne Soederberg. 2012. "Gender Equality as Smart Economics? A Critique of the 2012 World Development Report." *Third World Quarterly* 33(5): 949–968.

Sensoy, Özlem, and Elizabeth Marshall. 2010. "Missionary Girl Power: Saving the 'Third World' one Girl at a Time." *Gender and Education* 22(3): 295–311.

Shain, Farzana. 2013. "'The Girl Effect': Exploring Narratives of Gendered Impacts and Opportunities in Neoliberal Development." *Sociological Research Online* 18(2). www.socresonline.org.uk/18/2/9.html.

Summers, Lawrence. 1992. "The Most Influential Investment." *Scientific American* 267(2): 132.

Summers, Lawrence. 1994. "Investing in All the People." World Bank Institute Resources. Washington, DC: The World Bank. http://elibrary.worldbank.org/doi/abs/10.1596/0-8213-2323-7.

Switzer, Heather. 2013. "(Post) Feminist Development Fables: The Girl Effect and the Production of Sexual Subjects." *Feminist Theory* 14(3): 345–360.

UNFPA. 2011. "Unleashing the Power and Potential of Adolescent Girls | UNFPA – United Nations Population Fund." Press Release. Published 2 March 2011. http://www.unfpa.org/news/unleashing-power-and-potential-adolescent-girls.

UNGEI. n.d. "United Nations Girls' Education Initiative – About Us." Last accessed June 18 2017. http://www.ungei.org/whatisungei/.

United Nations Foundation. 2009. "World Economic Forum Gives Adolescent Girls a Voice on the Global Stage." Press Release. Published 30 January 2009. www.unfoundation.org/news-and-media/press-releases/2009/world-economic-forum-gives.html.

United NationsFoundation. 2010. "United Nations Foundation: United Nations Foundation Launches Girl Up." Press Release. Published 30 September 2010. www.unfoundation.org/news-and-media/press-releases/2010/united-nations-foundation-launches-girl-up.html.

Unterhalter, Elaine. 2017. "A Review of Public Private Partnerships around Girls' Education in Developing Countries: Flicking Gender Equality on and off." *Journal of International and Comparative Social Policy* 33(2): 181–199.

USAID. n.d. "Let Girls Learn." *Let Girls Learn*. Last accessed 24 January 2016. https://letgirlslearn.gov/.

White, L. 2011. "The Internationalization of Early Childhood Education and Care Issues: Framing Gender Justice and Child Well-Being." *Governance* 24(2): 285–309.

World Bank. 2009a. "The World Bank Launches Private-Public Initiative to Empower Adolescent Girls." World Bank. Press Release no. 2009/109/PREM. http://go.worldbank.org/83L2MOFND0.

World Bank. 2009b. "Gender and Development: Adolescent Girls in Focus at the World Economic Forum." World Bank. Published 26 February 2009. http://go.worldbank.org/QWPUUOPVY0.

World Bank. 2012. *World Development Report 2012: Gender Equality and Development*. Washington, DC: World Bank. https://openknowledge.worldbank.org/handle/10986/4391.

6 Human Capital, Private Profit

Introduction

Can everyone "do development"? Development provides a powerful ideological framework for understanding relationships between North and South. Its conceptual ambiguity and aspirational position in culture create space for a wide range of people and entities to participate: school and university students go off on volunteer-tourist trips to do development projects in the weeks of their summer holidays; celebrities do development by travelling across the world as Goodwill Ambassadors and attracting media attention to various humanitarian causes; companies do development through social media campaigns to raise awareness of a particular social issue or through a social enterprise they fund through a corporate foundation. Today, the range of actors involved in development is diverse and shifting. Where once the process called development was the purview of states, multi-lateral institutions and non-profit organizations, a variety of other non-state actors have stepped in to perform these functions. These are changes taking place across the landscape, not least in Gender and Development where gender equality as growth discourses have provided a source of legitimacy for older development agendas. Development as a project has faced crises of legitimacy across the years; today its crisis of legitimacy comes in the form of a crisis of authority and funding. Changing patterns of funding and financial power in development have translated into changing sources of authority and changing modes of development governance. This chapter examines how girls and women have been used in this shift, as a legitimizing mechanism for new power relations in development. As such, it addresses the material effects of human capital theory in Gender and Development governance.

Throughout this book, I have argued that the widespread embrace of human capital logic in development has allowed women to become legible as key agents for global development. It has done so, I have shown, by providing an analytical framework in which girls' and women's lives and bodies can be calculated as a resource for growth, and interventions prescribed to catalyse their economic productivity. It has created a mode of recognized agency for girls and women as development agents by putting them within accepted frameworks of profit and risk. This chapter demonstrates that the turn to human capital theory, as embodied in the "Gender Equality Smart Economics" agenda, has serious implications for the sources of authority – financial and epistemic – in development. First, it helps to legitimate new sources of authority in development, particularly private sector and profit-seeking actors. When girls and women are understood primarily as a site of investment, profit-making can be re-written as a positive incentive to achieve development outcomes, because firms presumably can identify good investments and have the most incentive to invest in profitable areas. This shift is underway in a range of public-private partnerships for empowerment that attempt to acquire legitimacy as development actors through a critique of public development failures and a valorization of profitmaking modes of operation. The rise of human capital theory has accorded girls and women visibility as ideal sites of development intervention, whose capabilities can be catalysed for growth. The analytic and programmatic axes of human capital point us to the relationship between identifying such idealized pre-empowerment subjects and legitimizing agents who can assert authority over subject formation in Gender and Development. On the programmatic side, a new range of private-sector entities are asserting authority to shape development agendas, lead development interventions, and produce development knowledge with regard to girls' and women's empowerment.

Second, the human capital turn has implications for concerns about the democratic politics of development, or the role of the public in relation to private sector actors. The construction of an easy synergy between gender equality and private profit works to put the private sector in a position of greater authority because it legitimizes the idea that the profit motive can and will drive development, with less input from public authorities. Moreover, the equation of private sector innovation with development and gender equality provides a framework in which business can avoid binding regulatory changes by offering to regulate itself. The assertion that the goals of the private sector and development goals are organically aligned has important effects on the kind of corporate governance that is possible. Thus the logic of Smart Economics is employed to re-draw development processes as relationships between entrepreneurial individuals and innovative firms. The human capital turn in Gender and Development has helped to re-structure the shape of the development field by re-making the sources of authority, the development priorities, and the relationship between individual and social. Although these trends are not the sole product of human capital's embrace in Gender and Development, they demonstrate that the conceptual transformations discussed in earlier chapters have concrete manifestations in the governance of development.

This chapter addresses changing governance patterns in Gender and Development in relation to questions of development authority, accountability, and knowledge production. It does so through an examination of three instances of public-private hybrid development initiatives that have emerged from the "Gender Equality as Smart Economics" agenda: Corporate

Social Responsibility, cause related marketing, and Bottom of the Pyramid enterprise. These three incarnations of private-sector development not only demonstrate the changes in development authority (who produces knowledge about development) or governance (who actually does the work of development), but they demonstrate how particular discourses about girls and women have been essential to legitimizing and speeding the arrival of these new power relations. An account of Gender and Development today requires engagement with these new private development governance initiatives, because the way that girls have acquired visibility as idealized subjects of development is closely tied up with the rise of new forms of private power.

Private governance in gender and development

Today, public-private partnerships abound in Gender and Development. Collaboration with private sector actors has been embraced as an end in itself and to achieve gender goals: emergent public-private partnerships join together global development institutions and private multi-nationals for collaborative projects that serve the "double bottom line" of financial and social impact. To name just a few of such partnerships: The United Nations Global Compact, a voluntary code of principles signed by over 9,000 companies, added a list of Women's Empowerment Principles in 2010 to empower women in the workplace. In 2010, Coca Cola partnered with UN Women on the 5by20 initiative to train and mentor women entrepreneurs in the global South who worked in the Coca Cola supply chain. In 2012, the United Nations Foundation partnered with the ExxonMobil Foundation to produce a report on investments in women's economic opportunity. This "roadmap for empowerment" provided suggestions for governments and NGOs on interventions that can "successfully increase women's productivity" (ExxonMobil Foundation 2013). In 2016, UN Women joined with MasterCard on a pilot scheme to provide women in Nigeria with ID cards to allow them to access electronic banking and other financial service (see Sato 2016; Prügl 2016; Roberts 2015b). Public-private partnerships are relatively new in the area of Gender and Development: although they have been prevalent in areas of global public health and environmental sustainability since the 1990s, public-private partnerships have emerged as a major force in GAD since the year 2000 (Bexell 2012). Nonetheless, observers of this trend have noted that the rhetorical prominence of gender equality-centred development partnerships might in fact outstrip the funds dedicated to supporting relevant programs. The UN Fund for International Partnerships reports that children's health and environmental issues are the two areas that receive the most funding, followed by gender and population programs which receive 13% of all funding contributed (Prügl and True 2014: 3).

Private sector partnerships and cross-sector collaborations are on the rise for a few reasons that reflect underlying crises in development governance and funding. First, development institutions operate in a context where private sector values and principles are prized as the most efficient operational mode for any and every institution. Responding to the critique of public sector institutions as outmoded and inefficient, private sector efficiency is held up as a model for all organizations (McGoey 2014; Mitchell and Sparke 2016). States and public institutions are increasingly expected to model themselves after firms and to conduct themselves in this way, giving priority to the current and future value of their capital by attracting investors and behaving as entrepreneurs. In practical terms, this pressure is translated into collaborative modes of cross-sectoral governance that emphasize partnerships and cooperation in place of regulation, as well as an emphasis on the moral agency of corporations (Brown 2015; O'Laughlin 2008; Shamir 2008). Second, development institutions face a funding challenge and look to private sector partnerships or philanthropic donors for the capital to continue on-going operations. Collaboration with private sector firms (or philanthropic organizations) not only provides a funding source but also allows public institutions to distance themselves from critiques of bloated and wasteful public spending. Advocates for this mode of collaborative governance argue that voluntary cross-sector partnerships will promote deliberation and better outcomes by harnessing the expertise of public and private institutions to identify areas for win-win collaborations and provide collective goods (see for example, Ruggie 2002; Reinicke 1998). Third, a public crisis of confidence in development aid has created enormous public pressure to reduce development expenditure, increase its efficiency, and demonstrate the "value for money" of foreign aid (see Harman and Williams 2014). The reliance on business rhetoric by global and national development agencies can be traced to this pressure, and the uptake of investment rhetoric in girls and women is linked to this trend. This can mean pressure for public development institutions, especially national governments, to demonstrate the value for the taxpayer at home. In short, on-going crises of legitimacy facing development institutions, combined with a governing ontology that prioritizes market-orientation, have created a political context in which public-private partnerships are on the rise.

Partnerships between public and private sector institutions for development goals have seen an increase in their power and authority, both in terms of the financial resources they wield and the influence in knowledge production they have. Yet, the diversity of actors and structures involved in public-private partnerships can make the search for precise definitions elusive and somewhat futile: public-private partnerships take numerous forms depending on the actors involved and the project at hand, but can be broadly defined as "hybrid governance structures" in which non-state actors govern alongside state actors to provide goods or perform functions that were previously state functions (Schaeferhoff et al 2009: 451–452). Private-sector partners here can include corporations, corporate philanthropic foundations, and private philanthropists. They are therefore indicative of broader trends associated with globalization, where state power is changing form and being re-scaled into quasi-governmental and non-governmental bodies; this form of collaborative and multi-stakeholder governance is characteristic of reformed, roll-out neoliberalism that involves the extension and expansion of market logics into new sectors. Partnerships with the private sector are especially common in the provision of public goods (see Unterhalter 2017; Schaeferhoff et al. 2009). While private giving on development issues has not outstripped public spending on development, private partners attract greater visibility for their contributions and exert significant agenda-setting influence on the process; the participation of high-profile private donors further attracts state funding to their chosen causes (McGoey 2014; 2016). These changes raise serious questions about power and control in development governance, because public-private partnerships have seen corporate actors take on the new mantle of public-minded institutions who operate in the public interest (Prügl and True 2015). In essence, public-private partnerships are notable because they signal a growing role for private, for-profit business in public policy and demonstrate broader transformations in the field that are shifting the locus of development knowledge production.

The cross-sectoral convergence on gender inequality as an issue for economic growth has produced a rhetorically popular rationale for investment in girls and women. While the "Gender Equality as Smart Economics" message is mainly targeted at development institutions and national governments, its private sector complement is a narrative of the "Business Case for Gender Equality" that uses a similar instrumentalist account of girls and women as producers and consumers whose labor and market can be captured (Calkin 2016). A 2006 headline in *The Economist* captured this spirit: "Forget China, India, and the internet: economic growth is driven by women." The "Business Case" account of gender equality has emerged through firms' emphasis on the double bottom line of financial and social impact, so that investment in girls and women expands the pool of available workers and consumers. The "Business Case", oriented around the interests and concerns of the private sector, has been further developed by a range of studies carried out by financial and accounting firms. It has gained particular strength in the wake of the 2007 global financial crisis, because efforts to avoid another crisis have produced a mini-industry of "Womenomics" literature that links the causes of crisis to macho-business culture. By extension, it aims to identify the intrinsic qualities of financial prudence and risk-aversion that women possess (Roberts 2012; 2015a; 2015b; see also Prügl 2012; Murphy 2017). The Business Case for Gender Equality takes many forms, and cannot be located in one single firm, initiative, or partnership. The initiatives discussed in this chapter sit at the convergence of the trends outlined above: the growing power of the private sector to assert authority in development, the pressures faced by states and public institutions to collaborate with the private sector in development, and the recognition of girls as unique subjects of "untapped" economic agency. Together, these trends converge to produce a wide range of public-private partnerships and Corporate Social Responsibility initiatives (broadly defined) that revolve around the "Business Case" for the empowerment of girls and young women.

Corporate social responsibility

Development institutions currently face a political and economic climate that creates pressure for private sector partnerships, but why do multi-national corporations join such partnerships? Their incentives stem from perceived obligations for firms to demonstrate their engagement with the social context in which their profits are made, through Corporate Social Responsibility (CSR). Corporate Social Responsibility has proliferated since the 1990s when increased scrutiny of business practices and backlash against corporate abuses prompted firms to take steps to demonstrate their concern for the communities in which they work (Ponte et al. 2009). At the most basic level, Corporate Social Responsibility describes a company undertaking "voluntary and discretionary" activities in the interest of social or environment goals, which is to say that it involves a company undertaking activities that are not *legally* required (Banerjee 2008: 60). Equipping a factory building with the legally-mandated fire safety equipment, for instance, does not constitute CSR; providing a voluntary career mentorship scheme for workers does. CSR builds from the premise that social good can also contribute to a firm's overall profitability in the long term, so that profit objectives need not be sacrificed for the achievement of social goals. Yet, beyond this core principle, debates over the definition of CSR offer broader and narrow conceptions of the concept. A narrow definition of CSR limits it to the "integration of environmental and social considerations into core business strategies" (Jenkins 2005: 540). This definition stands in contrast to broader definitions that encompass actions taken outside of the core business, including activities like corporate philanthropy. In recent years, the understanding of "legitimate CSR activity" has undergone a shift, expanding the circle for those represented as beneficiaries, and changing ideas about the kinds of benefits they receive (Ponte et al 2009: 302; see also Richey and Ponte 2008). Given the changing shape of this field and the hybrid forms of public-private collaboration that are emerging, it is essential to understand CSR in broad terms as involving a range of activities within the corporation, its supply chain, its environmental impact, its cause-related marketing, and corporate philanthropy efforts. Public-private hybrid initiatives in Gender and Development reflect this blurring of boundaries, where CSR takes diverse forms and evolves over time, challenging the boundaries of conventional categories for corporate social responsibility activity. This broadened understanding allows for useful connections to be made between a firm's philanthropic activity, upgrading within its core business, and branding efforts to attract "ethical" consumers.

Corporate Social Responsibility has emerged from two interconnected trends. The first is the growing power of multi-national corporations and the ability of capital to move across borders. Lengthening supply chains, mobile capital, and competition between states to create business-friendly regulatory environments tip the balance of power between states and firms. As such, increased corporate power has translated into excesses and abuses to which consumers have responded with anger. Concern with environmental pollution or poor working conditions, for instance, has provoked a backlash against corporate power and created pressure for firms to acknowledge their responsibilities to the contexts in which they operate (Dauvergne and Lebaron 2014). The second trend is a broader mode of collaborative governance that encompasses these economic processes: reformed neoliberalism is characterized by a logic of self-regulation in which states are permitted to intervene only to make markets operate more efficiently (O'Laughlin 2008; Soederberg 2007). Growing corporate power occurs in a context in which there is less state capacity (or willingness) to enforce compliance on firms, in part because some states lack the capacity to do so and in part because the pressures on states to compete to attract investment create climates in which states must cater to firms, rather than restrict them. As a corollary, NGOs and private voluntary organizations intervene to curb business excess and mediate between states and firms. This mode of governance is characterized by an emphasis on collaboration between public and private sectors, in place of legally binding rules.

The combined effect of this turn to voluntary governance raises concerns: even advocates of CSR acknowledge that while CSR may achieve gains in specific issue areas like environmental protection, it is unlikely to contribute to broader social justice. Substantive political empowerment, insofar as it requires redistribution of resources, is not aligned with CSR goals and therefore unlikely to result from it (Utting 2007). As such, CSR can be better understood as a "legitimizing mechanism" rather than a development tool in its own right (Blowfield 2007: 690; Soederberg 2007). CSR stems primarily from business obligations, or internalized perceptions of business obligations, rather than altruistic commitments to act as agents of development. CSR not only serves to legitimize existing business practices, but it gives them a moral gloss (Shamir 2008; 2010). This is because CSR functions to legitimize a broader paradigm of ideological neoliberalism, in which firms are attributed a prominent role in social and political structures. Corporate social responsibility, often labelled "corporate citizenship", advances an understanding of the firm as a rights- and duties-bearing individual with a conscience. It frames corporations as moral actors who pursue particular aims from a sense of moral responsibility advances the idea that corporations respond to norms, rather than regulations; this leads to the conclusion that corporations can be trusted to pursue social good out of an enlightened self-interest. Furthermore, attributing the corporation a conscience provides a moral legitimacy to the profit drive. If the pursuit of social aims is framed in terms of win-win "Business Case for Gender Equality" that benefits all parties, then the pursuit of profit comes to affirm "the moral side of business" (Shamir 2010: 536). The equation of private profit with gender equality is the *raison d'etre* of the new spate of women's empowerment CSR initiatives.

How is this process manifested in Gender and Development governance today? The World Bank's Global Private Sector Leaders' Forum provides an instructive example. The Global Private Sector Leaders Forum (GPSLF) was a World Bank initiative, launched in 2008 at the World Economic Forum, where it was pitched as a facility for using private-sector expertise to expand economic opportunity for women. The GPSLF was also introduced a tool for speeding up the implementation of the Bank's 2007–2010 Gender Action Plan; for this reason, it formally ended in 2011. The Forum was structured as a partnership between the Bank and twenty-one of "the world's leading private sector companies" including Goldman Sachs, Cisco, Boeing, Nike, Hindustan Unilever, and others[1] who would act as "ambassadors" for the Bank's Gender Acton Plan (World Bank 2009a; 2009b; 2009c). Membership of the Forum did not carry specific responsibilities, but members made two general commitments. First, the Forum's members gathered to share "best practices and lessons learned" on gender equality in business. In doing so, they would present evidence to "support the business case for increasing women's opportunity" in the private sector and to strengthen connections between gender policies in the Bank and private sector (Ehrenpreis 2011). Second, the Forum's members were asked to launch programs in their own organizations to promote economic opportunity for women. These programs could work within the corporate structure, the Corporate Social Responsibility division, or broader corporate philanthropy. No specific projects were required for membership, so the commitments that resulted took a variety of forms, from mentoring within the corporate headquarters to education programs outside of the supply chain. For example, on the corporate side, the international recruitment firm Heidrick and Struggles committed to including at least one woman on every corporate board shortlist. Boeing committed to increase the women-owned businesses in its supply chain by spending $2 billion on products from women-owned businesses from 2011–2014 (GPSLF 2009; 2011; n.d.). On the CSR side, Goldman Sachs introduced its "10,000 Women" initiative to provide entrepreneurship and management training to female small-business owners in the global South. When the 2007–2010 Gender Action Plan ended, the GPSLF stopped meeting, although several of the firm's members still include their membership in the list of their current CSR engagements.

Gender equality-oriented CSR presents a site of profitability and authority for firms, not only because it allows them to burnish their brand, but because it legitimizes a broader corporate-led mode of collaborative governance. The mode of governance that CSR represents relies on ideas of self-interested collaboration and win-win convergences between governments, businesses, and consumers. In practice, this constitutes a shift in the way that authority is deployed to govern firms. Collaborative governance models substitute laws and regulations for guidelines, principles, and codes of conduct; law becomes "a shared problem-solving process coded by notions such as 'multi-party cooperation', 'constructive dialogue', 'multi-stakeholder consultation', 'task sharing' and 'democratic participation' rather than an ordering activity" (Shamir, 2008:7). It endorses a collaborative process of knowledge sharing and validation for the development of best practices by business, on the assumption that these incentives will produce better results than binding forms of enforcement. This mode of executive-level commitments and best-practice sharing is common to the field of gender CSR: the UN's Women's Empowerment Principles, for example, represent the same mode of voluntary commitment. Adherence to the principles is not legally enforced, but is tracked by the United Nations, best practice examples are publicized, and leadership awards are given (Prügl and True 2015; Bexell 2012). Its logic is evident in the GPSLF: because members do not commit to any core principles or practices, their commitments are limited to initiatives designed and introduced by the firms themselves. Its members are called upon to share "best practices and lessons learned" in order to inspire others and show leadership in the field (GPSLF n.d.). They are not subject to audit or enforcement of these commitments, nor are the commitments required to relate to core business practices. In fact, it shores up the legitimacy of collaborative and voluntary forms of corporate governance by advancing the argument that enforcement of any key commitments or principles would dampen creativity. The GPSLF places emphasis on the emergence of best practice lessons from members sharing with each other, driving innovative gender equality solutions through inspiration rather than regulation:

> "The peer-to-peer exchange [of the GPSLF] evolved from a knowledge sharing exercise to a cross-industry and geographic pollinating incubator and is resulting in some innovative collaboration that will help drive women's economic empowerment."
>
> (World Bank 2011)

For Forum members, global development outcomes and company profits go hand-in-hand. The GPSLF articulates a vision of firms as development authorities both because they are driven by self-interest to achieve recognition in the field, but also because they are guided by moral principles. The moralizing function of CSR discourses, which serves to conflate profit motives with social initiatives, is evident in the GPSLF discursive construction of its membership as innovative leaders in their field: these companies are "enlightened" (World Bank 2011; 2012); they are "recognized leaders and role models" who gain advantages from their "first mover" position (Ellis 2010); and they engage in ambitious and innovative practices that are "not for the faint-hearted or short-sighted" (Neath and Varma 2008: 15). Commitments to gender equality are thus secured through positive incentives, like benefits to brand reputation or competitiveness, rather than enforcement mechanisms because the firms engaged in the Forum's work are attributed a set of progressive values associated with leadership in the field.

Goldman Sachs provides an illustrative example of the changing role of corporate power in development, especially in relation to its embrace of gender equality and empowerment projects. Goldman Sachs was a high-profile member of the GPSLF, whose CSR work was routinely showcased as representing the best practices to emerge from the Forum. In 2008, the same year it joined the GPSLF, Goldman Sachs launched the "10,000 Women" initiative. Initially, the program was designed to provide MBA-style business education at low cost to women entrepreneurs around the global South. Through partnerships with many universities, research institutes, and business schools, "10,000 Women" focuses on financial literacy and business-skills training for women (GPSLF n.d.; Goldman Sachs 2008). It currently operates in 56 countries with 30 academic partners; a 2014 expansion of the program introduced a loan facility to provide credit to female entrepreneurs. The role of Goldman Sachs in the GPSLF and its continued partnership with the World Bank on the "10,000 Women" project raises two issues. First, Goldman's engagement with women's empowerment issues arose out of concerns about external crises and its brand reputation. Goldman Sachs' partnership with the World Bank on women's empowerment themes evolved during 2007–2008, in the midst of the global financial crisis for which Goldman was receiving substantial blame, and with the Bank under the leadership of Robert Zoellick, who was a managing director at Goldman before and after he was president of the World Bank.[2] The World Bank's 2007–2010 Gender Action Plan that developed a "Business Case" for gender equality resonated with Goldman's long-term promotion of its "Womenomics" investment theme that stresses the need to see women as markets for credit (Roberts and Soederberg 2012).

In the wake of the financial crisis, Goldman was facing enormous public anger for its role in the sub-prime mortgage crisis and was facing pressure to reform its practices. Echoing the dominant tropes of the "Business Case" discourse, CEO Lloyd Blankfein emphasized the firm's commitment to the initiative is "not philanthropy" but a commercial decision for the firm, because it represents a source of growth for Goldman. He emphasized that Goldman's efforts to increase credit provision to women would drive economic growth around the world and thereby create a "virtuous circle" of production and profit (Korngold 2009). In more practical terms, "10,000 Women" served a public relations function for the firm's reputation and its position in landscape of financial institutions. Blankfein explained that "10,000 Women" helped the firm retain workers who would otherwise leave to go into public service, by allowing them to engage in mentoring and social-oriented activities: the firm's gender CSR "makes people feel more complete and fulfilled" (quoted in Korngold 2009). Moreover, he added, it increases the firm's competitiveness and provides investment returns that allow the firm to meet its fiduciary duty to shareholders. In this context, its turn to women's empowerment CSR materialized: the "10,000 Women" initiative was pitched as part of a longer-term investment strategy to invest in women's entrepreneurship and thereby emerging markets in the global South (Prügl and True 2015). Its gender-oriented CSR commitments serve multiple functions for Goldman Sachs, improving its reputation among the general public and satisfying employee's desires to have positive social impact, all while meeting its primary commitment to shareholders.

Second, Goldman's partnership with the Bank and its role in "10,000 Women" has provided it with a larger platform to position itself as a development authority. In 2014, it launched the Women's Entrepreneurship Opportunity Fund, a partnership between the IFC, Goldman Sachs and the Overseas Private Investment Corporation, the US government's development finance institution. At its launch, World Bank president Jim Kim emphasized the Bank's "extremely significant" agreement with Goldman on gender equality issues, and urged others to follow Goldman's lead. Kim explained that the partnership combined "expertise and resources" with the long-term intention of demonstrating the value of investments in women to "businesses and financial institutions alike". Kim also echoed Blankfein's argument that pitched their partnership against philanthropy: "it's not just philanthropy: we're appealing to the commercial interests of people and will provide the commercial opportunity for people to invest in women" (Goldman Sachs 2014). The equation of Goldman with the World Bank, as development partners, has raised concerns about transparency and accountability in the governance of such partnerships. Existing studies of "10,000 Women" projects highlight an absence of public data from which to draw concrete conclusions about the way the project is run, the groups who might benefit from it, the level of involvement of various partners, and the effects of project implementation (Prügl and True 2015). Access to these projects is notoriously difficult: researchers report being declined multiple interviews over long periods of time and strict conditions put on the disclosures they can make from interviews about such development activities (Allison et al 2017). In some cases, the project participants themselves are bound by non-disclosure agreements that prevent them conducting research altogether, as Allison and colleagues found in the Goldman Sachs "10,000 Women project" (Ibid.). A lack of transparency here amounts to the absence of public accountability in hybrid public-private development ventures, whose influence continues to outpace its credibility.

The move from public villain of the 2008 financial crisis to vaunted partner in international development has been accomplished at Goldman Sachs in part thanks to its embrace of gender equality and women's empowerment projects in its Corporate Social Responsibility work. Goldman took a leading role in public-facing development initiatives like the GPSLF and positioned itself as a leader in empowerment projects that served distant beneficiaries in shareholders. In so doing, it also demonstrated the blurred boundaries of CSR where beneficiaries of corporate philanthropic giving could become customers and help to grow the business. This move is facilitated by the prevailing consensus around the organic confluence of gender equality and private profit that offers private firms a larger role in funding development activity and directing development agendas. Gender and Development governance appears as a realm where firms can work to rehabilitate their public image, because private sector involvement in development is welcomed by consumers and public institutions alike. Its relationship to core business practices may be tenuous, or largely disconnected, but Corporate Social Responsibility and

Corporate Citizenship initiatives represent a popular mechanism for private-sector firms to fulfil a variety of objectives. The broader climate in development, where pressure for private-sector partnership and funding is growing, means such collaborations are set to increase in number and scope.

Cause-related marketing

The growing power of multi-national corporations, matched with increasingly public reporting of corporate misconduct (whether financial, environmental, labor-related, or political), has prompted a public backlash against corporate abuses. This is a backlash of which firms are well aware and are engaged in strategizing a response. In 2008, Shell acknowledged this "dilemma" for its growth, asking: "How do we increase global reach and build on global brands while recognizing and responding to the popular antipathy towards big business and globalization?" (Shell quoted in Dauvergne and Lebaron 2014: 34). Alternatively, this dilemma has been interpreted as an opportunity for growth: consumers' desire to purchase ethically sourced products creates new markets for firms to access. A growing culture of stakeholder capitalism has changed norms around consumption, so that consumers expect to drive change on social and environmental issues through individual acts of "conscious consumption." This calls upon consumers to use their purchasing power to make a difference, for instance by buying products backed with eco-certifications or associated with matching charitable donations (Richey and Ponte 2008: 721–722). This, too, creates opportunities for firms to capitalize on consumers' desired products and to articulate a new mode of engagement between consumer and corporation. The move to associate a brand with charitable causes or contributions to global development takes a number of forms: it might mean partnering with global development institutions in public-private partnerships (Bexell 2012; Gregoratti 2010); collaborating with and funding NGOs who work on relevant issues and have previously been critical of the firm (Dauvergne and Lebaron 2014); and cause-related marketing, advertising products whose proceeds partly go to fund charitable causes (Sato 2016; Ponte et al. 2009). Firms can use CSR and cause-related marketing to legitimate their activities or to disburse charitable funds, but CSR does not, by definition, need to form a core component of the brand; it is, however, integral to the branding and marketing of certain businesses. This points to a larger flaw in CSR and cause-related marketing, which can give firms the gloss of social responsibility and at the same time hide the way that profits are made (Charkiewicz 2005).

Gender equality and women's empowerment represent a popular focus through which to associate global development issues with a brand identity. Gender equality is a recognized source of value for firms and their brands, promoted by consultancies who advise firms on the "Business Case" for equality. Women are particularly targeted by cause-related marketing campaigns because advertisers perceive them as caring, compassionate consumers who will be receptive to such campaigns (Hawkins 2012). Association with empowerment rhetoric has a notable impact on a brand's perception: in 2014, after several high-profile ad campaigns that used girl-power motifs to sell products, the marketing magazine Ad Age reported that a majority of consumers felt these ads promoted a positive message for women and had "a strong, positive impact on the brands" (quoted in Zeisler 2016: 26). This advantage with consumers is much-discussed in the "Business Case" policy literature. In its report, *The Business of Empowering Women*, GPSLF member McKinsey & Co. argued that "investing in making life better for women in developing countries can be an effective way to enhance a company's reputation and brand" (McKinsey & Co. 2010: 14). McKinsey's report suggests that firms can stake out an early advantage on the issue, because so few companies "appreciate the potential of women's economic empowerment to spur economic growth or contribute to their companies' success" (Ibid.: 10). This echoes the discussion of brand reputation featured in the Bank's 2012 World Development Report which suggests that a brand's association with gender equality is a "desirable trait that customers and investors look for" and encourages corporations to see CSR as an opportunity to differentiate their product and "capture the loyalty of women's growing market power" (World Bank 2012: 36). Gender equality branding is recognized as an effective tool to appeal to feminist-minded (or at least female) consumers in the global North, and to grow markets of female consumers in the global South. However, as the above discussion of voluntary corporate governance demonstrates, the association between gender equality commitments and core business practices is often tenuous; the same is true for cause-related branding. The association of a firm with a public-private partnership a CSR initiative, or an empowerment-centered marketing campaign does not necessarily entail changes in business practices that would improve the lives of female workers or women in the community where the business operates. In fact, it may serve to displace pressure for these kinds of changes.

The Girl Effect, introduced in the previous chapter, serves as an instructive example of cause-related marketing by Nike Inc. and contributes to debates about cause-related marketing in the context of corporate Gender and Development partnerships. Nike Inc. has a well-publicized history of labor abuse charges, public backlash, reform efforts, and branding efforts to combat public criticism. Nike is the world's largest athletic shoe manufacturer and also manufactures clothing and sports equipment; it does so through hundreds of overseas suppliers who manufacture its goods, while its small US-based workforce designs and markets products. For much of the 1990s, Nike was plagued by scandal because its products were sourced from factories with extremely low wages and poor conditions, across a range of South East Asian countries (Locke et al 2007). Its CEO Phil Knight admitted that the "Nike product has become synonymous with slave wages, forced overtime, and arbitrary abuse" (quoted in Cushman 1998) and set out steps to change the company's working practices (and by extension, its reputation). In 1996, following the publication of further allegations of child labor, Nike opened its Corporate Social Responsibility office (Zadek 2004). It has since implemented a series of codes of conduct for suppliers and instituted new audit mechanism to ensure compliance, but continues to face charges of labor abuses (see Nadvi 2008; Lund-Thomsen and Coe 2015). The Nike brand has been troubled by continuous accusations of labor abuses and consumer boycotts for decades, although it has taken steps to recuperate the brand by engaging in charitable giving and CSR initiatives. In 2004, Nike Inc.'s charitable foundation re-launched itself with a single focus: it sought to raise awareness of the role of girls in anti-poverty and development.[3] The Girl Effect campaign began four years later. Although the Girl Effect became an independent NGO in 2015, from 2008 until 2015 it was run by the Nike Foundation and closely linked to Nike Inc.

The Girl Effect functions as a component of Nike's cause-related marketing: this is first evident in Nike's corporate strategy and branding is the relationship between the firm and its foundation. Even while it was run through the Nike Foundation, the Girl Effect campaign positioned itself outside of Nike Inc., as an initiative that aimed to draw on the corporate culture, funds, and resources of Nike Inc. but not as a commercial enterprise. Its Creative Director stressed its function as a charitable initiative that uses Nike's "unique approach to innovation" to solve the problem of girls' disempowerment, an issue which stands "outside of the company's commercial interests" (Kylander 2011: 2). The Nike Foundation aims, she explained, to leverage its resources in order to create attention and demands behind gender equality issues, in contrast to other corporate foundations who are "interested in their corporate brand image" (Emily Brew, quoted in Kylander 2011: 2). There are, however, some obvious tensions in this approach that undermine this claim and significant inconsistencies that seem to reflect a confluence of Girl Effect, Nike Foundation, and Nike Inc. brands. The Nike Foundation's brand is heavily featured in the Girl Effect campaign, appearing in Girl Effect campaign videos and on promotional material (Girl Effect 2008a; 2008b; 2010). By virtue of their shared name, Nike Inc. is associated with the Girl Effect, as their shared name means there is little distinction for the general public. Similarly, two out of three original Girl Effect campaign videos are animations rendered entirely in Nike corporate colours: orange, black and white (Girl Effect 2008a; 2010). These two videos, in Nike Inc. corporate colours, were shown in high-profile forums like the Clinton Global Initiative, World Economic Forum, and the Oprah Winfrey Show; the main "Girl Effect" video ad is still featured on Oprah's website. Girl Effect promotional publications and appearances also used Nike corporate colours and emphasized the Nike Foundation's relationship to Nike Inc. Its CEO Maria Eitel[4] explains that the "Nike corporation is all about people living up to their human potential… and the Nike Foundation is about adolescent girls and people being able to live up to their human potential" (Eitel 2010). Since 2015 when the Girl Effect became an independent NGO, its branding has been changed to remove

Nike corporate colours and to include fewer references to Nike, though Maria Eitel remains Chair of Girl Effect and Co-Chair of the Nike Foundation.

The second indication of the Girl Effect's role is apparent in its purported function for Nike Inc. When the Nike Foundation re-launched as a foundation dedicated to girls' empowerment, Nike's CEO Phil Knight declared that the Nike Foundation's "investments in human capital will spark a positive cycle of development and complements NIKE, Inc.'s efforts around improvements in our fundamental business practices" (Nike 2005). During Nike's engagement with the World Bank's Global Private Sector Leaders Forum, Knight touted the Girl Effect as a prime example of the kind of gender equality commitments encouraged in the forum. He explained the company's newfound focus on girls and women in terms of the convergence between development and corporate goals:

> "In [Nike Inc. and the Nike Foundation], a realization took hold several years ago that women were being underserved and underrated – whether as consumers of sports apparel or as people who could help break the cycle of poverty in poor nations. A new kind of thinking has made women more central to Nike's strategy on both fronts."
>
> (GPSLF n.d.)

By calling upon the idea of a global community of women who are Nike customers, business owners, athletes, and engines of economic development, Knight's message aims to shore up Nike's brand image with reference to a synergistic discourse of empowerment and market expansion. Nike's engagement with (and leadership in) the girl-power development discourse serves a core business function of appealing to new markets of consumers, even as it performs the function of a charitable foundation. Despite claims that its charitable work exists outside of the business, commercial goals are explicitly highlighted in the Girl Effect's work. For example, its Global Brand Manager identifies Nike's consumers as a key audience for the Girl Effect, alongside other audiences like NGOs, Nike employees, and the general public in the global South. Consumers in the global North, she suggests, have power "beyond the dollar" and will create public support for the Girl Effect's message (Kylander 2011: 4). Public support for the Girl Effect's brand is equated with support for Nike's business, and building loyalty to the brand is a task that the Girl Effect approaches with the tools of Nike corporate. The Nike Foundation aims to "own the brand" of the Girl Effect, by which it means having a monopoly on the discourse of girl-powered development. As the Senior Portfolio Manager at the Nike Foundation explains it, the Girl Effect brand exists in competition with Girl Up and similar girl-powered development campaigns, whose use of similar branding might cause confusion and "dilute" its impact (Kylander 2011: 7). These charitable initiatives serve multiple functions: they engage consumers concerned with "ethical" brands, expand into new markets of women consumers, and pursue a profitable growth strategy through association with development causes.

The Girl Effect serves as cause-related marketing for Nike Inc. to shield its brand from criticism, recuperate it from scandal, and promote it to female consumers. This is perhaps an unsurprising observation, given the prevailing climate of stakeholder capitalism. In fact, this kind of cause-related marketing is a very common strategy. Profit will be, invariably, the main motivation for business in all its activities, so the pursuit of profit itself is an insufficiently broad reason to critique all CSR and philanthropic endeavors (Blowfield and Dolan 2014). However, the Girl Effect merits additional scrutiny for its role in relation to Nike Inc. because it serves more than a branding strategy to associate the Nike logo with girls' empowerment. Indeed, it serves to divert attention from on-going labor abuses and to relieve pressure on the firm to change its core business practices. Nike Inc.'s involvement in CSR endeavors like the GPSLF and Girl Effect campaign allow it to publicly advertise its CSR activities and, in doing so, publicize its role in philanthropic endeavors. In regard to its role as a marketing tool, the Girl Effect allows Nike Inc. to cultivate its brand image in a way that masks the way its profits are made. This elision is evident in the kind of empowerment stories presented by the Girl Effect. For instance, in its most popular promotional video (and one that is illustrated entirely in Nike's black-white-orange colours) the vision of a girl's empowerment proceeds as follows: the empowered girl buys a single cow, subsequently builds a herd of cows and later opens a small business (Girl Effect 2008b). It is notable that her empowerment happens through agricultural activity and entrepreneurship, rather than employment along a supply chain that might end in a Nike product. She does not take a job at a Nike factory or similar manufacturing plant: her empowerment story takes place in a world wholly outside of Nike's supply chain or its profit-making structure. The children who have been continually found working in Nike's supply chain are not the children featured in the Girl Effect videos or promotional material. As such, Nike products can be marketed alongside the Girl Effect videos without acknowledging the tensions therein or without alerting consumers to the contradiction between the visualization of empowerment featured here and the lived realities of children within Nike's supply chain and neighboring communities.

Furthermore, this closure is important because it points to a tension in the relationship between the Girl Effect's vision of empowerment and the processes through which Nike Inc. makes its profits. Nike Inc. has long been a notorious example of those mobile firms who move across the global South in search of cheaper wages. From South Korea, to China, to Vietnam, Nike Inc. has continually relocated its manufacturing when wages rise; additionally, much of its sub-contracted manufacturing workforce is female (Locke et al 2007). As such, there is a notable contradiction between the vision of empowerment that Nike sells through the Girl Effect and the kinds of female labor it seeks out. These are fundamentally at odds because, as feminist political economist scholars have demonstrated, companies like Nike depend on the persistence of particular constructions of femininity – docile, "respectable" women – which make female labor in the global South cheaper. When workers along its supply chains demand higher wages or resist management practices, the company relocates to other countries where it can exploit a new workforce (Enloe 2004; Wright 2006). The labor practices at the heart of Nike Inc.'s business model have exploited gender inequalities around the world while marketing products to its consumers through the language of empowerment. The vision of empowered female entrepreneurs who exercise agency in their communities and workplaces is at odds with the way that Nike Inc.'s profits are made, and yet these tensions are hidden through the girl-powered development discourse it deploys in order to market its products. Nike Inc.'s use of the Girl Effect as a piece of cause-related marketing points to the wider implications of this tactic: it not only hides business practices from the consumer, but makes efforts to position the firm itself as a leader in development knowledge. Encapsulating the function of CSR and cause-related marketing as a legitimizing tool for private sector power in development, it speaks to the broader politics of development knowledge: global development institutions' partnerships with such firms clearly serve to authorize them as private sector leaders who can contribute to development goals.

The seemingly superficial efforts of the firms to brand themselves with girls' and women's empowerment rhetoric is, in fact, representative of larger changes in the governance of development and its knowledge production apparatus. Private sector actors, like Nike Inc., increasingly claim authority as leaders in Gender and Development activity, because of the prevailing assumption that public development and private profit goals are compatible and reinforce each other. Private sector power in development governance means new funding streams and mechanisms for awareness raising on a variety of issues, but it also means a re-imagining of development goals. On the issue of gender equality, the growing power of private-sector actors to position themselves as development leaders depends on the equation of gender equality with private profit, and firms' profitability with the increased ability to activate the dormant power of female labor and purchasing power.

Bottom of the Pyramid development

The role of the private sector in development is in transition: the above discussions about CSR and cause-related marketing have provided examples of how firms are becoming more engaged in development. Traditional CSR is generally understood as representing a so-called "defensive" approach to development (Ponte et al 2009). For instance, CSR efforts might represent a defensive effort to guard against damage to a firm's reputation or to respond to consumer anger about business practices. The Girl Effect and its relationship to Nike Inc.'s brand provides a representative example of this, as does Goldman Sachs' use of the "10,000 Women" initiative to deflect criticism of its business practices in 2008. In contrast, another model for private sector engagement in development has emerged: firms are taking a more aggressive stance and positioning themselves as "development agents" in their own right (Blowfield and Dolan 2014: 25). As a result, new partnerships, financial instruments, and for-profit development initiatives have emerged under the umbrella of "Bottom of the Pyramid" development. These initiatives re-imagine poverty as a business problem that can be best addressed by the private sector, because it has the necessary technical skills and the right incentives to lead more effective development interventions than the public sector. Reflecting the broader changes discussed at the beginning of this chapter, Bottom of the Pyramid development provides a further manifestation of changing power relations in development with significant conceptual and practical implications.

Bottom of the Pyramid development imagines the world's poor both as profitable consumer groups to be accessed with the right products, as well as powerful entrepreneurs who can lift themselves out of poverty if given access to capital and resources. As such, it sees a natural alignment between the goals of business and the goals of development: investors can address existing social problems which earning return on investment – both social return and financial (McGoey 2016: 81). The Bottom of the Pyramid development approach has entered development by way of management literature, promoting the idea that the world's poorest should be viewed by corporations as consumers constituting a market, rather than mere recipients of aid (Elyachar 2012). Although the term does not describe any single formally coordinated project, it reflects a coherent set of efforts to re-conceptualize poverty "as a frontier of profit and accumulation" (Roy 2012: 106). Bottom of the Pyramid (BoP) initiatives are perhaps most closely associated with microfinance, but also include diverse fair trade, direct sales, impact investing and social entrepreneurship schemes. BoP development is representative of a broader turn to for-profit business in development, related to similar ideas like "bottom billion capitalism", "creative capitalism," "inclusive business," and "making markets work for the poor" (Dolan and Roll 2013; Blowfield and Dolan 2014: 23). Given this emphasis on targeting populations in the global South who are not currently recognized as development agents, and populations with untapped purchasing power as consumers, women occupy a special place in this new development paradigm. As has been argued throughout this book, women have acquired visibility in development policy through the argument that they are uniquely productive and altruistic subjects, and this discourse has been especially important in animating the current themes of the "Business Case" for women. While men living in poverty are often depicted as feckless, irresponsible, and risky subjects, women are conversely represented as resilient and flexible subjects who will readily "downgrade" their work to provide for their families, while their husbands will stay at home (see Chapter 4). This is particularly so in BoP initiatives, where women are represented as ideal entrepreneurial subjects, because they are understood as gatekeepers to their communities where they influence consumption choices and have the social networks to increase the sale of a product (Dolan and Roll 2013; Roy 2012). Women's visibility as development agents derives, yet again, from their association with a variety of gender essentialisms about female economic subjectivities.

"Bottom of the Pyramid" ventures that focus on the purchasing power of women and girls encapsulate some of the most significant changes in global development theory and practice, representing a powerful new site of convergence between private sector-led development and girl-powered development (Calkin 2017). The Girl Effect Accelerator is one such initiative which is representative of the trend: launched by the Nike Foundation in 2014, the Girl Effect Accelerator represents a continuation of the Girl Effect movement, re-articulated through the structures and languages of the American tech industry and its focus on start-ups which "disrupt" and "innovate" to solve social problems. In the parlance of the tech industry, an accelerator is a forum to "accelerate" the growth of existing start-ups, where (within a limited timeframe) companies are given access to mentors and investors to achieve a set of fundraising goals. The Girl Effect Accelerator provides these resources to ten selected start-ups whose work appeals to the aims of the Girl Effect. For this initiative, the Nike Foundation is partnered with the Unreasonable Group, the charitable wing of a venture capital firm (the Unreasonable Institute) focused on social entrepreneurship; the Nike Foundation and Unreasonable Group provide the venue and resources for the Accelerator itself, but do not invest in the projects. Enterprises were selected to participate in the Girl Effect Accelerator on the basis of the following main criteria: 1) the start-ups are for-profit; 2) their annual revenue exceeds $500k; 3) they demonstrate the potential to scale up; 4) they are committed to the "Girl Effect vision"; 5) their impact on girls is measurable; and 6) the majority of their teams live and work in the countries where they operate (Girl Effect Accelerator n.d.; Girl Effect 2014). On the basis of these criteria, ten start-ups were chosen for the Accelerator project, which launched with a conference where the start-ups were matched with mentors, potential financiers, and a support network; subsequent investor gatherings will allow the ventures to attract funding from larger investment funds and philanthropists. In the longer term, the ventures will be evaluated on the investment they attract, the growth in their business, and their impact on girls, the measurement of which is tailored to each venture. The first round of start-ups selected for the Girl Effect Accelerator include off-grid electricity devices, low-cost healthcare products, and several mobile apps for banking, education, and direct retail, among others. Unlike the Girl Effect NGO, the Accelerator is focused exclusively on private capital and investment, without public institutions as partners: with mentorship and investment from GEA partners, the enterprises can "scale globally and unleash the girl effect" (Unreasonable 2014).

The model of girl-driven change endorsed by the Girl Effect Accelerator draws on the "ripple effect" model found in wider Girl Effect discourses; its vision for the structure of this change is notable, however, because it involves a pointed critique of public development institutions and an enthusiastic promotion of the values and logics of venture capitalists. Much of the rationale for the Accelerator and the wider Girl Effect movement is premised on the familiar claim that girls are invisible to policymakers, investors, and entrepreneurs. It proposes to solve the problem of girls' invisibility in global development. Its stated goal is to "put girls on the global agenda and drive massive resources to them" (Unreasonable 2014). This invisibility is articulated in terms of development funding: the Accelerator material frequently argues that only two cents in each "development dollar" goes to girls, which represents a major missed opportunity. The GEA uses this claim about money spent on girls as a proxy for their invisibility in development and argues that its project will correct this oversight by making girls visible "to the entrepreneurial, business, and investment worlds" (Girl Effect Accelerator n.d.). To this end, the GEA re-states a common critique of development assistance: despite so many billions of dollars spent in aid, with little effect:

> "Every year, more than $120 billion is spent in international development assistance, yet this system has yet to produce the game-changing results we all desire for girls and the world. This program is designed to bring new problem solvers to the table: entrepreneurs. The Girl Effect Accelerator will support solutions that are measurably benefiting girls in poverty: market based solutions that are locally driven, aid-independent, financially sustainable, and that have the potential to be scalable globally."
>
> (Girl Effect Accelerator n.d.)

The GEA's representation of gendered poverty – and the 250 million girls living in poverty who are its targets – is based on this implicit critique of state-led development, which it sees as having failed to recognize girls' potential. By extension, it endorses the private governance of development and the re-alignment of development with corporate values and structures. This critique of public failures in global development is therefore tied to an endorsement of the corporatization of development, on the assumption that the private sector can achieve results that the public sector cannot. This is a logic which is common to BoP development, which has employed a post-development critique of development failures to attack the state and seized upon opportunities to access the informal markets and social capital of the poor outside of state structures (Elyachar 2012). The GEA presents a critique of development as unconcerned with girls (by allocating insufficient resources to them) and ineffective in creating change (by spending billions of dollars inefficiently). Instead, it urges that the logic and values of the private sector must be applied in the area of global development, because investors demand returns and will not support inefficient ventures. Its critique of inefficient public spending is tied to the assertion that private firms and investors are best placed to drive global development change, because today's investors and their "demanding capital" expect returns on investment and reward for their risks (Roy 2010: 26–27). This is a belief reflected in the GEA's assertion that its entrepreneurs are the "new problem solvers" who can correct for years of ineffective development spending, satisfying the expectations of investors' "impatient capital" (Girl Effect Accelerator n.d.). In the early years of CSR, firms responded defensively to accusations against them and sought to engage in projects to redeem their reputations. Today there is no sense of reluctance when business acts as a development agent: "The only sin is insufficient expansion into untouched realms" (McGoey 2015: 85).

In Bottom of the Pyramid development, the terms upon which development problems are articulated sets the boundaries for their proposed solutions; the ways in which the causes of poverty are imagined works to shape and constrain the interventions proposed to eradicate poverty (Blowfield and Dolan 2014). In the Girl Effect Accelerator specifically, this equates to an understanding of gender inequality as driven by the absence of particular products and services. The GEA identifies start-ups as the actors who are best placed to "experiment" with solutions to "unlock the potential of girls around the world" and to do so in a way that generates revenues for investors (Girl Effect Accelerator n.d.; Unreasonable 2014). Tayo Ovioso, CEO of a mobile payment app selected by the GEA, explained how the program had changed his understanding of the gender issue:

> "I actually came in here thinking: 'What can we do to help girls?' That thinking has been completely refined, and turned on its head, and the question should actually not be, 'What can we do to help girls?' but rather, 'If girls were a target market for your business, how do you unlock that today?' I think that's going to really help our business bring The Girl Effect to life."
>
> (Unreasonable 2014)

Shaifali Puri of the Nike Foundation describes the Accelerator's mission in similar terms:

> "We're unleashing huge, hardest-to-reach markets. We think of this market as something that is necessary to address, not just nice to address. It's not, 'That's just about girls.' It's about transforming the way businesses operate."
>
> (quoted in Zax 2014)

Poverty, and gendered poverty in particular, is understood as a function of the market and especially as the inability of girls to access the market. The GEA deploys a market rationale to re-imagine poverty as the absence of material resources that provides the opportunities for entrepreneurs to intervene with suitable products; its theory of girls' visibility in development turns on the idea that girls will be ignored until they can be acknowledged as a powerful consumer market. The Girl Effect Accelerator envisions development as a process that progresses when girls get access to the kinds of products and services that will allow them to access online education, mobile banking, virtual marketplaces, and other products developed by its start-ups; it proposes a development process based on the direct connection between the individual girl and the business who sells the product she requires. In doing so, it envisions a model of development that can bypass the kind of infrastructure or institutions that the state would build in order to ensure universal provision of services (Calkin 2017). This is evident in the emphasis on the "leapfrogging" potential of innovations. In the parlance of start-ups, "leapfrogging" means creating a new technology that bypasses prior technology or eliminates the need for an older technology. For instance, mobile banking can be said to "leapfrog" because it allows customers to manage money in previously inaccessible places and in doing so eliminates the need for bricks-and-mortar banks to be built in those areas. The GEA is premised on this kind of innovation: its entrepreneurs are lauded for "leapfrogging the absence of electrical grid systems, leapfrogging the absence of schools, leapfrogging the absence of banks" (Nike 2014). Innovative technologies can bring about major improvements, but combined with attacks on state development and assertions that private sector motives are more conducive to achieving transformative results, the valorization of this kind of innovation raises concerns about state infrastructure and capacity. Here, the GEA cuts out the public sector altogether, deploying the familiar rhetoric about the enhanced efficiency and innovative style of private sector firms, while abandoning any references to the importance of public institutions (Calkin 2017). Its vision of the Girl Effect is less tethered to gender equality than it is to an individual's empowerment: the Girl Effect can assist girls to become educated and entrepreneurial, so long as they have the resources to access these products in the first place.

The Girl Effect Accelerator evidences two important trends at work in the private governance of Gender and Development, which echo the other forms of private-sector involvement detailed above. First, the ability of private firms to make claims about their superior ability to achieve development goals and eradicate poverty hinges on the assumption that public institutions have tried, and failed, to effect change. Critiques of public failures become folded into endorsements of private-led efforts. Second, the critique of public development failures is evidenced in these discourses through a narrative about girls' and women's "untapped" human capital resources. Private intervention, it is argued, can most effectively unlock these resources and trigger economic growth because private firms have the most relevant skills, resources, and incentives to achieve gender equality. They are animated by the shared contention that women can be empowered as entrepreneurs, consumers, and anti-poverty engines. Increased private sector power in development, growing recognition of the "Business Case" for gender equality, and widespread uptake of a human capital logic for anti-poverty action have converged to produce a distinctive set of public-private partnerships that aim to empower women through the market.

Conclusion

Many conversations about the co-optation of feminism start from the recognition that feminist language, images, or messages are used to sell a wide range products, services, and ideas. Many of the things that are sold through feminist packaging appear to be incompatible with, or at least in tension with, a feminist ethos. Others appear to hold only a tenuous relationship to actual improvements in working conditions or wages. The power of the female consumer to drive change through ethical shopping is an important component of current empowerment discourses. Can you be empowered by purchasing a certain clothing label? Can you empower a female entrepreneur in the global South by purchasing a particular brand of coffee? Can your matched donation to a charitable cause offset the harm done in the manufacturing process? These questions are the starting points for many conversations about "market" or "neoliberal" feminism, and they challenge us to think about the work being done by the association of particular brands or products with gender equality.

This chapter pushes the conversation further: it's not merely the case that gender equality is commodified and employed to sell things, although this is surely true. It is more important to note the way that the human capital logic of girls and women as untapped resources is employed to legitimize new forms of corporate authority in the development process. Human capital theory's ascendance in development policy and discourse has not been a purely discursive process by which the conceptual framings for gender equality are transformed. Its material effect on development interventions is evident in the range of initiatives and programs organized around the goal of shaping and training girls' and women's behavior to be compatible with market norms; it is further evident in the kinds of power relationships that are legitimized in Gender and Development today, where the over-arching push to identify and unlock female human capital creates new spaces for private sector involvement.

This is accomplished through the claim that investment in girls' and women's productive capacities will produce returns for early investors, be they states, firms, or private individuals. This equation of gender equality with private profit is a powerful rhetorical tool that is used to legitimize a range of business practices: it forms the conceptual basis for public-private partnerships in Gender and Development, which serve the function of Corporate Social Responsibility work, cause-related marketing, and Bottom of the Pyramid enterprise. In practice, these projects serve to distance companies from public scandals about abuses and misconduct, associate brands with gender equality while hiding the process through which profit is made, and legitimize private sector actors as preferred authorities on development issues. The logic at work in these shifts, as it relates to gender equality, is made possible by the dominance of human capital theory and its re-imagining of girls and women as dormant resources whose economic agency must be catalyzed by private intervention. As girls and women have become visible through human capital's calculative logic, the task of empowering them has been opened up to a wider range of actors that expand Gender and Development activity beyond its traditional institutional boundaries.

Notes

1 Press releases issued over the course of the GPSLF sometimes contained variations in membership. Compiled from GPSLF sources dating 2009–2011, and including all members identified as members from 2008 to 2011, the full membership list of the GPSLF and an indication of the company's business is as follows: Goldman Sachs (Finance), Boeing International (Manufacturing), Belcorp (Cosmetics), INSEAD (Business School), Accenture (Accountancy), Cisco Systems (Technology), Norfund (Finance), Tupperware Brands (Retail), Heidrick and Struggles (Recruitment), Sungjoo Group (Retail and export), Women Private Equity Fund (Finance), PriceWaterhouseCoopers (Accountancy), Carlson Industries (Hotel and Travel), Finansbank Turkey (Finance), Hindustan Unilever (Consumer goods), Nike (Atheltic equipment), Standard Chartered (Finance), Ernst and Young (Accountancy), Grupo Inter Quimica (Chemicals), Sun Media (Media), Shalakany Law Office (Legal services). Information compiled from World Bank 2009b; 2011; GPSLF n.d.).

2 Robert Zoellick served as World Bank president from 2007–2012. He re-joined Goldman Sachs in 2013 after his term as World Bank president ended.

3 Nike Inc. still maintains an in-house CSR department, called "Sustainable Innovation." The Nike Foundation is a private, grant-making foundation established by Nike.

4 Girl Effect CEO Maria Eitel joined the Nike Foundation as its CEO after serving as the first Vice President of Corporate Social Responsibility for Nike, when Nike opened this CSR office in the wake of a child labor scandal.

References

Allison, Katherine, Catia Gregoratti, and Sofie Tornhill. 2017. "From the Boardroom to the Workshop: Methodological Challenges in Research on Transnational Business Feminism." Presented at the 11th Pan-European Conference on International Relations, Barcelona, September.

Banerjee, Subhabrata Bobby. 2008. "Corporate Social Responsibility: The Good, the Bad and the Ugly." *Critical Sociology* 34(1): 51–79.

Bexell, Magdalena. 2012. "Global Governance, Gains and Gender: UN–Business Partnerships for Women's Empowerment." *International Feminist Journal of Politics* 14(3): 389–407.

Blowfield, Michael. 2007. "Reasons to Be Cheerful? What We Know about CSR's Impact." *Third World Quarterly* 28(4): 683–695.

Blowfield, Michael, and Catherine S. Dolan. 2014. "Business as a Development Agent: Evidence of Possibility and Improbability." *Third World Quarterly* 35(1): 22–42.

Brown, Wendy. 2015. *Undoing the Demos: Neoliberalism's Stealth Revolution*. Cambridge, MA: MIT Press.

Calkin, Sydney. 2016. "Globalizing 'Girl Power': Corporate Social Responsibility and Transnational Business Initiatives for Gender Equality." *Globalizations* 13(2): 158–172.

Calkin, Sydney. 2017. "'Disrupting' Disempowerment: Neoliberal Feminism and the Private Governance of Gender and Development." *New Formations* 91: 69–86.

Charkiewicz, Ewa. 2005. "Corporations, the UN and Neo-Liberal Bio-Politics." *Development* 48(1): 75–83.

Cushman, John. 1998. "Nike Pledges to End Child Labor And Apply U.S. Rules Abroad." *The New York Times*. Published 13 May 1998. www.nytimes.com/1998/05/13/business/international-business-nike-pledges-to-end-child-labor-and-apply-us-rules-abroad.html.

Dauvergne, Peter, and Genevieve Lebaron. 2014. *Protest Inc*. Cambridge: Polity Press.

Dolan, Catherine, and Kate Roll. 2013. "Capital's New Frontier: From' Unusable' Economies to Bottom-of-the-Pyramid Markets in Africa." *African Studies Review* 56(3): 123–146.

Ehrenpreis, Malcolm. 2011. "The Global Private Sector Leaders Forum." *World Bank*. Published April 2011. http://go.worldbank.org/KP4AMC7PH0.

Eitel, Maria. 2010. "Maria Eitel, Nike Foundation." *Rainmakers TV*. Uploaded 1 October 2010. http://rainmakers.tv/maria-eitel-nike-foundation-cgi-2010/.

Ellis, Amanda. 2010. "World Bank Group Action Plan (GAP): Global Private Sector Leaders Forum (PSLF)." Presentation delivered at Global Summit of Women 2010, Beijing. www.globewomen.org/summit/2010/Presentation/Amanda%20ellis%20Linking%20Business%2030.pdf.

Elyachar, Julia. 2012. "Next Practices: Knowledge, Infrastructure, and Public Goods at the Bottom of the Pyramid." *Public Culture* 24(1): 109–129.

Enloe, Cynthia. 2004. *The Curious Feminist: Searching for Women in a New Age of Empire*. Berkeley: University of California Press.

ExxonMobil. 2013. "United Nations Foundation and the ExxonMobil Foundation Release New Report on Most Effective Programs for Women's Economic Empowerment." Press Release. Published 16 September 2013. http://news.exxonmobil.com/press-release/united-nations-foundation-and-exxonmobil-foundation-release-new-report-most-effective-.

Girl Effect. 2008a. "The Girl Effect: I Dare You to See I Am the Answer." The Girl Effect. www.youtube.com/watch?v=-Vq2mfF8puE.

Girl Effect. 2008b. "The Girl Effect." The Girl Effect. www.youtube.com/watch?v=WIvmE4_KMNw&feature=youtube_gdata_player.

Girl Effect. 2010. "The Girl Effect: The Clock Is Ticking." Girl Effect. www.youtube.com/watch?v=1e8xgF0JtVg&feature=youtube_gdata_player.

Girl Effect. 2014. "These Aren't Your Average Silicon Valley StartUps." Girl Effect. www.girleffect.org/what-girls-need/articles/2014/11/these-arent-your-average-silicon-valley-startups/.

Girl Effect Accelerator. n.d. "Girl Effect Accelerator." *Girl Effect Accelerator*. First accessed 20 January 2016 [Website content changes often] http://girleffectaccelerator.com.

Global Private Sector Leaders Forum (GPSLF). n.d. "Promoting Women's Economic Empowerment." Washington, DC: World Bank. Www.un.org/en/ecosoc/phlntrpy/notes/world_brochure.pdf.

Goldman Sachs. 2008. "10,000 Women: Education. Empowerment. Economic Opportunity." Goldman Sachs. www.goldmansachs.com/our-thinking/investing-in-women/bios-pdfs/10000-women-summary.pdf.

Goldman Sachs. 2014. "Goldman Sachs 10,000 Women, IFC To Raise Up To Dollar 600 Million to Support Women Entrepreneurs." Published 5 March 2014. Goldman Sachs. www.goldmansachs.com/citizenship/10000women/news-and-events/10000women-ifc.html.

Gregoratti, Catia. 2010. "UNDP, Business Partnerships, and the (UN)democratic Governance of Development." In *Democracy and Public-Private Partnerships in Global Governance*, edited by Magdalena Bexell and Ulrika Mörth, 190–212. Basingstoke: Palgrave Macmillan.

Harman, Sophie, and David Williams. 2014. "International Development in Transition." *International Affairs* 90(4): 925–941.

Hawkins, Roberta. 2012. "A New Frontier in Development? The Use of Cause-Related Marketing by International Development Organisations." *Third World Quarterly* 33 (10): 1783–1801.

Jenkins, Rhys. 2005. "Globalization, Corporate Social Responsibility and Poverty." *International Affairs* 81(3): 525–540.

Korngold, Alice. 2009. "Goldman Sachs at CGI: Women Offer the 'Highest ROI.'" *Fast Company*. Published 24 September 2009. www.fastcompany.com/1372489/goldman-sachs-cgi-women-offer-highest-roi.

Kylander, Nathalie. 2011. "The Girl Effect Brand: Using Brand Democracy to Strengthen Brand Affinity." Cambridge MA: Hauser Center for Nonprofits, Harvard University. www.hks.harvard.edu/hauser/role-of-brand/documents/girleffect.pdf.

Locke, Richard, Fei Qin, and Alberto Brause. 2007. "Does Monitoring Improve Labor Standards? Lessons from Nike." *ILR Review* 61(1): 3–31.

Lund-Thomsen, Peter, and Neil Coe. 2015. "Corporate Social Responsibility and Labour Agency: The Case of Nike in Pakistan." *Journal of Economic Geography* 15(2): 275–296.

McGoey, Linsey. 2014. "The Philanthropic State: Market–state Hybrids in the Philanthrocapitalist Turn." *Third World Quarterly* 35(1): 109–125.

McGoey, Linsey. 2016. *No Such Thing as a Free Gift: The Gates Foundation and the Price of Philanthropy*. London: Verso Books.

McKinsey & Company. 2010. *The Business of Empowering Women: Where, Why and How*. McKinsey & Company. http://mckinseyonsociety.com/the-business-of-empowering-women/.

Mitchell, Katharyne, and Matthew Sparke. 2016. "The New Washington Consensus: Millennial Philanthropy and the Making of Global Market Subjects." *Antipode* 48(3): 724–749.

Murphy, Michelle. 2017. *The Economization of Life*. Durham, NC: Duke University Press.

Nadvi, Khalid. 2008. "Global Standards, Global Governance and the Organization of Global Value Chains." *Journal of Economic Geography* 8(3): 323–343.

Neath, Gavin, and Vijay Sharma. 2008. "The Shakti Revolution." *Development Outreach*. Washington, DC: World Bank. https://openknowledge.worldbank.org/handle/10986/4541.

Nike. 2005. "Nike Foundation Steps on to New Field." *Nike News*. Published 08 March 2005. https://news.nike.com/news/nike-foundation-steps-on-to-new-field

Nike. 2014. "Meet the Innovators Who Put Girls First in the Fight Against Poverty." *Nike News*. Published 14 November 2014. http://news.nike.com/news/meet-the-innovators-putting-girls-first-in-the-fight-against-poverty.

O'Laughlin, Bridget. 2008. "Governing Capital? Corporate Social Responsibility and the Limits of Regulation." *Development and Change* 39(6): 945–957.

Ponte, Stefano, Lisa Ann Richey, and Mike Baab. 2009. "Bono's Product (RED) Initiative: Corporate Social Responsibility That Solves the Problems of 'distant Others.'" *Third World Quarterly* 30(2): 301–317.

Prügl, Elisabeth. 2015. "Neoliberalising Feminism." *New Political Economy* 20(4): 614–631.

Prügl, Elisabeth, and Jacqui True. 2015. "Equality Means Business? Governing Gender through Transnational Public-Private Partnerships." *Review of International Political Economy* 21(6): 1137–1169.

Reinicke, Wolfgang. 1998. *Global Public Policy: Governing without Government?* Washington, DC: Brookings Institution Press.

Richey, Lisa Ann, and Stefano Ponte. 2008. "Better (Red)TM than Dead? Celebrities, Consumption and International Aid." *Third World Quarterly* 29(4): 711–729.

Roberts, Adrienne. 2012. "Financial Crisis, Financial Firms… And Financial Feminism? The Rise of 'Transnational Business Feminism' and the Necessity of Marxist-Feminist IPE." *Socialist Studies/Études Socialistes* 8(2): 85–108.

Roberts, Adrienne. 2015a. "Gender, Financial Deepening and the Production of Embodied Finance: Towards a Critical Feminist Analysis." *Global Society* 29(1): 107–127.

Roberts, Adrienne. 2015b. "The Political Economy of 'Transnational Business Feminism.'" *International Feminist Journal of Politics* 17(2): 209–231.

Roberts, Adrienne, and Susanne Soederberg. 2012. "Gender Equality as Smart Economics? A Critique of the 2012 World Development Report." *Third World Quarterly* 33(5): 949–968.

Roy, Ananya. 2010. *Poverty Capital: Microfinance and the Making of Development.* Abingdon: Routledge.

Roy, Ananya. 2012. "Ethical Subjects: Market Rule in an Age of Poverty." *Public Culture* 24(1): 105–108.

Ruggie, John G. 2002. "The Theory and Practice of Learning Networks." *Journal of Corporate Citizenship* 2002(5): 27–36.

Sato, Chizu. 2016. "Two Frontiers of Development?: A Transnational Feminist Analysis of Public-Private Partnerships for Women's Empowerment." *International Political Sociology* 10(2): 150–167.

Schaeferhoff, Marco, Sabine Campe, and Christopher Kaan. 2009. "Transnational Public-Private Partnerships in International Relations: Making Sense of Concepts, Research Frameworks, and Results." *International Studies Review* 11(3): 451–474.

Shamir, Ronen. 2008. "The Age of Responsibilization: On Market-Embedded Morality." *Economy and Society* 37(1): 1–19.

Shamir, Ronen. 2010. "Capitalism, Governance, and Authority: The Case of Corporate Social Responsibility." *Annual Review of Law and Social Science* 6: 531–553.

Soederberg, Susanne. 2007. "Taming Corporations or Buttressing Market-Led Development? A Critical Assessment of the Global Compact." *Globalizations* 4(4): 500–513.

Unreasonable Group. 2014. "Inaugural Girl Effect Accelerator Video." Uploaded 19 December 2014. https://vimeo.com/114992307.

Unterhalter, Elaine. 2017. "A Review of Public Private Partnerships around Girls' Education in Developing Countries: Flicking Gender Equality on and off." *Journal of International and Comparative Social Policy* 33(2): 181–199.

Utting, Peter. 2007. "CSR and Equality." *Third World Quarterly* 28(4): 697–712.

World Bank. 2009a. "The World Bank Launches Private-Public Initiative to Empower Adolescent Girls." Press Release no. 2009/109/PREM. Washington, DC: World Bank. http://go.worldbank.org/83L2MOFND0.

World Bank2009b. "World Bank Group Private Sector Leaders Forum Announces New Measures to Improve Women's Economic Opportunities." Press Release

No. 2010/084/PREM. Washington, DC: World Bank. http://go.worldbank.org/RW25VJYWJ0.

World Bank 2009c. "World Bank Calls for Expanding Economic Opportunities for Women as Global Economic Crisis Continues." Press Release no. 2009/214/PREM. Washington, DC: World Bank. http://go.worldbank.org/8G1SVWMY70.

World Bank2011. "The Global Private Sector Leaders Forum." *World Bank*. May 25. www.worldbank.org/en/news/feature/2011/05/25/the-global-private-sector-leaders-forum.

World Bank 2012. *World Development Report 2012: Gender Equality and Development*. Washington, DC: World Bank. https://openknowledge.worldbank.org/handle/10986/4391.

Wright, Melissa W. 2006. *Disposable Women and Other Myths of Global Capitalism*. Abingdon: Taylor & Francis.

Zax, David. 2014. "The Girl Effect Accelerator Launches, Aiming To Help Girls Earning Less Than $2 A Day." *Fast Company*. Published October 7 2014. www.fastcompany.com/3036691/for-girls-living-on-2-a-day-the-nike-foundation-launches-the-girl-effect.

Zadek, Simon. 2004. "The path to corporate responsibility." *Harvard Business Review* 82(12): 125–132.

Zeisler, Andi. 2016. *We Were Feminists Once: From Riot Grrrl to CoverGirl, the Buying and Selling of a Political Movement*. London: Hachette UK.

Conclusion

What do the Trump and al-Saud families have in common? It might surprise you to learn that they are united by a professed commitment to empowering the world's female entrepreneurs. In the summer of 2017, the Trump family and Saudi royal family both made news for their involvement in the World Bank's Women Entrepreneurs Finance Initiative (known as We-FI). The fund, popularly dubbed the "Ivanka Fund" was launched at the G20 in Hamburg, where Ivanka Trump publicly led its bid to attract funders. The fund will provide increased access to financing and technical resources for small and medium sized enterprises owned by women in developing countries, much like the Women Entrepreneurs Opportunity Fund led by the World Bank and Goldman Sachs. After meetings with members of the Trump family at the G20, Saudi Arabia and the United Arab Emirates committed funding to We-FI, amidst speculation that they were using the issue to curry favour with the Trump administration (MacBride 2017). The idea for the fund reportedly emerged from conversations between Ivanka Trump, Canadian PM Justin Trudeau, and World Bank president Jim Kim. For his apparent willingness to work with the Trump administration and Trump family, Jim Kim has also come in for criticism, because the Trump administration is seeking to dramatically reduce the American aid budget and withdraw the USA from a variety of multilateral institutions (Chilkoti 2017). Even in this fraught context, financing for women's entrepreneurship appeared as a consensus issue among the parties. At the We-FI launch, Kim touted its prospects to potential funders:

> "I'm confident that We-FI can harness the tremendous enthusiasm to unlock finance for women entrepreneurs in developing countries, and break down the legal and regulatory barriers that prevent women from starting and growing businesses. Our mission – to end poverty and increase prosperity – can't be accomplished unless we tap the full potential of women entrepreneurs."
>
> (World Bank 2017)

Women's empowerment may seem, at first glance, an unlikely cause for such parties to champion. The Trump administration is not known for its eagerness to engage in multilateral development projects, nor is the Saudi royal family known for a preoccupation with women's economic independence or labor force participation. Yet, as the preceding chapters in this book have demonstrated, it should not surprise us that the cause that unites such resolutely anti-feminist actors is women's entrepreneurship and the economic potential therein. The equation of gender equality with global development, poverty eradication, and economic growth has sped its arrival as a consensus issue on the global stage. Everyone can agree, it seems, that women's empowerment is good for business and good for national economies. This consensus has led to a politically diverse array of proponents for women's economic empowerment, including surprising figures previously known for their virulent and violent misogyny. We might say, in other words, that "Gender Equality as Smart Economics" has created such a low bar for engagement that there is no actor who cannot align themselves with gender equality, nor any ideology that cannot mould women's empowerment for its own use. The idea that women and girls possess special entrepreneurial potential, and represent as-yet-untapped resources for growth, is widely held. It is an idea that is rooted, as this book had demonstrated, in the ascendance of human capital theory and its promotion of a particular account of economic agency, which in turn has helped to cultivate the idea of gender equality as economic growth. It advances the powerful notion that if women's entrepreneurship could be unlocked, and their potential shaped to comport with market norms, the resulting economic benefits would align with the objectives of a range of powerful actors.

Girls and women have gained visibility as political and economic actors of consequence, albeit in ways that have raised concerns about emergent corporate, neoliberal, market, or managerial feminisms. This book opened by articulating the uneasy sense that feminist efforts to put gender equality on to the global agenda have been transformed by conservative and neoliberal forces. This anxiety is characteristic of the "Gender Equality as Smart Economics" development agenda and encapsulated in the We-FI initiative. Women's empowerment is a central goal of today's Gender and Development agenda, but empowerment to what end? This book seeks to make an intervention in this space, by asking what we might understand about Gender and Development governance if we looked past the mirage of market feminisms, and started with human capital theory to unpack the logics that structure the Smart Economics agenda and examined the forms of interventions that it authorizes.

Neoliberal manifestations of feminism cannot be explained away as instances of co-optation for pre-existing political agendas. The forms of gender equality governance that are characteristic of the "Gender Equality as Smart Economics" agenda must be understood as a distinct set of governance interventions that take women as idealized neoliberal subjects and seek to shape their behavior accordingly. Human capital theory underpins this orientation to gender equality because it understands inequality as the product of insufficient investment in female capital and potential gains to be "unlocked" from women's empowerment. A feminist critique of human capital theory, inspired by Foucault's treatment of the subject, demonstrates that the narrative of Smart Economics depends on essentialist visions of women's unique entrepreneurial and altruistic qualities, coupled with the call to equip them with appropriate skills and attitudes for market success. The reconciliation of productive and reproductive work is central here, because women's reproductive capacities are valorized as producing a distinctively female mode of economic agency, but also continually imagined as a threat to their productive capacity. The feminist critique of human capital in this book has emphasized the relationship between analytical and programmatic axes of human capital: ideal subjects of human capital are discursively constructed, identified, and authorized as pre-empowerment subjects. The practical effects of human capital theory in Gender and Development, I have argued, are to economize gender equality issues, legitimize a broader privatization of development government, and re-write structural inequalities in terms of women's failure to become fully empowered and economically active.

Human capital logics are influential across the geographical and ideological spectrum, underpinning a range of governance interventions across the world. Smart Economics discourses in gender equality policymaking are one area of influence, but by no means the only one. A robust critique of the effects of human capital theory and its effects, however, should start from a position that acknowledges the gendered underpinnings of the theory and the gendered effects of its operation. It must acknowledge that human capital theory functions as a powerful influence on policy because of the relationship between the analytical and programmatic axes: it works to define the problem in terms of the preferred solution. In Gender and Development, this means identifying women's idealized, but "untapped" economic agency and authorizing a range of interventions to capitalize on it. This narrative of gender inequality's causes and remedies has proven salient across institutions and sectors, providing a popular brand for a wide range of entities to unite behind a purported commitment to empowerment. The pervasive language of women's empowerment is seductive, precisely because it hints at power without actually promising it. So too does Smart Economics provide an appealing grammar for discussing gender equality issues, because it identifies gender inequality as an oversight and promises that we can improve the lives of everyone by unleashing women's economic power. The form of female agency it offers, however, is a profoundly truncated and individualized agency that is antithetical to feminist solidarity and collective action. It is my hope that the feminist critique developed in this book will provide relevant conceptual tools to understand the complex and gendered power relations of development governance, and to help us think creatively about feminist futures in political economy.

References

Chilkoti, Avantika. 2017. "With World Bank Initiative, a Change in Tone for Trump Administration." *New York Times*. Online. Published 19 July 2017. www.nytimes.com/2017/07/19/us/politics/world-bank-initiative-multilateral-institutions.html.

MacBride, Elizabeth. 2017. "Ivanka Trump's We-Fi fund initiative could spark a $1.7 trillion market around the world." *CNBC.com*. Online. Published 19 September 2017. www.cnbc.com/2017/09/19/ivanka-trumps-we-fi-fund-initiative-to-unlock-billions-for-women.html.

World Bank. 2017. "Statement on Women's Entrepreneurship Finance Initiative (We-FI)." World Bank Press Release 2018/046/EXC. Published 12 October 2017. Washington, DC: World Bank. www.worldbank.org/en/news/press-release/2017/10/12/statement-on-women-entrepreneurs-finance-initiative-we-fi.

Index